contents simplicity sewing book

Simplicity Pattern Co. Inc., 200 Madison Avenue, New York, N. Y. 10016
In Canada, Dominion Simplicity Patterns Ltd., 120 Mack Ave., Scarborough, Ontario

chapter 1

equipment

You're about to embark on an exciting journey into the world of sewing. Bring along your imagination, add a little patience and practice, and before long you'll be setting fashion trends. Sounds great? It is. Come on along. We'll show you the basics and you take it from there. To start you off, turn the page for helpful hints on setting up your sewing area.

sewing area

Welcome! Come into our cheery sewing room. You will find the two special features of this room are comfort and convenience. Comfort because working in an attractive room and having all the essential equipment at hand helps to make sewing a truly enjoyable experience. Convenience because, when you have a special sewing area, your work and tools can be left without having to gather up everything each time you must interrupt your sewing. Our sewing room is full of lots of great ideas that you can use in your own sewing area.

A high level of illumination in the working areas is essential to keep eye fatigue at a minimum. Daylight is the ideal light for sewing, but there are electric light sources which give the type of light needed for working indoors. The "high intensity" lamps and the color balanced fluorescents are brilliant and closely simulate natural sunlight.

The ironing board and pressing equipment should be set up near the sewing machine so that pressing is only an arm's length away.

Your cutting surface should be high enough for you to work on it comfortably in a standing position. Cutting fabric on the floor or on top of a bed interferes with the accuracy of your work because of the uncomfortable position of your body.

A full length mirror should be close by for checking the fit and appearance as you progress.

Notions and equipment should be arranged and stored in an orderly manner to save time when you need them again. See-through plastic boxes can be found in many shapes and sizes. Notions and findings fit into shoe boxes; fabrics are more easily stored in blanket boxes.

The importance of being able to leave work and equipment undisturbed between working periods cannot be over emphasized. Many of your free moments can be utilized if your work is ready to take-up where you left-off. A decorative folding screen can be used to shut off your sewing area from the rest of the room.

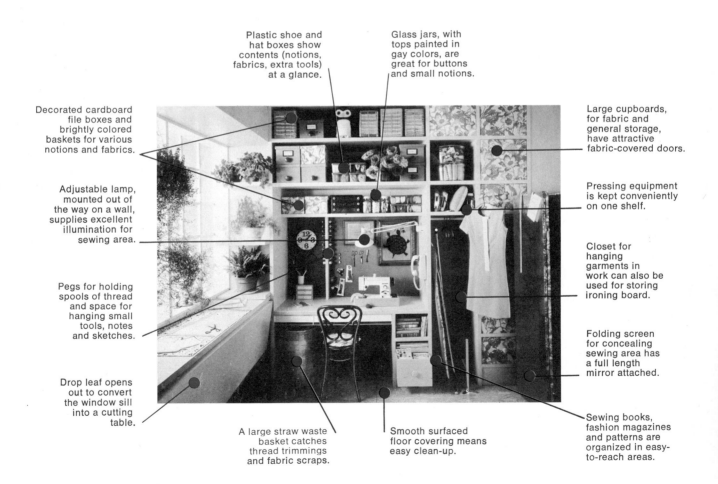

Plastic shoe and hat boxes show contents (notions, fabrics, extra tools) at a glance.

Glass jars, with tops painted in gay colors, are great for buttons and small notions.

Decorated cardboard file boxes and brightly colored baskets for various notions and fabrics.

Large cupboards, for fabric and general storage, have attractive fabric-covered doors.

Adjustable lamp, mounted out of the way on a wall, supplies excellent illumination for sewing area.

Pressing equipment is kept conveniently on one shelf.

Pegs for holding spools of thread and space for hanging small tools, notes and sketches.

Closet for hanging garments in work can also be used for storing ironing board.

Drop leaf opens out to convert the window sill into a cutting table.

Folding screen for concealing sewing area has a full length mirror attached.

A large straw waste basket catches thread trimmings and fabric scraps.

Smooth surfaced floor covering means easy clean-up.

Sewing books, fashion magazines and patterns are organized in easy-to-reach areas.

cutting tools

Scissors and shears are greatly responsible for the accuracy of your work. Buy only the best grades; use them only for fabric, never to cut paper. Fine scissors and shears will last a lifetime but they are precision tools. Have them sharpened at the first sign of dullness to insure accurate cutting.

Many types and sizes of scissors and shears are available. Those displayed here are the ones most essential for your sewing.

1 Bent-handled shears are the best to use for cutting fabric because the blades rest flat on the cutting surface, and you do not have to lift the fabric when cutting around the pattern. The 7 or 8 inch lengths are most commonly used. Left handed models are available in the better grades.

2 Trimming scissors are good for trimming and clipping seams and for general use. The 6 inch length is the easiest to handle and is the most versatile trimming scissor.

3 Sewing and embroidery scissors have pointed blades, and are good for cutting buttonholes, threads and other small jobs. The 4 or 5 inch lengths are recommended.

4 Pinking shears cut a zigzag edge and are used for finishing hem edges, seams, etc. Never use them for cutting out the garment. Left handed models are available in the better grades.

5 Scalloping shears cut a scalloped edge instead of a zigzag edge and can be used for the same purposes as the pinking shears. If pinking or scalloping shears become dull, it is best to return them to the manufacturer for sharpening.

6 The seam ripper is a handy little tool for taking out seams and removing stitches, but it must be used carefully so as not to cut the fabric.

7 The cutting board is a most helpful piece of equipment. It opens flat to be placed on top of your cutting surface, to enlarge and protect it, and folds up easily and compactly for storage. Because it is made of lightweight cardboard, fabrics can be pinned securely to the cutting board to prevent them from slipping. One-inch square markings help you to insure on-grain placement of the fabric.

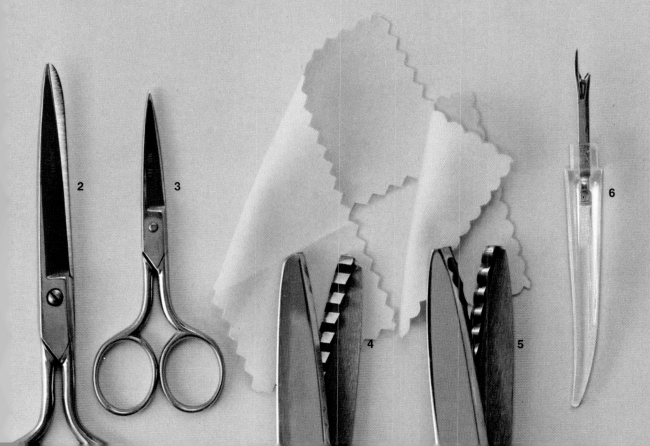

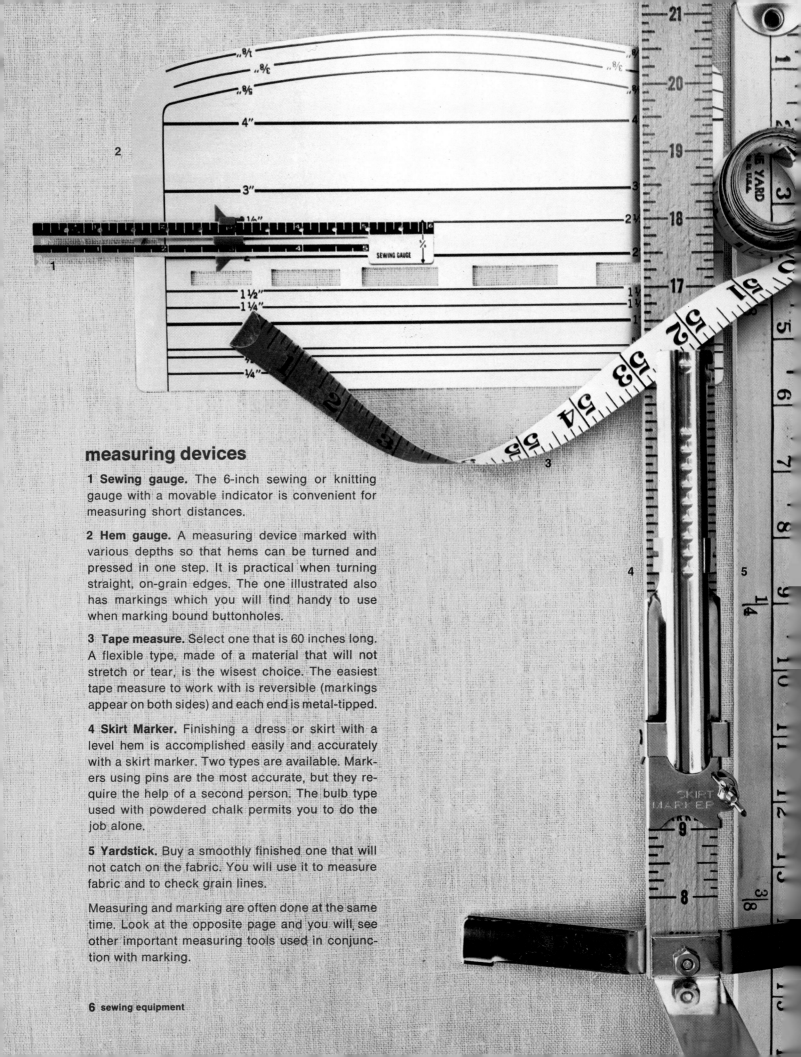

measuring devices

1 Sewing gauge. The 6-inch sewing or knitting gauge with a movable indicator is convenient for measuring short distances.

2 Hem gauge. A measuring device marked with various depths so that hems can be turned and pressed in one step. It is practical when turning straight, on-grain edges. The one illustrated also has markings which you will find handy to use when marking bound buttonholes.

3 Tape measure. Select one that is 60 inches long. A flexible type, made of a material that will not stretch or tear, is the wisest choice. The easiest tape measure to work with is reversible (markings appear on both sides) and each end is metal-tipped.

4 Skirt Marker. Finishing a dress or skirt with a level hem is accomplished easily and accurately with a skirt marker. Two types are available. Markers using pins are the most accurate, but they require the help of a second person. The bulb type used with powdered chalk permits you to do the job alone.

5 Yardstick. Buy a smoothly finished one that will not catch on the fabric. You will use it to measure fabric and to check grain lines.

Measuring and marking are often done at the same time. Look at the opposite page and you will see other important measuring tools used in conjunction with marking.

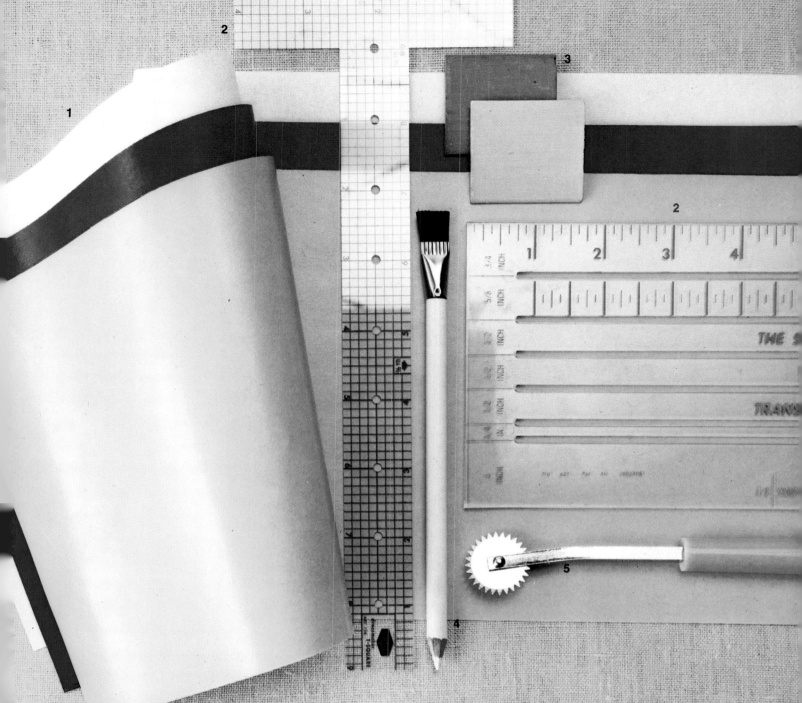

marking aids

1 Dressmaker's tracing or carbon paper can be used to transfer pattern markings to underlinings and to some fabrics. Use a color close to your fabric color. A package of assorted colors is most convenient to have on hand.

2 Transparent rulers come in a variety of shapes and sizes. Use them with a tracing wheel or chalk pencil for marking lines for pattern alterations, darts, pleats or any straight line markings.

3 Tailor's chalk is used on fabrics which cannot be marked with carbon. Because the chalk rubs off easily, it is used for temporary markings, such as

grain lines on garment sections. While the chalk comes in four colors, white and blue are used most often as they are less likely to stain the fabric.

4 Chalk pencils are available in white, pink and blue. Because these pencils can be sharpened to a point, they give a thin, accurate line.

5 Tracing wheels having teeth or dull points are recommended for use with carbon paper. To get a better impression from the carbon and to protect your working surface slip a piece of heavy cardboard under the fabric before starting to use wheel.

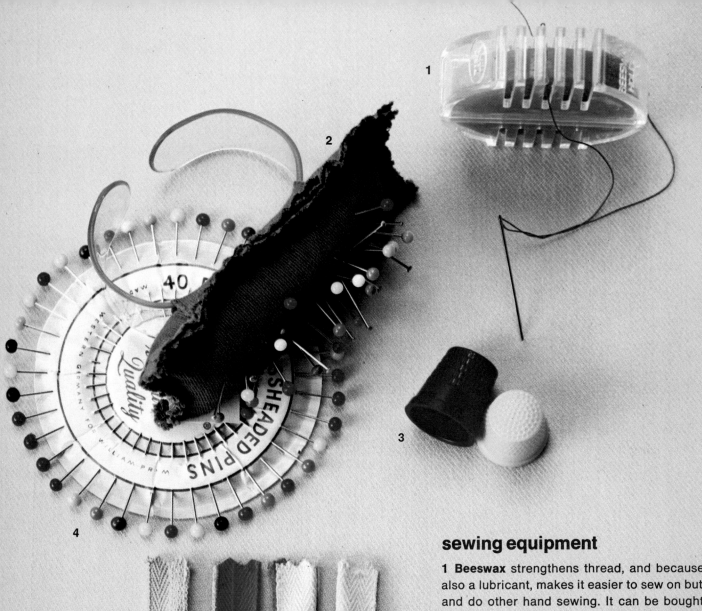

sewing equipment

1 Beeswax strengthens thread, and because it is also a lubricant, makes it easier to sew on buttons, and do other hand sewing. It can be bought in a holder having grooves through which thread is pulled for waxing.

2 Pin cushions come in all shapes and sizes. For convenience use the type having an elastic or plastic wrist band to hold it in place on your wrist.

3 Thimbles are made of either metal or plastic. Select one that fits the middle finger snugly. This is a must for hand sewing.

4 Pins with brilliantly colored glass heads are practical to use in many cases because they are easy to see and handle. Use fine, non-rusting dressmaker pins for fine fabrics.

5 Zippers are the most popular fasteners in use today. They are made with synthetic coils or with metal teeth. The latest version of the metallic type has a fabric covering which renders the zipper invisible. Whatever kind of zipper you need, you will find it in an infinite number of colors and lengths.

More essential sewing equipment is listed on p. 10.

The sewing machine. The purchase of a sewing machine should be approached carefully from several angles. There are two basic types of machines, straight stitch and zigzag.

A straight stitch machine sews only in a straight line, backward or forward, and is adjustable for length of stitch. Attachments are available which expand the usefulness of this machine, so if the initial cost is an important factor in your choice, the straight stitch machine might be the one to buy. The zigzag machine is a different story altogether. There are a great number of models in a wide range of prices. The best way to choose is to visit sewing centers maintained by the various manufacturers, and try the machines under supervision. As a rule the more the machine can do, the more it will cost. When making your selection, remember you will be using the machine for many years.

Give some thought to buying it as a console. It has the advantage of an adequately sized, flat working surface, and the machine is always ready for use. Tables into which a portable model can be set are available; they also provide ample working surface. If you buy a used machine, be sure to get it from a reputable source.

A sewing machine, cared for according to the manufacturer's manual, can last a lifetime.

An adjustable zipper foot, which replaces the standard foot on the machine, is a necessity. It permits stitching close to a raised edge, such as the line of the zipper, welting or cording.

The seam guide, adjustable for various seam widths, aids in sewing straight, even seams.

Machine needles come in sizes 9 (finest) to 18 (coarsest). Buy in three groups: Fine, medium and coarse; this also indicates weight of fabric to be stitched. Always select brands with the same name and model number of your machine.

more sewing equipment

Needle and thread are the two words which mean "sewing" to everyone. There is a large variety of needles and threads available to you.

Mercerized cotton thread can be used on light and medium weight fabrics. It is available in over 150 colors, in size 50, on both large and small spools. Colors are added or dropped depending on fashion trends. "Heavy duty" is a stronger version used for heavier dress fabrics and home furnishings. It is made in about 50 colors on large spools. Two colors come in a range of sizes. White — size 8 (coarsest) to size 100 (finest). Black — size 8 to size 70. They are available in various sized spools.

Button and carpet thread is extra heavy for hand sewing only. It comes in ten colors and on large spools only.

Silk thread can be used on silk and fine wool fabrics. It comes in one size only (A), in approximately 100 colors. Be sure to check thread tension on your machine before using it to stitch.

Buttonhole twist is a strong, silk thread with a special twist for making hand-worked buttonholes, sewing on buttons and decorative hand or machine stitching. It comes in about 100 colors.

Synthetic thread is a nylon or a cotton covered polyester thread recommended for use on knits, permanent press and wash-and-wear fabrics. Its elasticity makes it compatible with knits and other stretch fabrics. It comes in one size, in a wide range of colors on regular sized spools.

Hand-sewing needles come in sizes from 1 (coarsest) to 10 (finest) and in several types to suit different sewing needs. Packaged assortments are available in sizes 3-9 and 5-10.

"**Sharps**" — all-purpose, round-eyed needles of medium length.

"**Betweens**" — short, round-eyed needles used for very fine sewing.

"**Milliners**" — round-eyed, long and slender; they are used for basting, hand-shirring and similar sewing tasks.

"**Crewels**" — medium length with long eyes that make threading easy, and they can carry several strands of thread as used for embroidery.

"**Calyx-eyed**"—open at the top for quick threading.

pressing equipment

Careful pressing is essential to a perfectly finished garment. You must use these tools of a professional if you are to press like a professional

Iron. A combination steam-dry is best. Make sure the temperature control indicates synthetic and wash-and-wear fabrics. Follow carefully its directions for use, especially how to keep the base clean and polished.

Ironing board. A board that is adjustable for various heights is preferred. It should be well padded, and the cover should be kept clean.

1 Sleeve board. A small ironing board that enables you to press small areas easily.

2 Tailor's board. This provides a number of differently shaped surfaces for pressing points, curves and various shaped contours and surfaces. It is made of hardwood, and can be used with or without a padded cover designed for it.

3 Tailor's ham. A firm, rounded cushion for pressing areas that need shaping such as curved darts or seams at shoulder, bust or hip line.

4 Velvet or needle board. A length of canvas, covered with fine, upright wires which is used for pressing nap and pile fabrics. The pile side of the fabric is pressed over the wire side of the board preventing it from matting or flattening

5 Press cloths. These cloths are used to prevent fabrics from getting a "shine" which occurs when fabric comes into direct contact with a hot iron. **Cheesecloth** in grade 70 is recommended. Use it dampened if extra moisture is needed in addition to the vapor of the steam iron. **Drill cloth** is a firm, heavy cloth for protecting fabrics from iron-shine. **Wool press cloths** are used with steam to prevent flattening texture or nap of woolens. They are usually combined with drill cloth. **Steam iron cloth** is non-woven and designed especially for use with a steam iron

6 Seam roll. A narrow, cylindrical cushion used for pressing seams and small areas. It prevents ridges from forming on the outside of the garment when seams are pressed open.

7 Pounding block or tailor's clapper. This shaped length of wood is used to pound and flatten seams and faced edges as they are steamed.

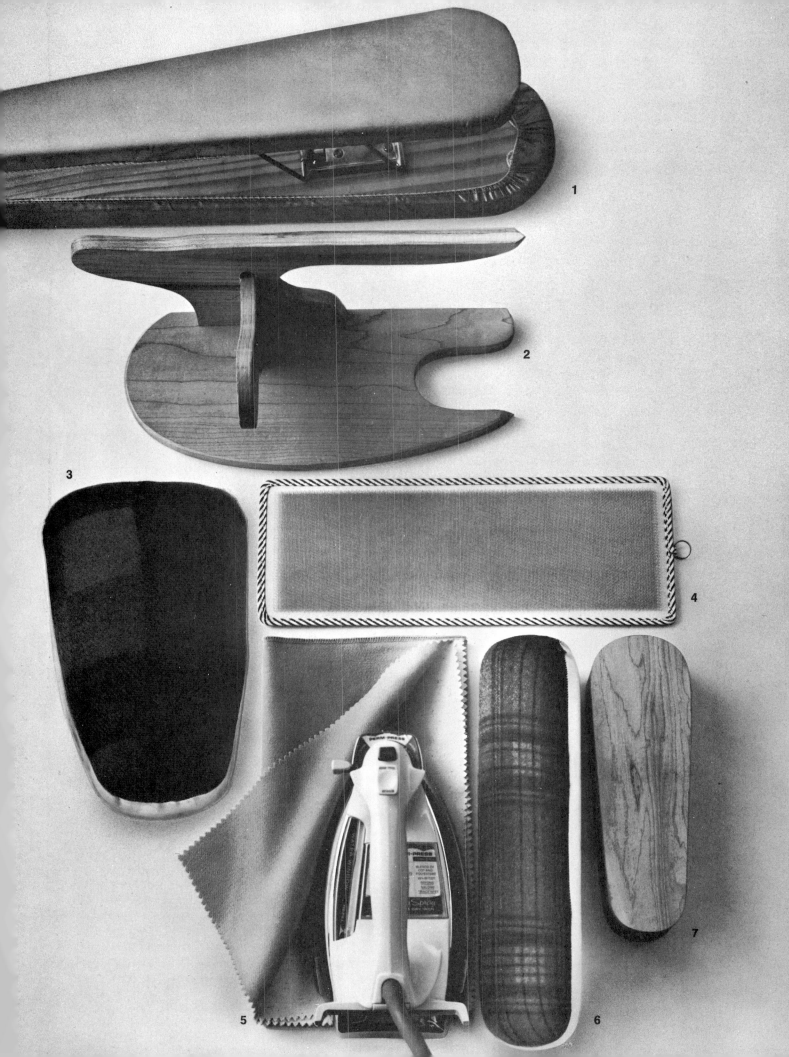

2 picking a proper pattern

Obviously you want to learn how to sew your own clothes so, without any further to-do, let's take the first important step toward that goal, the selection of your pattern.

Your pattern envelope contains much more than a tissue paper pattern. Fashion design, good taste, construction know-how and expertise in every phase of fashion are right there at your fingertips. How well you utilize this wealth of information for your own best advantage depends, first of all, on picking the proper pattern. Carefully analyze the charts and information in this chapter before making a final decision on just which figure type and pattern size you are. Because pattern size and figure type determine the fit of a garment, using the correct size eliminates much pattern adjustment and garment alteration.

You have such a wide range of choices in patterns, styles and fabrics that you are truly your own custom designer. Each garment you make should enhance your figure, suit your personality and reflect the originality of your creative efforts.

what figure type are you?

From observing a group of women or girls, you can see that the feminine figure varies greatly in shape. As a result, patterns are grouped under nine figure types according to height and proportion. Although they seem to do so, most of the figure types do not refer to age groups. However, the Young Junior/Teen and the Junior Petite are designed to be fashionwise for that age group. Ready-to-wear fashions are similarly grouped according to figure type, and the type you wear in ready-to-wear clothing may be right for you in a pattern, too.

Determining Your Figure Type
Your figure type is based on two measurements — your height and your back waist length. In addition to knowing these measurements before you can choose your type, you must analyze your own body proportions and shape; then compare your figure with the descriptions and illustrations of the figure types on the right. Observe the profile of your body silhouette in a mirror and decide which type you are most like before you choose a pattern size.

If you are unsure of your figure type, you can pretest one or more types by using basic patterns (see Chapter 13).

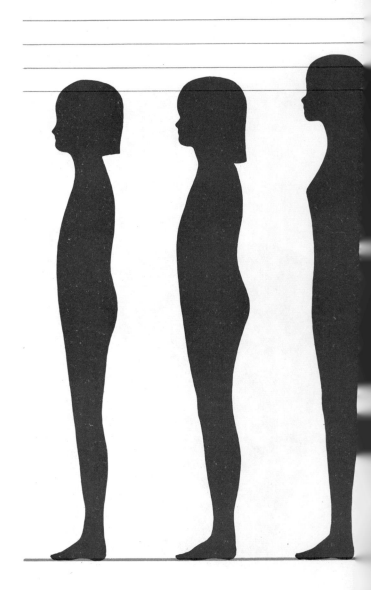

Girl (from 4'2" to 5'1") is the smallest of the nine figure types. Because the bustline is not defined on this just-developing figure, no underarm dart is needed in the dress bodice.

Chubbie (from 4'2" to 5'1") is the growing girl who weighs more than the average for her age and height. Girl and Chubbie patterns are the same height in comparable sizes.

Young Junior/T (about 5'1" to designates the veloping teen pre-teen figure w has a very sr high bust wi waist larger in portion to the

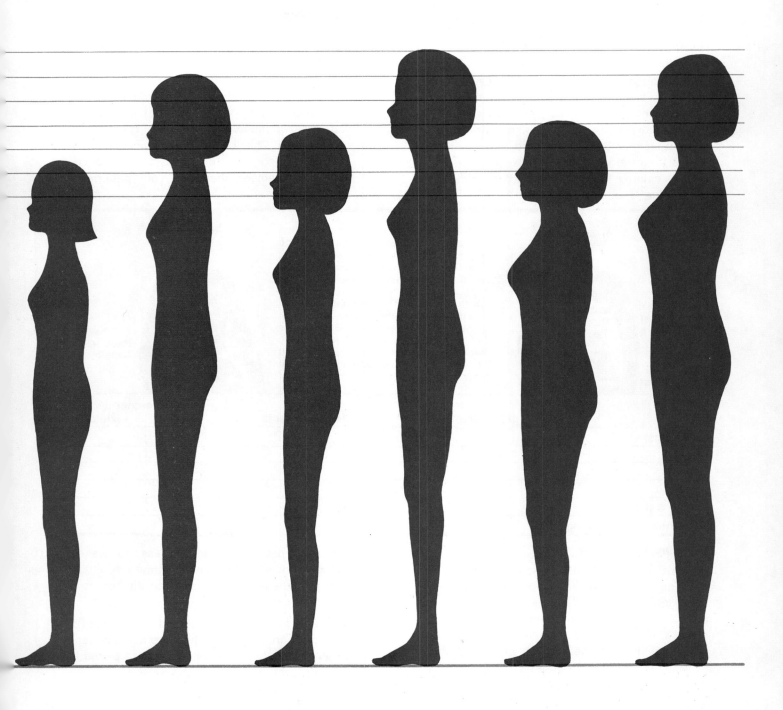

ior Petite (about
o 5′1″) is a short,
l-developed fig-
with small body
ucture and a
rter waist length
n any other type.

Junior (about 5′4″ to
5′5″) is a well-devel-
oped figure slightly
shorter than a Miss
in waist length and
in over-all height.

Miss Petite (about
5′2″ to 5′3″) is a
shorter figure than a
Miss with a shorter
waist length than
the comparable Miss
size, but longer than
the corresponding
Junior Petite.

Miss (about 5′5″ to
5′8″) is well-propor-
tioned, well devel-
oped in all body
areas, and is the
tallest of all figure
types. This type can
be called the "aver-
age" figure.

Half-Size (about 5′2″
to 5′3″) is a fully-
developed shorter
figure with narrower
shoulders than the
Miss. The waist is
larger in proportion
to the bust than in
the other mature fig-
ure types.

Woman (about 5′5″
to 5′6″) is a larger,
more mature figure
of about the same
height as a Miss.
The back waist
length is longer be-
cause the back is
fuller, and all meas-
urements are larger
proportionately.

what size are you?

Pattern sizes are determined by horizontal body measurements. They are not always the same as ready-to-wear sizes because there is little consistency in ready-to-wear. New Sizing was developed for patterns by the Pattern Fashion Industry to help you get a better fit and to correspond more closely to standard ready-to-wear sizes, but a difference still remains. You must determine your correct pattern size by comparing your own body measurements to the standard body measurements from the chart on the next page or in the pattern catalog. Pattern sizes are always the same from issue to issue.

Taking Body Measurements

Body measurements are the actual measurements of your body. They are not the measurements of the pattern. Have someone help you take your body measurements over a slip and the foundations that you will wear with your garments. Measure the body at the points designated by holding the tape measure comfortably snug but not tight. Record your measurements and the date taken on the chart below. Check your measurements periodically and record any changes in order to keep your measurement chart and your pattern size up-to-date.

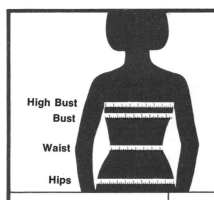

High Bust: Directly under the arms, then straight across the back bringing tape above the fullest part of the bust.
Bust: Across the fullest part of the bust.
Waist: Around the natural waistline.
Hips: Around the fullest part of the body which is usually 9″ below natural waistline for Misses, Women's and Juniors; 7″ below for Miss Petite. Half-Size, Junior Petite and Young Junior/Teen figures.
Back waist Length: From the prominent bone at the back neck base to the natural waistline.

	Your Measurements	Pattern Measurements	Difference Plus	Minus
High Bust				
Bust				
Waist				
Hip				
Back Waist Length				
Finished Garment Length				

Selecting Your Pattern Size

Now you are ready to determine your pattern size by using your own measurement chart. If you are going to make a dress, blouse, suit or coat select the size that has the bust measurement nearest to yours. Compare your bust measurement with the high bust measurement on the chart. In most cases, there should be about a 2″ difference. If there is a difference appreciably more than 2″ between your high bust measurement and your bust measurement this means your bust is full in relation to your frame and you may select the pattern size according to the high bust measurement. Alter it to fit the bust measurement if necessary. Selecting the pattern according to the high bust measurement will give you a better fit through the chest, neckline, shoulders and armholes, areas that are more difficult to alter than the bustline.

Suit jacket patterns include the ease for wearing the jacket over a lining and a lightweight blouse. Coat patterns include the ease for the coat to be worn over a dress.

Skirt and pants patterns should be selected by waist measurement. If the hips are much larger in proportion to the waist, select the size by the hip measurement, and alter at the waist.

If the pattern includes more than one type of garment, such as a wardrobe pattern or a blouse and pants pattern, select your pattern by bust measurement. If your bust and hip measurements require two different sizes, make adjustments in the hip area.

If your measurements should fall between two sizes, select the smaller size if you are small-boned, or pick the larger size if you are large-boned or full-bodied.

To Alter Or Not To Alter

Determine whether any pattern alterations are necessary by comparing your body measurements to the standard body measurements, not by measuring the pattern pieces. By comparing these measurements you will maintain the necessary pattern ease, and will avoid having to make alterations on the finished garment.

Complete the chart on the opposite page by filling in the standard body measurements for the pattern size you have selected. Include your personal finished garment length and the finished garment length found on the back of the pattern envelope. Compare the two sets of measurements, and note any differences in the plus or minus columns. This indicates where alterations must be made.

Misses'

Size	6	8	10	12	14	16	18	20
Bust	$30^1/_2$	$31^1/_2$	$32^1/_2$	34	36	38	40	42
Waist	22	23	24	$25^1/_2$	27	29	31	33
Hip	$32^1/_2$	$33^1/_2$	$34^1/_2$	36	38	40	42	44
Back Waist Length	$15^1/_2$	$15^3/_4$	16	$16^1/_4$	$16^1/_2$	$16^3/_4$	17	$17^1/_4$

Miss Petite

Size	6mp	8mp	10mp	12mp	14mp	16mp
Bust	$30^1/_2$	$31^1/_2$	$32^1/_2$	34	36	38
Waist	$22^1/_2$	$23^1/_2$	$24^1/_2$	26	$27^1/_2$	$29^1/_2$
Hip	$32^1/_2$	$33^1/_2$	$34^1/_2$	36	38	40
Back Waist Length	$14^1/_2$	$14^3/_4$	15	$15^1/_4$	$15^1/_2$	$15^3/_4$

Junior

Size	5	7	9	11	13	15
Bust	30	31	32	33½	35	37
Waist	21½	22½	23½	24½	26	28
Hip	32	33	34	35½	37	39
Back Waist Length	15	15¼	15½	15¾	16	16¼

Junior Petite

Size	3JP	5JP	7JP	9JP	11JP	13JP
Bust	$30^1/_2$	31	32	33	34	35
Waist	22	$22^1/_2$	$23^1/_2$	$24^1/_2$	$25^1/_2$	$26^1/_2$
Hip	$31^1/_2$	32	33	34	35	36
Back Waist Length	14	$14^1/_4$	$14^1/_2$	$14^3/_4$	15	$15^1/_4$

Women's

Size	38	40	42	44	46	48	50
Bust	42	44	46	48	50	52	54
Waist	34	36	38	$40^1/_2$	43	$45^1/_2$	48
Hip	44	46	48	50	52	54	56
Back Waist Length	$17^1/_4$	$17^3/_8$	$17^1/_2$	$17^5/_8$	$17^3/_4$	$17^7/_8$	18

Half-Size

Size	$10^1/_2$	$12^1/_2$	$14^1/_2$	$16^1/_2$	$18^1/_2$	$20^1/_2$	$22^1/_2$	$24^1/_2$
Bust	33	35	37	39	41	43	45	47
Waist	26	28	30	32	34	$36^1/_2$	39	$41^1/_2$
Hip	35	37	39	41	43	$45^1/_2$	48	$50^1/_2$
Back Waist Length	15	$15^1/_4$	$15^1/_2$	$15^3/_4$	$15^7/_8$	16	$16^1/_8$	$16^1/_4$

Boys / Teen-Boys

Size	7	8	10	12	14	16	18	20
Chest	26	27	28	30	32	$33^1/_2$	35	$36^1/_2$
Waist	23	24	25	26	27	28	29	30
Hip (Seat)	27	28	$29^1/_2$	31	$32^1/_2$	34	$35^1/_2$	37
Neck	$11^3/_4$	12	$12^1/_2$	13	$13^1/_2$	14	$14^1/_2$	15
Height	48	50	54	58	61	64	66	68

NOTE: For Toddler and Little Boys (1 to 6) — See Toddler and Children's charts.

Young Junior/Teen

Size	5/6	7/8	9/10	11/12	13/14	15/16
Bust	28	29	$30^1/_2$	32	$33^1/_2$	35
Waist	22	23	24	25	26	27
Hip	31	32	$33^1/_2$	35	$36^1/_2$	38
Back Waist Length	$13^1/_2$	14	$14^1/_2$	15	$15^3/_8$	$15^3/_4$

Girls'

Size	7	8	10	12	14
Breast	26	27	$28^1/_2$	30	32
Waist	23	$23^1/_2$	$24^1/_2$	$25^1/_2$	$26^1/_2$
Hip	27	28	30	32	34
Back Waist Length	$11^1/_2$	12	$12^3/_4$	$13^1/_2$	$14^1/_4$
Approx. Heights	50"	52"	56"	$58^1/_2$"	61"

Chubbie

Size	8½c	10½c	12½c	14½c
Breast	30	$31^1/_2$	33	$34^1/_2$
Waist	28	29	30	31
Hip	33	$34^1/_2$	36	$37^1/_2$
Back Waist Length	12	$12^3/_4$	$13^1/_2$	$14^1/_4$
Approx. Heights	52"	56"	$58^1/_2$"	61"

Dress Lengths from Back Neck Base to Lower Edge

Size	½	1	2	3	4	5	6	6X
Child		17"	18"	19"	20"	21"	23"	25"
Toddler	14"	15"	16"	17"	18"			

Toddlers'

Size	½	1	2	3	4
Breast	19	20	21	22	23
Waist	19	$19^1/_2$	20	$20^1/_2$	21

Children's

Size	1	2	3	4	5	6	6X
Breast	20	21	22	23	24	25	25½
Waist	19½	20	20½	21	21½	22	22½
Hip			24	25	26	26½	
Back Waist Length	8¼	8½	9	9½	10	10½	10¾
Approx. Heights	31"	34"	37"	40"	43"	46"	48"

Men

Size	34	36	38	40	42	44	46	48
Chest	34	36	38	40	42	44	46	48
Waist	28	30	32	34	36	39	42	44
Hip (Seat)	35	37	39	41	43	45	47	49
Neck	14	$14^1/_2$	15	$15^1/_2$	16	$16^1/_2$	17	$17^1/_2$
Sleeve Length	32	32	33	33	34	34	35	35

NOTE: Height is approximately 5'10"

bonus basic patterns

If you are unsure of pattern size or puzzled about alterations, pre-test by making and fitting a garment using one of Simplicity's Bonus Basic Patterns, the waistline dress or the A-line dress, both with set-in sleeves. The Bonus Basic should be made in a firmly woven, lightweight cotton such as gingham. The checked pattern of the fabric makes it easy to see the fabric grain, and is helpful for layout, construction and fitting. Your completed Bonus Basic can be used as a guide for the selection and alteration of all your patterns.

pattern ease

No garment fits as snugly as the tape measure. In addition to standard body measurements, patterns include ease or tolerance which is the extra number of inches added to the pattern to insure wearing comfort. Without ease included, garments would be tight, uncomfortable and unattractive.

Some patterns also include design ease in addition to standard ease. Design ease is added to give various fashion effects, and varies from year to year according to the latest fashion trends. In a basic sheath dress with set-in sleeves the standard ease in a Simplicity pattern is as follows:

Bust: About $2^5/_8$" in Girls' patterns.
About $3^1/_4$" in Misses', Junior and Miss Petite.
About 3" in Junior Petite and Young Junior/Teen.
About 4" in Chubbie patterns.
About $4^1/_4$" in Half-Size patterns.
About $4^3/_4$" in Women's patterns.

Waist: About $1^1/_2$" in Misses', Junior, Miss Petite, Women's and Half-Size patterns.
About 1" in all other pattern types.

Hips: About 2" in Young Junior/Teen patterns.
About $2^1/_2$" in Misses', Junior, Miss Petite, Half-Size, Junior Petite and Girls' patterns.
About 3" in Women's patterns.
About 4" in Chubbie patterns.

Backwaist Length: About $1/_8$" in Junior Petite, Young Junior/Teen, Girls' and Chubbie patterns.
About $1/_4$" for Misses', Junior, Miss Petite, Half-Size and Women's patterns.

maternity patterns

Maternity patterns are selected in the same size that you would select for a regular dress. The pattern is designed to include the maternity ease that will be needed.

toddlers' and children's patterns

Toddler patterns are designed for a figure that is taller than a baby but shorter than a child. They have the same breast and waist measurements as do Children's patterns in the same size, but in Toddler patterns the bodice is about 1" shorter and the shoulders about $1/_2$" narrower than in Children's.

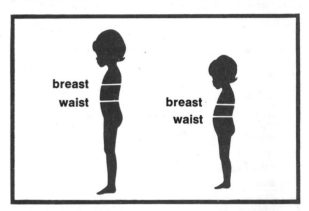

Keep in mind that the sizes of these pattern types are based on body measurements, not on age. There can be a great variation in height and girth among children of the same age.

men's and boys' patterns

Determine pattern size for a man or boy by taking the measurements as illustrated.

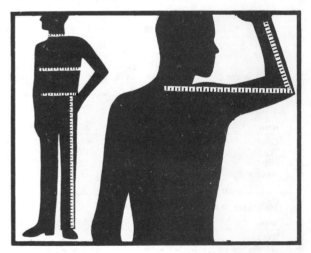

For a coat or jacket. Measure around the fullest part of the chest.
For shirts. Measure around the neck and add $1/_2$" for the neckband size.
For trousers. Measure around the waist and from the waist down the outside leg seam to get the outer leg measurement.
For sleeves. Measure from the back neck base, along the shoulder and down to the wrist.

3 what's in the pattern for you?

The fashion pattern is now in your hands. Study the entire package carefully before you do anything else. You will find that the illustrations are clearly coordinated with the instructions to help you with each step. It is your blueprint for successful sewing.

All three elements of the package — the envelope, the Cutting and Sewing Direction Sheet and the tissue pattern pieces — have been coordinated to make your sewing easy and accurate. Don't overlook a thing! The rewards are worth your efforts as you will soon see in the mirror.

the envelope front

The sketches and photographs show up-to-the-minute fashion trends by illustrating several views in a range of fabrics. A beginner should make one view exactly as illustrated. When you have more experience, you will learn how to combine features of several views.

Study the fabrics illustrated on the front, and the suggested fabrics on the back of the envelope. The illustrations indicate fabric characteristics of weight, texture and design suitable for the style so as to achieve the effect for which the dress designer aimed.

If a style is illustrated in a plaid or stripe, it means that the pattern definitely is suitable for these fabrics. If it is not illustrated in a plaid or stripe, check the box above the yardage block on the back of the envelope. This box lists any fabrics that would be unsuitable for the design.

Fabrics vary greatly in their characteristics. For example, linens, gabardines and poplins give a neat, tailored look when combined with straight line designs. A soft, feminine look is achieved when a rounded, flowing design is combined with a sheer or soft fabric. Study the sketches and develop a feel for the weight, body and draping characteristics of fabrics; it will aid greatly in the selection of your fabrics.

Identification information consisting of the pattern number, size, figure type and special labels such as "Jiffy" or "How to Sew" is included on the envelope front. Check to be sure that you have the correct pattern size and type.

the envelope back

Advice on Special Fabrics

If you intend to buy a nap, pile, plaid, striped or one-way design fabric, read the advice on special fabrics found in the box in the upper right corner. This box informs you if extra fabric is required and which fabrics are unsuitable for the design.

Standard Body Measurements

These are the measurements on which the patterns are sized. They are not the measurements of the pattern. They are always shown on the back of the envelope for easy reference.

The Number of Pattern Pieces

This is shown directly under the style number in the upper left corner. Usually the patterns with fewer pieces are easier and faster to sew.

Pattern Pieces

You will find them illustrated in scale against a colored background for easy identification.

Back Views

These line drawings illustrate details not easily visible in the fashion sketches or photographs.

The Yardage Chart

This chart shows the amount of fabric needed for the different views, fabric widths and pattern sizes. Yardages for lining, interfacing and trimmings (if any) are also listed on the chart.

Garment Description

Here you will find additional information on construction and design details.

Suggested Fabrics

A list of suggested fabrics is given for each style to help you in selecting the right fabric.

Sewing Notions

Notions are listed in the size and quantity needed. Buy them along with your fabric to save time and insure a close color match.

Finished Garment Measurements

These measurements appear below the yardage chart and include width of lower edge, finished back length, etc. Use them as a guide to help you determine pattern alterations for your figure.

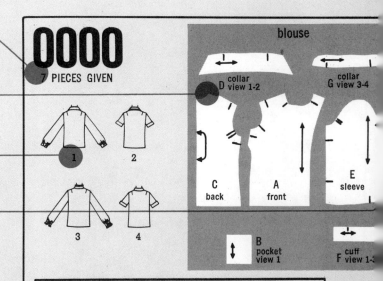

0000
7 PIECES GIVEN

blouse

1   2   3   4

D collar view 1-2   G collar view 3-4

C back   A front   E sleeve

B pocket view 1   F cuff view 1-

A PATTERN FROM SIMPLICITY'S "HOW-TO-SEW" SERIES

MISSES' BLOUSES WITH TWO COLLAR INTEREST: (INCLUDING TISSUE L CHART . . . "How to attach a stand-up collar.") The blouses have high neckline, front button closing and set-in sleeves. V. 1 and 2 have shir collar and optional top-stitching. V. 3 and 4 have "stand-up" collar. V. 1 have long sleeves gathered to buttoned cuffs. V. 2 and 4 have short s with turn back cuffs. V. 1 has button trimmed patch pockets. V. 2 ha trasting collar. V. 3 has lace edging trim.

Suggested fabric types — Cottons and blends; pique, gingham. Linen. Silks, syn and blends; poplin, cotton sateen, challis, chambray, crepe. V. 1 also in soft and blends; wool crepe, wool challis, printed woolens, wool jersey. V. 2 also i lengthwise stripes.

Sewing notions — Thread. View 1: Eight ½" buttons. View 2 and 4: Four ½" b View 3: Six ½" buttons.

How Much Fabric to Buy

Mark the view you are using. **2**
Mark your size. **10**
Mark the width of the fabric you intend to buy. **44″**
Draw a line across from the fabric width and a line down from your size.
Where the two lines cross you will find the yardage of the fabric needed. **1½**
Also note the lining, interfacing, or trimming yardage for your view. **⅝**

Notice the words "with nap" and "without nap" on the chart. They refer to any nap, pile or one-way fabric, all of which require the pattern pieces to be laid facing in the same direction and so require extra yardage. If a "with nap" yardage is not listed, determine the extra yardage needed by doing a trial layout. As a rule you will need ⅜ to ¾ of a yard extra depending on fabric width.

Plaids and fabrics that require matching also need extra yardage. See page 168 for additional information on plaids.

If you are planning to buy a fabric in a width not listed on the chart, buy the amount shown for the width nearest to your fabric.

inside information

Cutting and Sewing Direction Sheet

Line drawings of the fashion views are shown on the front of this sheet. Each view, designated by a circular symbol, is shown with the number of pattern pieces to be used and the identifying letters for the pieces. When sorting the pattern pieces, refer to this information. View symbols are also printed on the pattern pieces. If a piece does not have a view symbol printed on it, use it for all the views.

General instructions on "how to use your Simplicity pattern" give tips on the following: Preparing your pattern for cutting including basic lengthening and shortening alterations, preparing your fabric for cutting including how to straighten fabric ends and uneven grain, general pattern markings, laying out, cutting your pattern, marking fabric including how to mark single and double layers, and sewing your garment including tips on how to pin, baste, stitch and press. More detailed information will be found throughout this book.

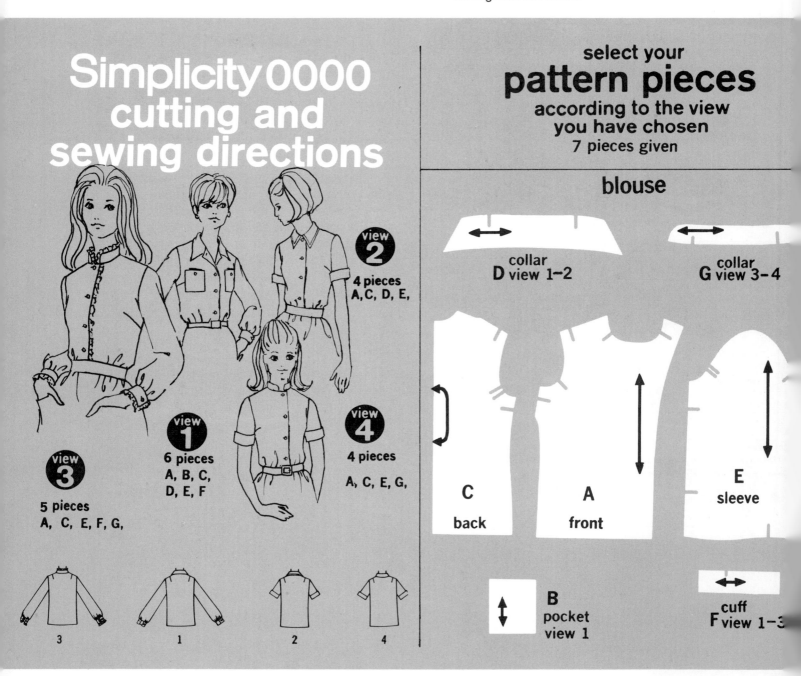

Cutting layouts are found on the bottom portion of the sheet. They show different pattern sizes on various fabric widths. Locate the diagram for your view, pattern size and fabric width. If you are using a nap, pile or one-way design fabric, be sure diagram is marked "with nap". Circle your diagram for easy identification and quick reference for future use.

The patterns themselves are shown as white shapes. The black area represents the fabric. If a pattern piece is shown as a white outline on the fabric, it means that the piece is cut twice. Reverse it for the second cutting. When pattern pieces extend beyond the fold of the fabric, cut out all pieces except the pieces that extend; then open out the fabric and on a single thickness, cut extending pieces on right side of the fabric in the position shown.

Read any special notes on cutting in this section.

They tell you when to cut fabric bias strips, interfacings and other pieces such as belt strips for which a pattern is not included.

Sewing directions are found on the reverse side of the sheet. These step-by-step directions illustrate the Unit System of Sewing, an easily followed method which greatly simplifies garment construction. This system is discussed fully on page 36.

Extra tissue charts are included in the "How-to-Sew" patterns. The "How-to-Sew" charts give more detailed instructions on basic techniques such as setting-in a sleeve or applying a neckline facing. Special finishing and sewing techniques such as the making of bound buttonholes or hand sewing a zipper are explained in the "Designer Touch" Leaflets included in the "Designer Fashion" patterns. For additional information on any phase of garment construction refer to other chapters of this book.

cutting layouts

Black area represents fabric

GENERAL NOTE: When pattern pieces extend beyond fold of fabric, cut out all pieces except pieces that extend; then open out fabric and on single thickness, cut extending pieces on right side of fabric in position shown.

blouse

5" 36" fabric
without nap
sizes 6, 8, 10, 12

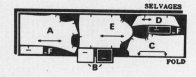

5" 36" fabric
without nap
sizes 14 16, 18

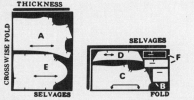

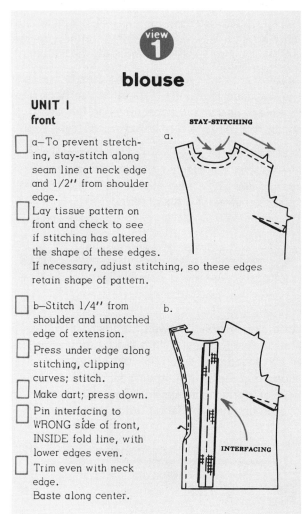

view 1
blouse

UNIT I
front

☐ a—To prevent stretching, stay-stitch along seam line at neck edge and 1/2" from shoulder edge.

☐ Lay tissue pattern on front and check to see if stitching has altered the shape of these edges. If necessary, adjust stitching, so these edges retain shape of pattern.

☐ b—Stitch 1/4" from shoulder and unnotched edge of extension.

☐ Press under edge along stitching, clipping curves; stitch.

☐ Make dart; press down.

☐ Pin interfacing to WRONG side of front, INSIDE fold line, with lower edges even.

☐ Trim even with neck edge.
Baste along center.

STAY-STITCHING

INTERFACING

reading the pattern

Patterns have a special language of their own for their markings. Look over the pieces to familiarize yourself with this language before you use the pattern because the markings are there to help you with the cutting, marking and sewing.

Identification markings are printed on each pattern piece and include the style number, size, identification letter and view number. The name of the piece and whether it is front or back are also shown. Look for this information when you are sorting pattern pieces.

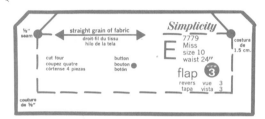

"Lengthen or shorten here" along with a double line is printed on those pattern pieces which may require this alteration. Information on how to use this lengthening or shortening line is on page 132.

Center front and center back are clearly marked. The waistline is usually marked on the back pattern piece and in some instances on the front. On pants, this is generally noted at the side seam.

Grainline markings are arrowhead symbols with instructions for placing the pattern on grain. A straight line with arrowheads at each end indicates "place on straight grain of fabric".

A bracketed grainline with the instruction "place line on fold" indicates that the pattern edge has to be placed exactly on the fold of the fabric that is on grain. Refer to Chapter 5 for detailed instructions on using these markings, and refer to Chapter 4 for information on fabric grain.

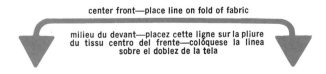

Cutting lines are the heavy outlines of the pattern. A cutting line may sometimes be shown within the pattern to designate the cutting of an alternate, shorter view, a lower neckline, a facing or a lining from the same piece. Special cutting instructions will be shown on the pattern if this should occur. Instructions will also indicate when a piece is to be cut more than twice.

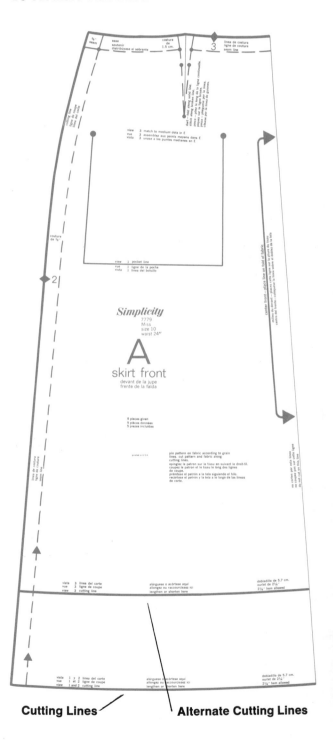

Cutting Lines / **Alternate Cutting Lines**

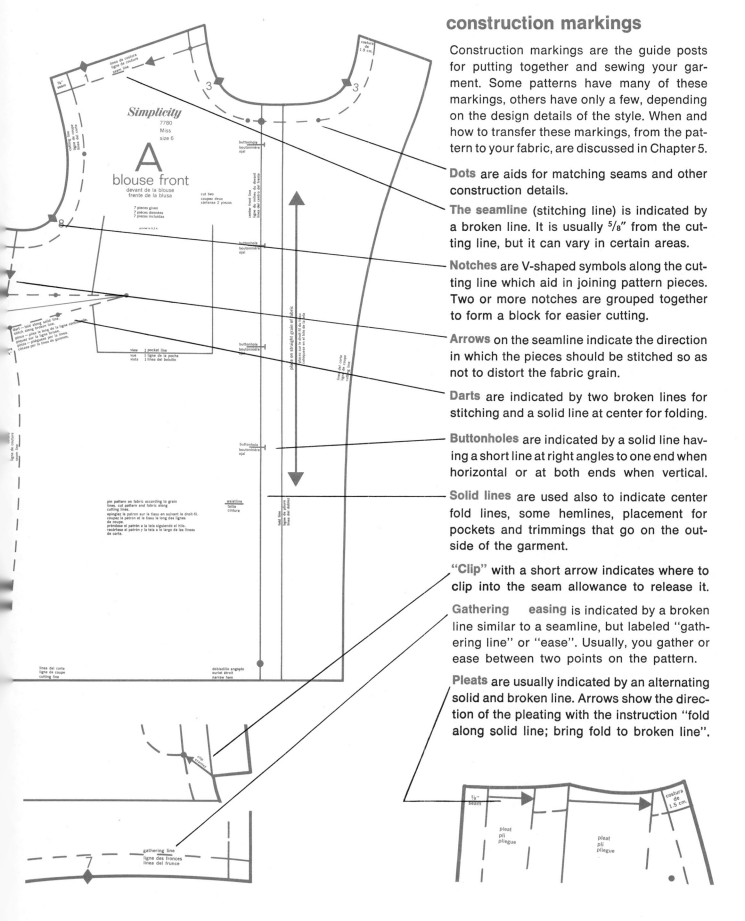

construction markings

Construction markings are the guide posts for putting together and sewing your garment. Some patterns have many of these markings, others have only a few, depending on the design details of the style. When and how to transfer these markings, from the pattern to your fabric, are discussed in Chapter 5.

Dots are aids for matching seams and other construction details.

The seamline (stitching line) is indicated by a broken line. It is usually $5/8''$ from the cutting line, but it can vary in certain areas.

Notches are V-shaped symbols along the cutting line which aid in joining pattern pieces. Two or more notches are grouped together to form a block for easier cutting.

Arrows on the seamline indicate the direction in which the pieces should be stitched so as not to distort the fabric grain.

Darts are indicated by two broken lines for stitching and a solid line at center for folding.

Buttonholes are indicated by a solid line having a short line at right angles to one end when horizontal or at both ends when vertical.

Solid lines are used also to indicate center fold lines, some hemlines, placement for pockets and trimmings that go on the outside of the garment.

"Clip" with a short arrow indicates where to clip into the seam allowance to release it.

Gathering   easing is indicated by a broken line similar to a seamline, but labeled "gathering line" or "ease". Usually, you gather or ease between two points on the pattern.

Pleats are usually indicated by an alternating solid and broken line. Arrows show the direction of the pleating with the instruction "fold along solid line; bring fold to broken line".

4 bias? on grain? we'll explain!

There are some very important things you'll need to know about fabrics before you make that first cut with the shears. If the fit, hang and appearance of your finished fashion are to give you a feeling of pride and satisfaction, it will be largely the result of proper preparation and handling of the fabric. So, read on and we'll tell you all about it.

fabric grain

Woven fabric is composed of two sets of yarns (threads) that run at right angles to each other. The lengthwise yarn (warp) runs vertically, and is called the lengthwise grain. The selvage is the finished lengthwise edge on each side of the fabric. The crosswise yarn (weft or filling) runs horizontally from selvage to selvage, and is called the crosswise grain.

Bias refers to any diagonal on the fabric. True bias is the diagonal edge formed when the fabric is folded so that the crosswise threads run in the same direction as the lengthwise threads. Fabric cut on the true bias has the maximum "give". Sometimes garments are cut on the bias for reasons of design, but generally they are cut on the lengthwise grain because it is the strongest and most stable grain.

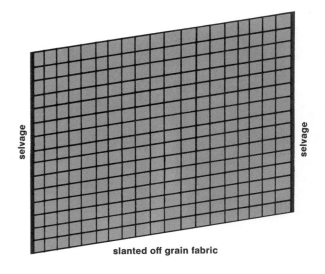

slanted off grain fabric

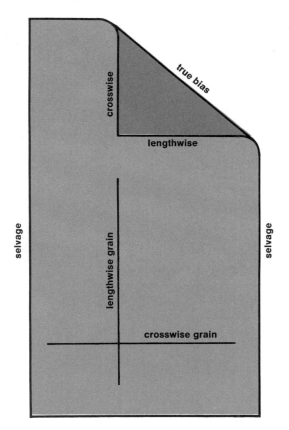

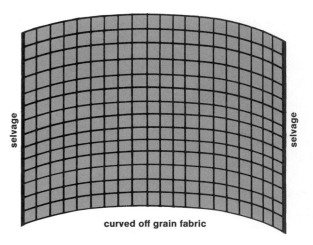

curved off grain fabric

A fabric is on grain when the lengthwise and crosswise threads run exactly at right angles to each other. When the two sets of yarn do not run at right angles to each other, or the crosswise yarn curves toward fabric's center, the fabric is off grain.

Garments which are cut correctly on grain hang well and retain their shape. Fabric grain is used as a guide in the Unit System of Sewing which is presented throughout this book. You will learn to cut, sew, press and fit in relation to grain.

Making Fabrics Thread Perfect

A fabric is thread perfect when a single thread runs across the cut or torn edge from selvage to selvage. Check to see whether your fabric is straight on both crosswise ends because thread perfect ends are basic for a grain perfect fabric. There are several ways to make a fabric thread perfect and they are shown here in the order in which they are most commonly used.

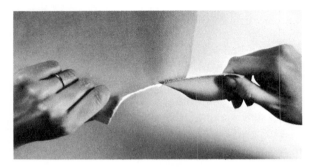

Tearing. If the fabric was not torn off the bolt at the time of purchase, check to see if it will tear. About an inch from the cut end clip one selvage with scissors, tear firmly and quickly to second selvage, then cut selvage. If fabric tears successfully, do the other end. The ends of evenly woven cotton and synthetics, some wools and silks, can be straightened by tearing. Never tear the crosswise edges of linen fabrics.

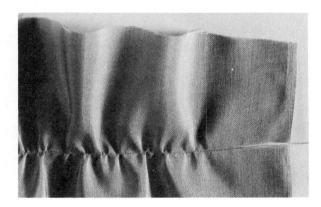

Drawn thread. Clip one selvage with scissors. Pick out one or two crosswise threads with a pin. Grasp thread with fingers and pull gently, slipping fabric along thread with other hand. Cut along the pulled thread as far as you can see it clearly. If the thread breaks, cut along line it has made until you can again pick up the end. Continue to pull and cut until reaching the opposite selvage. The construction of some fabrics makes it possible to draw a thread completely across the fabric before you start to cut.

Cutting along a thread. When a fabric has a prominent thread or rib or a woven pattern such as a plaid or check, it can be used as a guide for cutting from selvage to selvage.

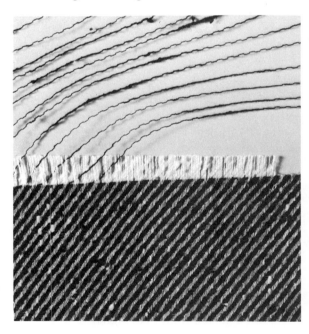

Pile or napped fabrics are also cut on a thread. On the crosswise edge unravel the threads until one thread can be drawn off the entire width. Cut off the uneven fringed edge.

Bonded and permanent press fabrics do not have to be thread perfect because the grain is locked into position during their processing, and cannot be straightened.

Evaluating Fabric Grain

After making your fabric thread perfect it is easy for you to evaluate the grain. Fold the fabric in half, lengthwise, and try to line up the ends with a table corner or the markings on a cutting board. If the fabric is on grain, the crosswise edges form a right angle with the selvages.

With an off-grain fabric, such as the one in the above photograph, the edges form a slanted angle.

Off-Grain Fabrics

There are many reasons which cause a fabric to be pulled off grain. If the fabric is rolled onto a bolt with uneven tension, or subjected to irregular pressures during printing and finishing, the finished product will be off grain.

There are a number of durable resin or stabilizing finshes which, when applied to fabrics during manufacture, give them many desirable characteristics. Wrinkle and stain resistance, wash-and-wear features, and water repellancy are a few of these benefits. Because some of these finishes are of a permanent nature they lock the fabric grain in place. Off-grain fabrics so treated are not a good choice for the beginner because the grain cannot be made thread perfect.

preparing fabrics for cutting

After making the crosswise ends of your fabric thread perfect, and having evaluated the grain, refer to the appropriate information below. It will guide you in the further preparation of the fabric.

Silk Fabric

(A) It does not need to be shrunk, and is ready for cutting when purchased.

(B) If silk fabric is off grain, straighten it by pressing with the steam iron.

Synthetic Fabrics

Rayon, acetate, triacetate, acrylic, nylon, polyester and many others.

(A) Most of these fabrics will not need shrinking. Check the manufacturer's label, or the end of the bolt to see if the fabric has been preshrunk, and for information on finishes. If the fabric does need to be shrunk, follow the method for cotton and linens.

(B) If these fabrics are off grain, but are labeled preshrunk, they can be straightened by pressing unless they have one of the permanent finishes that has been described previously.

(C) If straightening and shrinking are needed on a fabric blend containing one of the synthetic fibers and a larger percentage of wool, follow processing method for straightening and shrinking woolens.

Cotton and Linen Fabrics

(A) Good quality cottons and linens will be preshrunk, but check the manufacturer's label to be sure. If they need shrinking, follow method on the next page.

(B) If cotton or linens are found to be off grain, but are labeled preshrunk, try to straighten them by pressing unless they have a permanent finish. If you attempt to straighten by pressing and are unsuccessful, try the shrinking and straightening process described for cottons and linens p. 27.

Wool Fabrics

(A) On some woolens there is a finish which disappears with steam pressing, and it should be removed before cutting. To test your fabric for this finish press a corner using a damp cheesecloth. If the fabric surface then looks dull compared to the unpressed surface, or if it feels softer, shrink it to remove the finish entirely even though it may have been preshrunk and on grain. Follow the method described on page 28.

(B) If your fabric needs shrinking and/or straightening, follow the method on page 28.

processing methods

Straightening Fabric Grain By Pressing

If your fabric is preshrunk and not badly off grain, it can usually be straightened by pressing with the steam iron (except woolens). If it needs both shrinking and straightening, it can be done in one procedure as instructed later on.

Before pressing make ends thread perfect. Fold fabric in half lengthwise, right sides together. First, pin or baste selvages together, then the crosswise ends. If off grain, diagonal wrinkles and puckers will form as the doubled fabric is laid on a flat surface. The number of wrinkles will depend on how much the fabric is off grain.

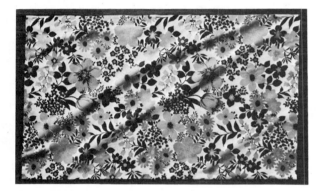

Dampen the underside of the folded fabric with a wet sponge. The steam iron will provide moisture on the topside. Press, moving the iron with the lengthwise grain. If the fabric is still off grain, it may help to press in the opposite direction, moving the iron on the crosswise grain. Avoid pressing on the center fold as this crease may be difficult to remove later.

Shrinking and Straightening

Linens or Cottons (or washable fabrics). Make the crosswise ends of your fabric thread perfect. Fold fabric in half lengthwise, right sides together. First, pin or baste selvages together, then the crosswise ends. Place pins about 6 inches apart, parallel and close to the edges.

Fold the length of fabric in accordian pleat folds about 8 inches wide. Place in warm water until thoroughly wet. Check wetness by looking between folds of the fabric.

Lift the fabric from the water. Remove excess water by pressing it out between your hands. Never wring the fabric. Excess water can also be removed by wrapping in a turkish towel. Place the fabric on a flat surface to dry, laying it on a sheet or a piece of plastic. Never hang it or drape it over a clothesline because it can stretch.

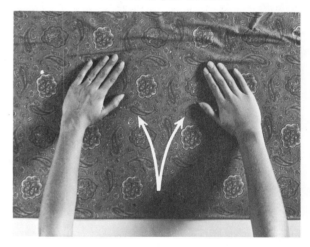

To straighten the grain, gently pull and smooth the fabric with your hands. It may be necessary to repeat the pulling during the drying time in order to keep the grain straight. When it is completely dry, press the fabric with a steam iron working on the lengthwise grain.

A cotton corduroy should be handled differently to avoid crushing the pile when wet. Make your fabric thread perfect, fold and soak it in water. Lift from water, and gently press it with the palms of your hands to remove excess moisture. Never wring it. Put the corduroy immediately in an automatic dryer. This helps to raise the pile, and as a rule no pressing is needed. If the corduroy garment is to be dry-cleaned only, and not washed, this special preparation is unnecessary, and the corduroy can be cut as purchased.

Woolens (or dry-cleanable fabrics). With this method of shrinking three things are accomplished at the same time: You straighten the grain, shrink and remove any surface finish.

Make the crosswise ends thread perfect by using one of the methods described previously. Leave the fabric folded in half lengthwise as purchased, right sides together. Keep edges even along selvages and crosswise ends, and then hand-baste the cut ends together.

Old sheets or any clean, absorbent cotton fabric are needed in which to wrap the fabric and keep it moist. Have enough cloths on hand to equal the length of your fabric, but they should be a few inches wider than the folded fabric.

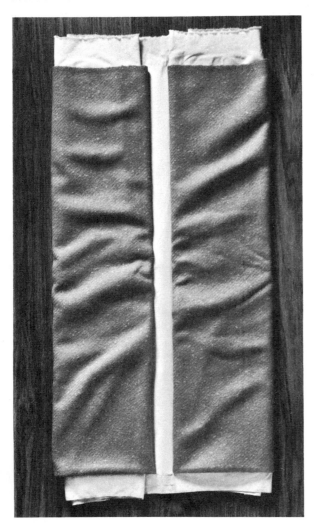

Wet the cloths thoroughly, and wring to remove excess moisture. Heavy fabrics need more moisture than lightweight ones. Lay the fabric on a flat surface, and place wet cloths over it. Start at one end by turning the lengths together in wide folds. Press down on the fabric as you fold it to push the moisture into it. From the opposite end fold fabric toward center in the same way. Cover the folded fabric with another wet cloth. Then wrap in plastic or place in a plastic bag to distribute moisture evenly throughout fabric. Allow to stand for two or three hours to be sure that the fabric has thoroughly absorbed the moisture.

Remove from plastic, and unfold the fabric on a flat surface to dry. Never hang it up! To straighten the grain pull and smooth gently with your hands. When surface is almost dry to the touch, turn fabric over to underside to help it shrink and dry evenly. Generally pressing will not be necessary, but if it should be needed, use a steam iron pressing on the lengthwise grain. If you are working with knits, follow the instructions on page 167.

Pressing Torn Edges

When fabric is torn, press the raw edges to restore a smooth grainline and flatten the rippled edges. The ends must be pressed even though the rest of the fabric is on grain.

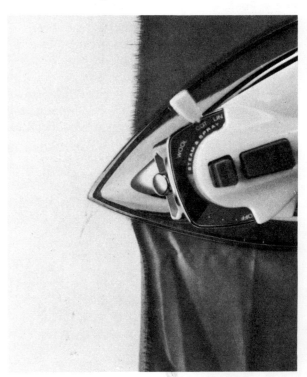

If the fabric has been torn in both directions, press lengthwise and crosswise edges. To keep the grain perfect, fold the fabric in half before you press.

5 from pattern to fabric to the unit system of sewing

So far, so good! Now we are going to show you how to make sense out of all those pieces of tissue in your pattern envelope; how to lay out and cut your pattern, and then how to transfer the pattern markings to your fabric. Speed will come with practice, but accuracy is what we are after at this stage. So be careful; take it easy. Remember that the sewing experts were once neophytes just like you, and now they are writing sewing books!

cutting

Begin by removing all the pattern pieces from the envelope, and select the ones for the view you are going to make. Put the extra pieces back into the envelope to avoid confusion. If small pattern pieces are grouped together on one tissue, cut them apart leaving a margin around them.

Tissue margins are left on all pattern pieces except when you are working with very bulky or slippery fabric. If you are going to work with one of these fabrics, cut the margins off before placing the pattern on the fabric because with these fabrics it is easier to cut along the edge of the tissue.

Use a warm, dry iron to press the wrinkles from your pattern pieces. Never use steam; it causes the tissue to shrink and pucker.

Press your fabric if it has noticeable creases or folds from being stored. Make sure that the center fold will press out by pressing a section of the fold with a steam iron, pressing on the crosswise grain. On a few fabrics, such as double knits and bondeds, the fold may not press out. If this is the case, refold the fabric in a way which will avoid the permanent fold when you are laying out the pattern for cutting.

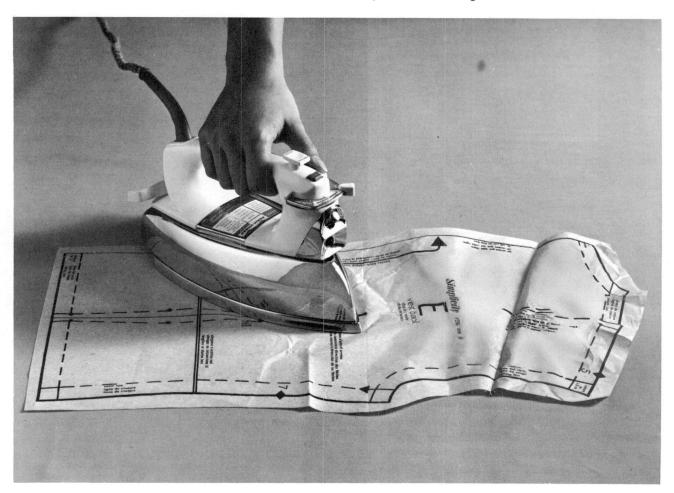

Folding the Fabric

Circle the cutting layout on the Cutting and Sewing Direction Sheet. Study the layout carefully before folding your fabric.

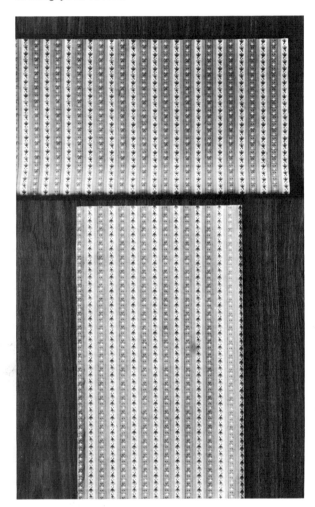

Fabric is usually folded in half on the lengthwise grain with the selvage edges meeting and right sides together. Follow the diagram exactly, however, because the layout may require a crosswise fold, a combination of crosswise and lengthwise folds or a single thickness of fabric. Regardless of its position, the fold should always be on grain, crosswise or lengthwise. The only exception to this rule occurs when the directions show a fold on the bias.

Do not let the fabric ends hang over the edge of the cutting surface while you are working. Keep the fabric folded on grain until you are ready to lay the pattern on it. A cutting board facilitates this phase of construction because of its large, slip-resistant surface area.

Pinning the Pattern

Place the pattern pieces on the fabric, following your cutting layout carefully. First pin pieces that are placed on the fold. Pin at 6 inch to 8 inch intervals along the folded edge and at right angles to it. Smooth out the pattern from the pinned line, and pin diagonally into the corners. Then pin the sides; set pins at right angles to the cutting edge, and points always toward pattern edge. Do not let the pinpoints extend past the cutting edge. Pick up only a few threads of the fabric with each pin so that the pattern will lie flat.

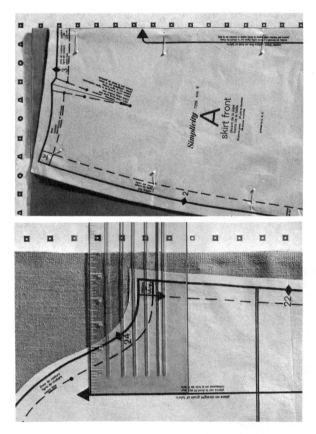

The remainder of the pieces must be placed on the fabric grain by measuring from the grainline symbol (indicated on each pattern piece by a line with arrowheads at both ends). Use the transparent ruler to measure from each end of the grainline to either the selvage or the fold of the fabric. The line must lie parallel to one of these edges. Pin near each end of the line, smooth out the pattern from the pinned line, and continue to pin as described above. Don't worry if the margins overlap; they will be cut away later. Pin all the pieces to the fabric before you cut, or check to see if they will all fit.

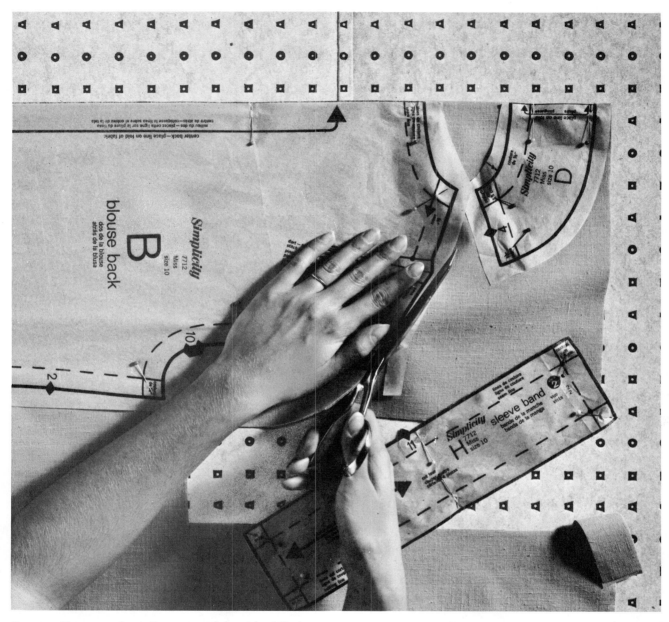

Easy cutting requires the use of bent-handled shears. Cut with long, firm strokes of the shears, the blades never quite closing completely. Use shorter strokes for cutting around curves. Cut precisely on the cutting line with the pattern piece always to your left as you cut. Hold the fabric flat on the table by placing your left hand on the fabric near the edge of the pattern. Never cut with pinking or scalloping shears.

Cut notches outward. Where pattern pieces are pinned on a fold, make a tiny snip, or cut a notch at both ends of the fold edge. This marks the center, and will help you to match it to other pattern pieces during construction.

A straight edge of a pattern piece can be placed on the selvage edge. The selvage will act as a seam finish or as a clean-finished edge. If the selvage ever becomes tight or pulled after the garment is laundered, snip it at intervals to release it.

After cutting leave the patterns pinned to the fabric for marking. Where there are interfacings and underlinings, markings will be transferred to these and not to the outer fabric.

One-Way Fabrics — Folding and Cutting

These fabrics present a problem because they have a surface texture or design that runs in a definite direction. When you lay out your pattern on a one-way fabric, all the pieces must run in the same direction. Special cutting layouts for nap or one-way fabrics are included on the Cutting and Sewing Direction Sheet.

Nap and Pile Fabrics. If the garment pieces are cut with the nap running in opposite directions, the sections of the completed garment will appear to have been cut from different shades of the same color. The direction in which you lay the pattern pieces depends on the fabric. Determine the direction of the nap or pile by stroking the fabric with your fingers on the lengthwise grain. If the surface feels smooth, you are stroking in the direction of the nap. If it feels rough, you are stroking against the nap. Mark nap direction with a chalk arrow on the back.

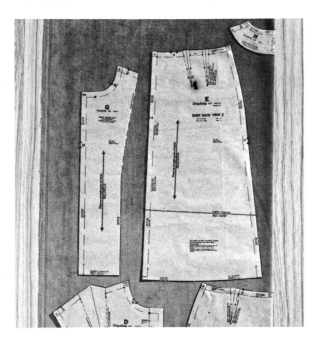

Short napped fabrics include velvet, velveteen, corduroy and suede cloth. The nap should run towards the top of the garment for the richest and darkest color. If the nap runs down, the color will have a silver cast to it.

Long napped fabrics, such as broadcloth, fleece, velour and camel's hair should have the nap run down toward the garment hem. This will help the nap to wear well, and will prevent it from unattractively "roughing up".

Fold pile and nap fabrics for cutting with the nap side out. If the fabrics are folded with nap sides facing, the fabric will shift as you cut.

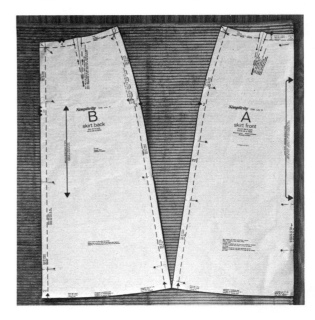

Wide wale corduroy can be cut folded on the crosswise grain for an unusual look. Be sure to match the wales at the seams.

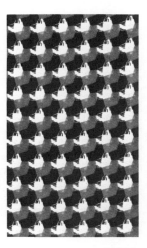

One-way Prints. Always analyze a print carefully to determine if it is a one-way design and to decide how it will look best in a finished garment. Lay all the pattern pieces one way on the fabric, in your chosen direction, and cut.

Other fabrics, such as satins and irridescents that reflect light differently, should also be cut with all pieces facing in the same direction.

Plaid and striped fabrics require special attention. Refer to page 168 for layout and cutting information.

marking

What to Mark

The word "mark" (or marking) as used in sewing, means the transfer of construction symbols from the pattern to the wrong side of the garment sections. If an underlining is used in a garment, markings should be transferred to the underlining only. Markings are your guide for sewing garment details neatly and accurately. Transfer all the construction markings that will help you to sew your garment.

It would be wise for a beginner to mark curved seamlines or seamlines which might be difficult to stitch with the seam guide. It is not necessary to mark straight seamlines.

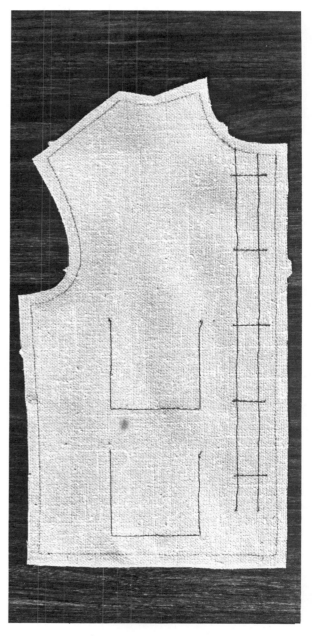

For darts, mark the stitching lines and the line through the center known as the fold line. Mark a line at right angles to the point of the dart. This serves as a visible guide for the end of the dart when the fabric is folded for stitching.

Mark position lines for buttonholes, pocket locations, trims etc. These markings have to show on the right side of the fabric. First, mark them on the wrong side and then transfer the markings to the right side by basting along the lines by hand or machine. Buttonholes and button placement should be transferred to interfacings only.

Mark pressed pleats down the entire length of the skirt, marking a termination point where the stitching ends and the pleat opening begins.

Mark dots for matching with a small cross that intersects at the center of the dot.

How to Mark

Tracing paper and wheel is the method most often used because it is fast, accurate and the easiest for most fabrics. Dressmaker's tracing paper and a tracing wheel are the items needed. Use small pieces of tracing paper except when marking two layers of fabric. Use a shade lighter or darker than the fabric to be marked. Checkerboard paper works well on multi-colored prints, tweeds etc. Before you mark, test mark on a scrap of the fabric to determine the amount of pressure needed to make a light, visible line.

Mark by following the lines on the pattern, rolling the wheel away from you. For straight lines use the transparent ruler as a guide for the wheel.

On a dart, mark the center line before marking the two outside lines to prevent the pattern from shifting as you mark.

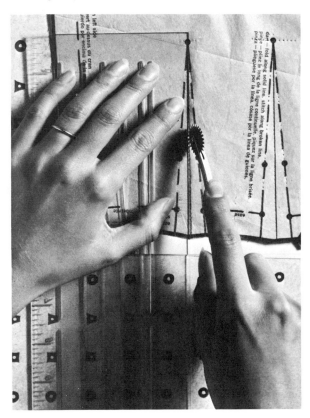

To mark two thicknesses of fabric with right sides together and pattern on top, use a strip of tracing paper about 3 inches by 10 inches. Fold coated sides together to make 3 inches by 5 inches. Insert one end of paper under bottom layer of fabric, and the other end between the fabric and the pattern, removing pins where necessary.

Lightweight and sheer fabrics usually do not need the tracing paper because the teeth on the wheel will leave visible marks in the fabric. Just follow pattern markings with the wheel, and use the ruler for straight lines.

Heavyweight fabrics, naps and tweeds may be marked one layer of fabric at a time. Place a piece of cardboard between the two layers of fabric at the place to be marked. To mark the top layer insert a single sheet of tracing paper, carbon side facing the wrong side of the fabric. To prevent the pattern from tearing, put cellophane tape over the marking lines before using the wheel on them.

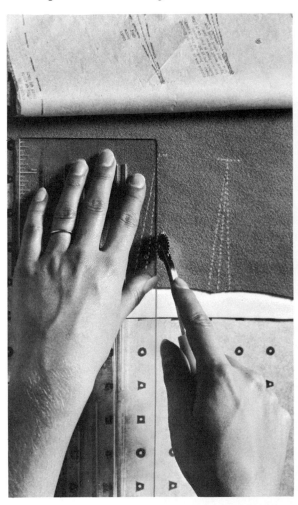

To mark the bottom layer of fabric remove tracing paper from under the pattern, and place it with carbon side facing the wrong side of the bottom layer. Remove the cardboard. Unpin the pattern at the place to be marked; then follow the markings on the top fabric layer with the wheel to transfer markings to the bottom layer.

Chalk and pins can be used on all fabrics because the chalk marks are not permanent. Start at the innermost point to be marked, and work toward the edge of the pattern. Stick small-headed, straight pins down through the tissue and both fabric layers. After all points are marked with pins, turn fabric over so that the points of the pins face up. Connect the pin markings by drawing lines with a sharp pointed chalk pencil and the transparent ruler. After the fabric side is marked, turn the section over so that the pattern side faces up. Remove the pattern carefully so as not to disturb the pins. Mark with chalk and ruler. Remove the pins after marking is completed.

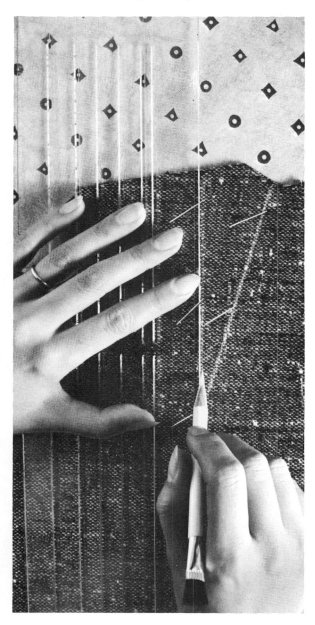

Tailor's tacks can be used for most fabrics and this method is sometimes the best one for marking bulky, spongy fabrics and some laces. It is best to work with darning cotton because it does not slip out of the fabric easily; however, a regular cotton thread will do. Work with a long, unknotted double thread. Place tacks at dots, or at intervals along marking line.

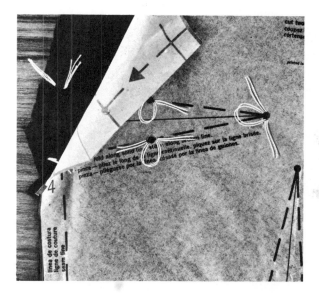

Take a small stitch through the pattern and both fabric layers leaving a thread end 1 inch long. Take a second stitch over the first, leaving a long loop. Cut thread leaving a 1 inch end. Cut through the top of the loop. Remove pattern very carefully so as not to pull out the threads.

Separate the fabric layers, clipping the threads between and leaving thread tufts on both layers.

the unit system of sewing

The Unit System of Sewing is an organized way of making a garment, unit by unit. The garment sections are arranged in units, including interfacings and underlinings, if used. The number of units and the number of pattern pieces in each unit depend upon the style of the garment.

As far as possible all stitching and pressing is completed on one unit before proceeding to the next unit. As the units are completed, they are joined to each other until the entire garment is assembled. Because you concentrate on sewing one unit at a time, short periods of time can be used to complete a unit. The unit can then be set aside until there is another opportunity for sewing.

This system not only is a time saver, but also it reduces garment handling to a minimum, thereby eliminating much wrinkling and stretching.

The garments illustrated in the following chapters are made according to the Unit System of Sewing.

Units in Your Basic Blouse

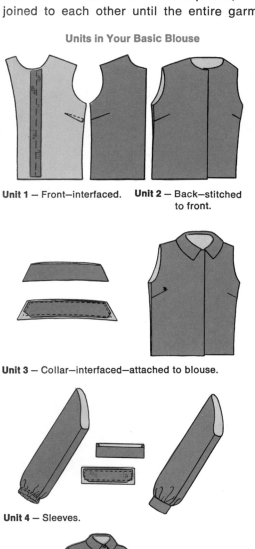

Unit 1 — Front—interfaced.   Unit 2 — Back—stitched to front.

Unit 3 — Collar—interfaced—attached to blouse.

Unit 4 — Sleeves.

Unit 5 — Cuffs—interfaced—stitched to sleeves. Sleeves stitched to blouse. Hem and finishing details added.

Units in Your Basic Skirt

Unit 1 — Front.

Unit 2 — Back—zipper attached—stitched to front.

Unit 3 — Waistband. Hem and finishing details added.

Units in Your Basic Dress

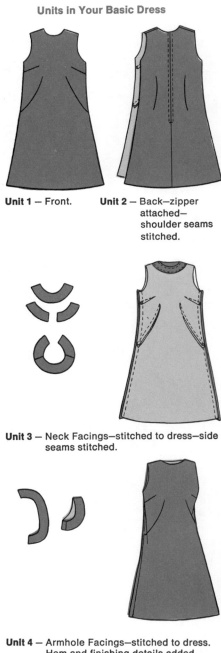

Unit 1 — Front.   Unit 2 — Back—zipper attached—shoulder seams stitched.

Unit 3 — Neck Facings—stitched to dress—side seams stitched.

Unit 4 — Armhole Facings—stitched to dress. Hem and finishing details added.

chapter 6 all this and sewing, too?

The only thing the latest zigzag machines can't do is to sew your seams while you're preparing dinner! Someone is probably working to correct <u>that</u> oversight right now.

Seriously though, a sewing machine is a precision instrument. It requires care. The instruction manual shows how to keep it in good working order, how to make simple adjustments and how to operate it. If you do not have the manual for your machine, the manufacturer can usually supply one even if the machine is not of recent manufacture. It pays to have the manual at hand as a reference for the names of the operating parts mentioned from time to time in sewing directions.

If you are not an experienced hand at the machine, operate it slowly enough to allow you to follow the marking lines exactly. In a short while you will find that you can sew at a much faster pace, but keep in mind that accuracy, not speed is our goal.

using the sewing machine

Stitch length, pressure and tension are the three variables that must be adjusted to the specific fabric you are going to use. Refer to the manual for the correct needle size and proper stitch length. The manual also shows how to adjust the pressure and tension on your machine.

Basic Stitch Lengths most generally used are:

<u>Regulation Stitch</u> — from 12 to 16 stitches per inch depending on fabric weight. Use the shorter stitch lengths for fine and lightweight fabrics.

<u>Machine-Baste</u> — the longest stitch on your machine. Used as a temporary stitching.

<u>Ease-Stitch</u> — about 10 stitches per inch. Used for easing-in fullness evenly.

<u>Reinforcement Stitch</u> — about 20 stitches per inch. Used for strengthening the stitching line at points of strain.

Pressure adjusted correctly on the presser foot holds the fabric firmly while the machine is stitching. The regulation of the pressure depends on various characteristics of the fabric such as fiber content, bulk or weight, texture or finish.

Tension on the thread, properly adjusted, results in a balanced stitch, exactly the same on both sides of the fabric. Improper thread tension can cause puckering or loose stitches. Once it is set properly, tension usually needs no further adjusting.

Once you have learned to handle your machine with the ease of an expert, you may try more complicated sewing techniques, or try some innovations of your own. However, a beginner should confine herself to the more simple, basic methods.

Be sure to thread the machine correctly, or breakage may occur. Your manual contains a diagram for correct threading of your machine. Cut thread at an angle to enable it to go through the eye of the needle more easily.

Testing a Seam for Tension and Pressure

From scraps of the fabric you are using cut two strips about 8 inches long on the lengthwise grain. Match the lengthwise edges, and pin together at each end with the pins at right angles to the lengthwise edge. Place the double layer of fabric under the presser foot, and start the stitching while guiding the fabric in front of the presser foot. If fabric does not <u>feed smoothly</u>, but feeds in a jerky manner, pressure on the presser foot is too light.

If fabric ripples as in the photograph, pressure on the presser foot is too heavy. If fabric puckers, the thread tension is too tight on both the needle and the bobbin. If stitching is out-of-balance, thread tension is either too loose on one side, or is too tight on the other side. Make any necessary adjustments and test the seam again.

Fastening Threads

Secure threads at the beginning and ending of a stitched seam with one of these methods:

Backstitching is done on many machines by simply moving a lever to "reverse". If your machine does not reverse, retrace stitching by lowering presser foot 1/2 inch from edge of fabric, and then lower the needle into the fabric. Raise presser foot slightly, and draw fabric forward (toward you) while you stitch backward to the fabric edge. Lower the presser foot, and stitch the seam. Repeat backstitch at end of stitching.

Tie thread ends by removing stitched fabric from under presser foot, and cut threads leaving 3 inch ends on fabric. Draw one thread through to wrong side of fabric, and tie both threads together with a square knot. Clip threads to 1/8 inch.

Lockstitching the threads at the beginning and ending of a seam can be used on firm, heavyweight fabrics. Before you start to stitch the seam, hold fabric in place with the left hand so that fabric does not feed through the machine. Raise the presser foot slightly with the right hand while making three or four stitches very slowly. At the end of the seam-line lockstitch the final stitch following the same procedure. Clip threads to 1/8 inch.

straight stitching

Stitching a Seam from Start to Finish

Thread your machine. Turn the hand wheel to raise the needle to its highest point so that thread will not slip out as stitching starts. Draw needle and bobbin threads under presser foot, extending threads about 3 inches behind it. Place fabric under the raised presser foot with the seam edge on the right and the bulk of the fabric to the left. Enough of the fabric should lay on the machine so that it will feed evenly without dragging.

Turn the hand wheel to lower the needle into the fabric about 1/2 inch in from the beginning of the stitching line. Hold thread ends while lowering the presser foot. Backstitch almost to end of fabric, and then slowly stitch forward at an even speed. The machine stitches best when it is run evenly without speed-ups or slow-downs. Reduce speed as you near the end of the seam so as not to go beyond the edge of the fabric. Backstitch to fasten the end of seam.

Raise the needle to its highest point by turning the hand wheel. Lift the presser foot, and draw the fabric toward the back of the machine. Cut threads on the machine's thread cutter, or clip threads close to the fabric with a small scissors. Leave about 3 inch lengths of needle and bobbin thread on the machine for future stitching.

Guiding Fabric

While the needle is stitching, guide the fabric only in front of the presser foot. This is usually sufficient to obtain smooth, even stitching.

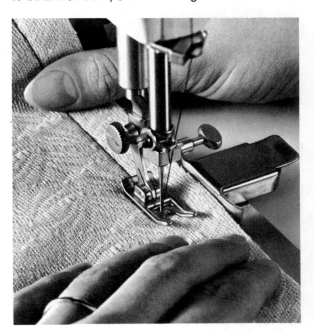

Filmy sheers, crepes, knits, tricots and some fabrics with unusual textures require additional support while they are being stitched if puckering and seam splitting are to be avoided. Hold the fabric gently with the right hand in back of the presser foot without pulling while the left hand guides the fabric in front of the presser foot.

Guidelines on the throat plate of the machine are spaced usually at $1/8$ inch intervals starting $3/8$ inch from the needle. These marks enable you to stitch $3/8$ inch, $1/2$ inch, $5/8$ inch and $3/4$ inch from the fabric edge.

Seam Guide. This accessory, either magnetic or a screw-on type, is used in relation to the presser foot. It helps to achieve a perfectly straight seamline and a uniform seam allowance. Use the guidelines on the machine throat plate to position the seam guide accurately. If there are no guidelines on the plate, use a tape measure to measure from the needle to the seam guide for proper positioning.

Stitching curves can best be done by first hand-basting all curved seams. Use a shorter machine-stitch than the one used for the straight seams.

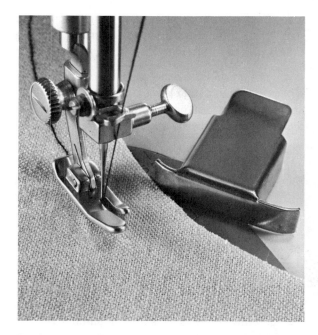

For both outside and inside curves the seam guide is set at an angle so that one corner of the end is in line with the needle. Guide the fabric edges lightly against the seam guide while stitching.

Pin-basting is used in place of hand or machine-basting for straight seams on easy-to-handle fabrics. Your machine <u>must</u> have a hinged presser foot for stitching over points of pins without distorting the stitching line. Never place pins on underside of fabric where they can come in contact with the feed dog on the machine.

Insert pins at right angles to the seamline. Take a very small "bite" in the fabric, inserting only the tapered point of the pin.

If you are going to use the seam guide, insert pins with <u>points</u> toward lengthwise edge of fabric. When seam guide is not used, the <u>heads</u> of pins are toward the lengthwise edge of fabric.

Machine-basting is done with the longest straight stitch or with a machine chain-stitch, now available on some machines. Machine-basting can be done quickly, and is easy to remove. Use it for basted fittings and other temporary stitching. This basting method is not recommended for pile fabrics such as velveteen because the needle marks may show if an area is altered.

Baste-marking uses the machine to transfer construction markings needed on the right side of the fabric. With the wrong side up stitch over the traced markings using a long stitch.

Reinforcement stitches are small stitches (about 20 per inch) used to strengthen points of strain such as a corner or point that is to be trimmed and turned, or an inside curve that is to be clipped.

Stitch the seamline to within ³/₄ inch of the point. Change to the finer stitch, and continue stitching to point. Pivot, and continue the same stitch for ³/₄ inch on other side of point. Change back to regulation stitch, and continue stitching seamline.

Corners of all angles, such as collars and lapels, are easier to turn and result in a smoother seam when a diagonal stitch or two is taken across the point. One stitch across the point is usually enough for lightweight fabrics, but use two or three small stitches for heavier fabrics.

Stitch slowly toward the corner, and use the hand wheel to take the last few stitches up to one or two stitch lengths from the corner. Lower needle at the exact pivot point. Raise presser foot, and turn fabric so that you can take a stitch diagonally across the point. Pivot again to bring the needle into the correct position to stitch the seam on the second side of the corner or point.

Ease-stitching is used to control a slight amount of fullness in a seam edge before it is joined to another seam edge which does not have any fullness. Using 8-10 stitches per inch place a single row of stitches on the seamline. When two rows of stitches are needed, as for the cap of a sleeve, stitch one row on the seamline and the second row in the seam allowance about $1/4$ inch from the first row. The bobbin thread is then drawn up to make the slight fullness. Adjust carefully between the pattern markings so that the fabric does not look gathered or puckered.

Ease-plus stitching can be used in some areas that require a moderate amount of easing. The fullness is controlled by crowding the threads of the fabric together while stitching with a regulation stitch. This method can be used on the back shoulder seam or for the top edge of a turned hem on a slightly flared skirt.

Press the index finger of the right hand against the back of the presser foot while stitching for several inches. Fabric will pile up against your finger. Lift finger to release fabric and repeat procedure until entire edge is eased.

Machine-gathering is used where controlled fullness is needed at the bodice or skirt waistline, a puffed sleeve and other places depending on the pattern style. Before stitching on the seamline as indicated on the pattern, loosen the upper (needle) tension slightly so that the bobbin thread will pull easily as you adjust the fullness.

Use a slightly longer than average stitch for sheer fabrics; use the longest stitch for heavier fabrics. For more uniform gathers make a second row of stitching in the seam allowance $1/4$ inch from the first row. Draw the thread ends through to the underside. At one end of stitching line tie threads with a knot. At the other end draw up the bobbin thread until gathers are the proper length, and tie thread ends.

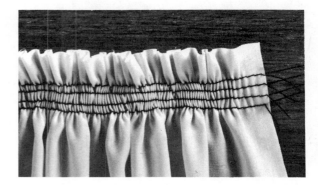

Shirring is several rows of gathers used for a decorative effect. The rows of stitching are made inside the seamline and are visible on the outside of the garment.

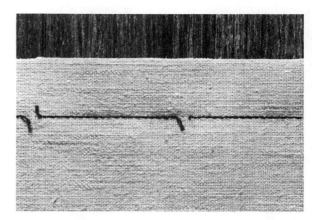

Removing stitches is never done by pulling the edges apart. Use a small scissors or a seam ripper to cut stitches at 2 inch intervals along one side of the seamline. Pull out thread on the opposite side. Remove any short threads that remain on the first side.

zigzag machine

The zigzag machine, with its infinite variety of stitches, has made possible whole new areas of achievement for sewing in the home. The ability of its owner to create designs for the decorative stitches of this machine is its only limitation.

In the paragraphs which follow are shown various uses for the zigzag stitches that apply to garment construction and some ideas for using the zigzag stitches decoratively.

Seams

Knit fabrics need a seam with "give" so that the stitches will not break during wear. A narrow, closely spaced zigzag stitch is recommended. Use the same stitch to stay shoulder and waistline seams with straight seam binding to prevent stretching in these areas. There are also machines that make special stretch stitches for use on knits.

Jersey knits do not need a seam finish to prevent raveling, but because of their stretch and tendency to curl under, a triple-stitch zigzag stitch may be used for a seam finish and on the edges of facings.

If you do not have a zigzag machine, support the fabric both in front and in back of the presser foot. See Guiding Fabric on page 38. A sewing thread, made with a polyester core and a cotton covering, is practical for sewing knit fabrics because it has flexibility and gives with the knit.

Sheer fabrics can be used more effectively when they are finished with fine, dainty seams. Because the hairline seam eliminates visible seam allowances it is excellent to use for the edges of collars and cuffs in sheer fabrics.

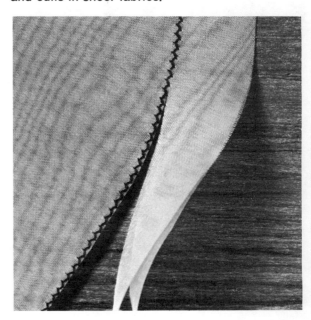

Lay right sides together and hand-baste. Stitch with a fine, narrow zigzag stitch. The stitching can be done over a filler cord to give additional strength to the seam. Trim close to the stitching line. Turn right side out and press.

Edge Finishing

Seam edges are finished to prevent raveling in use, to strengthen the seam and to give an improved appearance to the wrong side of a garment. Zigzag stitching is used on a pressed open, plain seam. Use a regular zigzag stitch along each seam edge, but do not let the stitch go over the edge. Trim close, but take care not to cut into stitches.

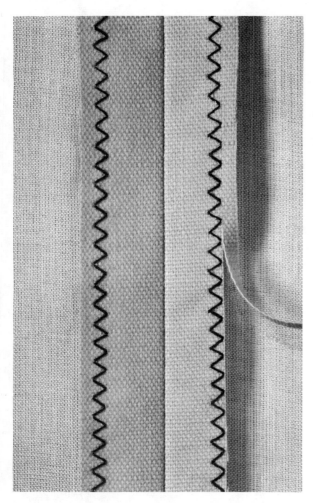

If your machine has a special zigzag stitch that sews an overedged finish, no trimming will be needed.

Facings in heavy fabrics are not turned under because of the extra bulk. Finish the edges with zigzag stitching as instructed above.

Hem Finishing

Hem edges in fabrics that ravel and in knits can be finished with the zigzag machine.

Use a multi-stitch or plain zigzag stitch near the free edge of hem, or use an overedge stitch in the same manner as instructed for seam edge above.

Machine blindstitching makes an almost invisible hem on the right side of a garment. The blindstitch is a combination of straight stitches alternating with a zigag stitch every 4-6 stitches. It is suitable for straight or slightly flared hems in medium-weight cottons or blends. It is not recommended for fine fabrics. Follow instructions for preparing and stitching this hem in your sewing machine instruction book.

Buttons and Buttonholes

Buttons can be sewn on by machine, and in some cases, it is possible to form a thread shank as you attach the button. Refer to your sewing machine instruction book for directions.

Buttonholes are made by zigzag machines very neatly on most fabrics. The sewing instruction book for each machine illustrates the type of buttonholes that the machine can make. Include the same number of fabric layers of the fabric you are using in your garment, and make a test buttonhole. You will learn the proper machine settings as well as which styles are best suited for your garment. Test the buttonhole opening to be sure that it can be cut easily without cutting the stitches.

Attaching Lace

Lace can be attached securely and attractively with the following method. Fold under the fabric edge about $3/8$ inch. Lap straight edge of lace over fabric fold $1/4$ inch and hand-baste. Set the machine for a narrow zigzag or a decorative stitch. Position the work under the needle so that the right edge of the stitching line is in the lace and fabric, and the left edge of the stitching line is in the fabric only. Trim excess fabric close to stitching line on the wrong side.

Gathered Lace. Draw the top thread of the straight edge, and ease lace along to make fullness. Space the gathers evenly. Baste over edge of fabric, and stitch as directed previously.

Attaching Elastic

Zigzag stitching can be used to apply elastic to waistlines of lingerie and pajamas because the stitching stretches with the elastic. Fit elastic around your waistline to the desired tension adding an extra inch for lapping the ends. Lap ends, and secure with zigzag stitching. Fold fabric edge 1/4 inch to the right side. Divide the waistline of the garment and the elastic band into 4 equal sections, and mark with pins. Overlap the turned edge of garment with edge of elastic, matching the marking pins. Stitch with a narrow, plain zigag stitch, stretching elastic between pins as you stitch.

Decorative Stitching

Many decorative touches can be achieved with the special stitches on the zigzag machine. The stitch patterns are built into the machine or achieved by adding cams or discs.

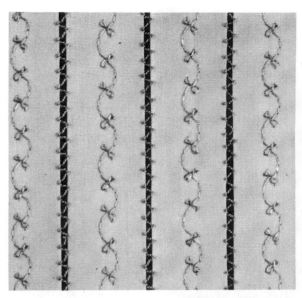

Decorative touches include scalloped edges on collars and cuffs; monogrammed initials or names on pockets, labels, etc.; borders of faggoting and appliqued designs. The satin stitch, usually used to applique, is a very close zigzag stitch. Rows of it, done in different color threads, will resemble decorative braid.

Embroidery, floral designs, script lettering and monogramming can be done with free-motion stitching without a presser foot; a hoop is used to control the fabric movement.

For detailed stitching directions and the application of zigzag decoration consult your sewing machine instruction book. It describes the stitches and techniques for your particular machine.

a glorious splurge

Fashion . . . made to perfection . . .
not only beautiful, but sensational fun.

Here are the exciting details of the
most important fashion trends.
Everything . . . skirts, blouses, dresses
and pants . . . have fabric and color
suggestions and you'll be able to sew
them all. Plot your look, select
your fabric and create the fashion
just for you.

Everyone ready?

for the soft look in blouses & skirts—
check chapters 7 and 9

to sew the blouse beautiful—
check chapter 8

shift dresses for afternoon and after—
check chapter 9

**changing effects with trimmings—
check chapter 19**

a shirtdress, no less—check chapter 9

**plaids and stripes forever—
check chapter 16**

to line it or underline it?—
check chapter 10

if you want to underline it—check chapter 10

if you want to line it—
check chapter 10

the shape of pants to come—
check chapter 12

pert skirt

Well! Here you are at chapter 7, and it is really about time you sewed your first seams! Remember that everything you learn at the start, no matter how simple it may be, you will use in almost every fashion you sew from now on. Anyone can make her own garments with a little practice, but to be truly proud of the garments you will make and wear takes practice, practice and still more practice so let's start with something simple, like the skirt shown on this page.

Choose a skirt pattern with a minimum of seams, darts and styling details. A firm, self-supporting fabric that doesn't need a lining would be a good choice. Avoid tricky plaids or one-way designs which require matching. Hopsacking, duck, poplin, cotton suiting and sailcloth are good for a starter.

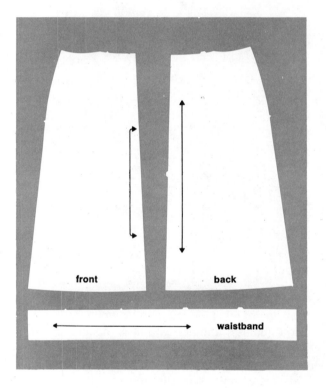

Every sewing project divides into two general work areas — the preliminary steps and the actual construction. The preliminary sequence is: Select pattern; select and prepare fabric; alter pattern if necessary; cut and mark the garment. Refer to the previous chapters for information on all of these points. Refer to Chapter 14 for pattern adjustments. Press your skirt during and after construction using the methods found in Chapter 15.

NOTE: For clarity in the photographs that follow, contrasting thread has been used and tracing paper markings are heavier than normal.

staystitching

Staystitching, the first step in the construction of any garment, is a line of regular machine stitching used to hold the fabric grain on bias or curved edges so that these edges will not stretch during construction of the garment.

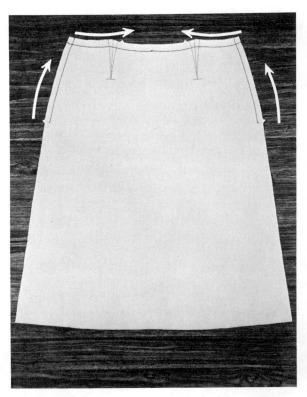

This line of stitching is made $1/2$ inch from the cut edge (unless another width is specified) with matching thread, through a single thickness of the seam allowance. On deep curves, at necklines and waistlines, staystitching is done on the seamline, $5/8$ inch from the edge. Staystitching must be done directionally, with the grain, as indicated by arrows on your Cutting and Sewing Direction Sheet.

Illustrations throughout this book show arrows and stitching lines which indicate the correct direction to use where staystitching is necessary.

skirt front unit

Staystitch $1/2$ inch from edge on sides of the skirt from the notch to waistline as shown by the arrows. Staystitch on the seamline of the waistline edge from side edges to center.

Stitch the darts. To make a dart, crease along the center line, right sides together. Match outside lines and begin pinning at point of the dart. Pin-baste with heads of pins toward fold of dart.

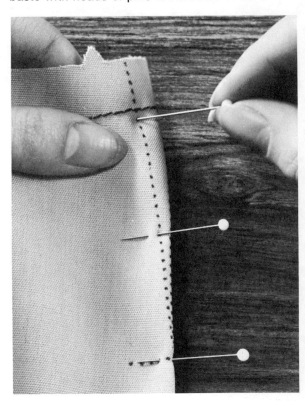

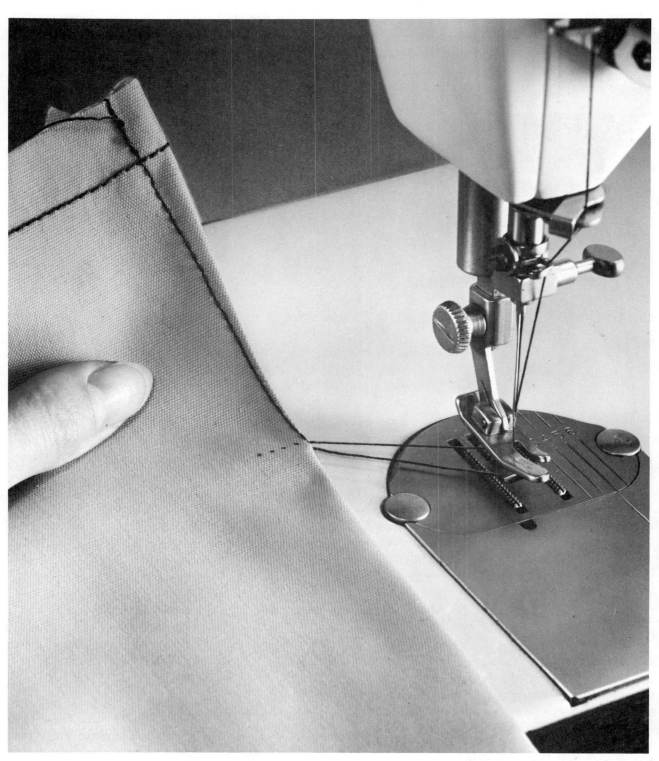

Place skirt on the machine with wide end of dart in line with the needle and the bulk of the fabric to the left of the presser foot. Stitch from the wide end to the point, removing pins as you stitch. At point of dart make the last stitches right on the fold. Clip thread ends about 2 inches long, and

tie in a square knot close to end of dart. Do not tie so tightly that the dart point puckers. Pin and stitch second dart in the same way.

Press the darts toward the center front. This completes the skirt front unit; set it aside until the back unit has been completed.

skirt back unit

Staystitch waistline edge and side seam edges of skirt from the notch up in the same direction as the front. Pin and stitch back darts; then press toward the center back. With right sides together, match notches of center back seam; pin and stitch.

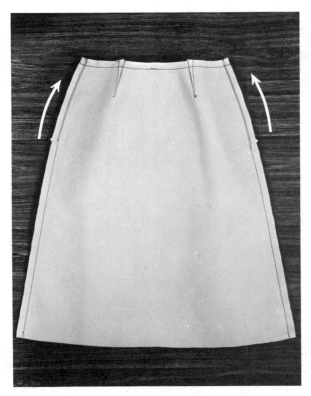

Side seams. (If you are uncertain of the fit of the skirt, you may machine-baste the seams and the waistband for a fitting before stitching permanently. See fitting a skirt details on page 123.) Place the front skirt unit and back skirt unit right sides together, and pin-baste side seams. Pins should be about 6 inches apart to prevent slipping. Stitch the right side seam from lower edge to waistline edge.

On the left side, where the zipper will be inserted, the length of the zipper opening should measure the length of the zipper plus 1 inch. A marking is indicated on the pattern to show where the bottom of the zipper is placed. Permanently stitch the seam up to the end of the zipper opening and backstitch. Then adjust the stitch regulator for machine-basting, and continue stitching on the seamline to the waistline edge.

Pink the seam edges, and press all seams open. Press directionally, from the lower edge up, as explained on page 156.

lapped zipper application

Replace the presser foot with the zipper foot, adjusting foot to right side of needle. Place skirt wrong side out on the machine with the top of opening toward you. Extend the right hand seam allowance (back of skirt) under the foot with the other seam allowance and skirt to the left.

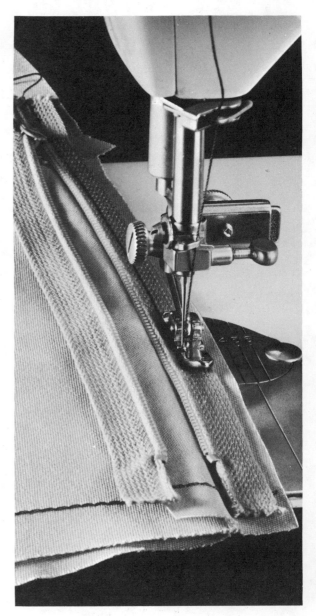

Place opened zipper face down over back seam allowance with top stop 1 inch from cut edge, and zipper coil or teeth on the seamline. The bottom stop should be at lower end of opening. Inserting pins crosswise of tape, pin tape to right hand seam allowance. Machine-baste from bottom to top along guideline on the zipper tape. Remove pins as you stitch.

Close the zipper, and turn it face up by folding under seam allowance with tape attached. Smooth away fabric from the zipper teeth. Move zipper foot to left of needle, and adjust stitch to regular length. Starting at the bottom, stitch through the fold to secure back seam allowance to zipper.

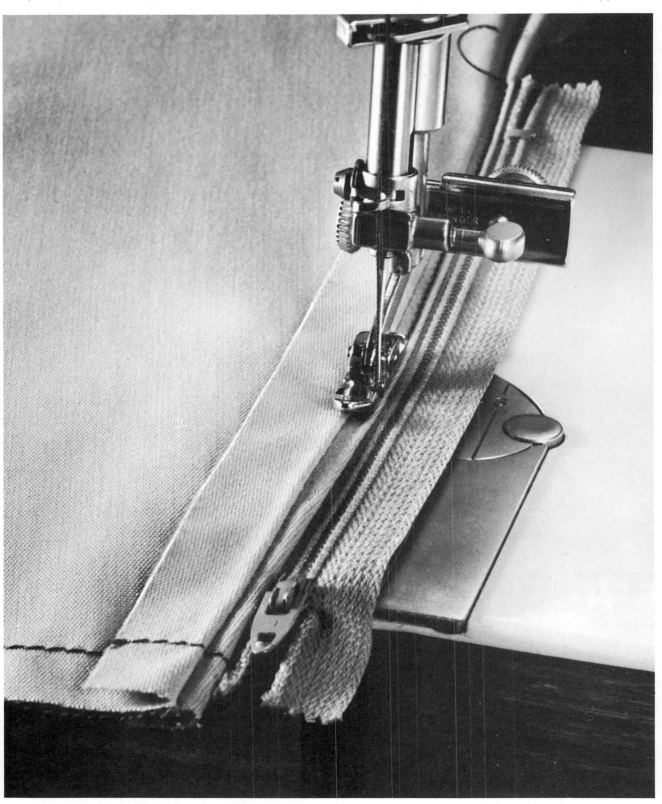

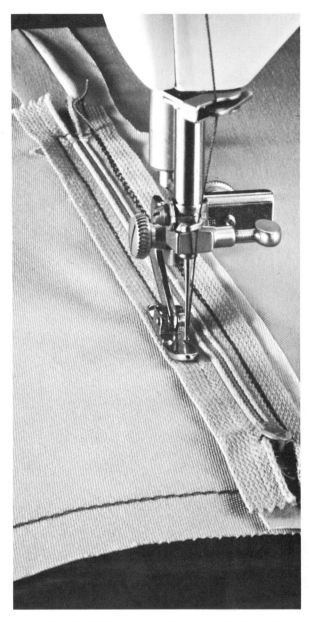

zipper. With the zipper closed press on the wrong side over a tailor's ham. If necessary, press on the right side using a press cloth to protect the fabric.

As you progress with your sewing projects, you will learn to insert zippers by hand. See page 91 . Hand-finishing a zipper application imparts a professional or custom look to your garments.

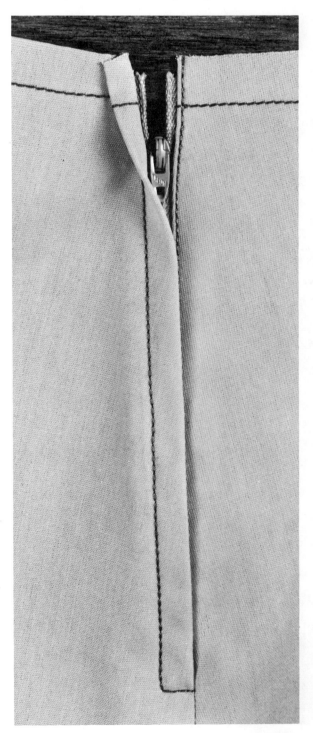

Spread out skirt, wrong side up, with the zipper face down over the left hand seam allowance (front of skirt). Smooth the zipper toward the left so that it lays perfectly flat, and a small pleat forms at the end of the zipper. Pin. Starting at the seamline, stitch across the bottom of zipper to the guide line, pivot and continue stitching up the other side of the zipper. You are stitching through three thicknesses—the zipper tape, seam allowance and skirt. This row of stitching shows on the outside.

At the bottom of the opening, draw the upper thread to the underside and tie thread ends. Working under the back seam allowance clip and remove machine-basting to open the seam over the

waistband unit

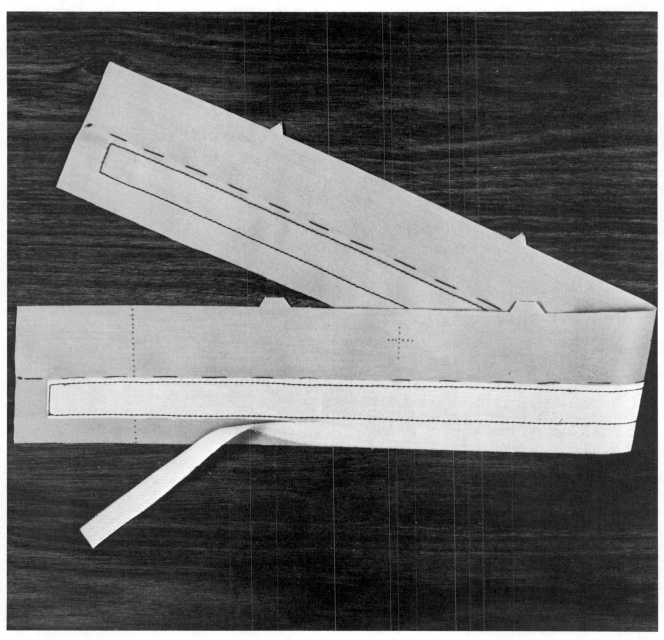

Interfacing the waistband prevents it from stretching. Cut a strip of firm interfacing on the lengthwise grain the same length as the waistband, but only half its width. Pin interfacing to wrong side of band along unnotched edge. Mark lengthwise fold with basting stitches, using edge of interfacing as a guide. Stitch $1/8$ inch from inner edge of interfacing. Machine-baste remaining edges to waistband $1/2$ inch from cut edge. Trim interfacing to stitching line along unnotched edge and on ends. Turn and press seam allowance on unnotched edge to the wrong side. Trim this seam allowance to $1/4$ inch.

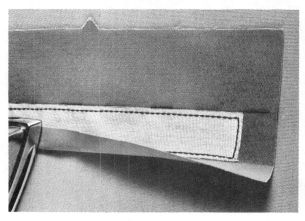

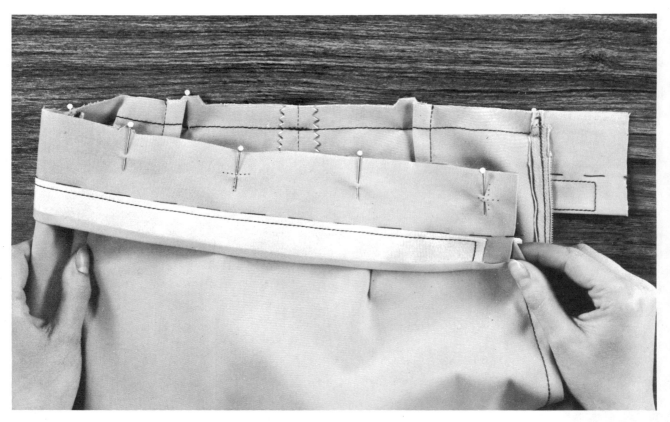

Attaching the waistband. With notched edge up, pin the waistband to the waistline of the skirt, right sides together. Match center fronts, center backs and single and double notches. Stitch, starting at one end of waistband and finishing at opposite end. Use backstitching to secure both ends of the stitching.

Fold waistband lengthwise along baste-marking with right sides together. Stitch $5/8$ inch seams across ends. This stitching in the front should be even with the folded edge over the zipper. On the back there is an extension to allow for the over-lapping. Trim seams and corners. Turn waistband right side out taking care to keep corners square

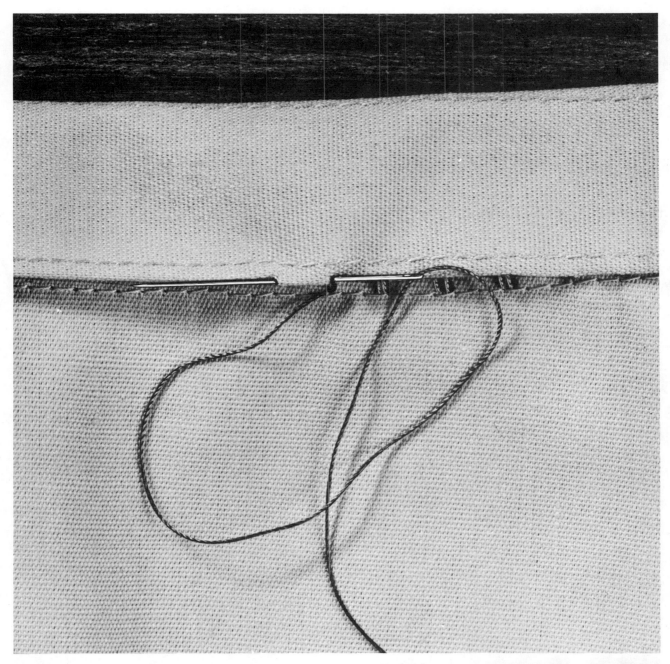

and smooth. Press. Pin the free turned-under edge of waistband over the seam allowance on inside of skirt. Slip-stitch turned-edge to waistline seam. To slip-stitch, catch up one thread on seam line; then slip the needle along for about $1/4$ inch in fold of turned-edge, continuing slip-stitching across back extension. Lap front end of waistband over back extension.

Hooks and eyes are used to hold lapped ends of waistband. Keep zipper closed when marking position with pins. Sew the hooks on the upper edge so the stitches go through the underside of band and interfacing only, not the outside of the band.

final fitting

Try on the skirt for final inspection while wearing undergarments and shoes with the same heel height you will wear with the finished skirt. Position waistband comfortably. Now check the skirt length. The length of your skirt is determined by current fashion trends and the best lines for your individual figure.

the hem

There are four steps in making a hem; the first three are the same for all hems, but the fourth step varies with the type of hem.

Mark the hemline. Have a second person mark the desired length with a skirtmarker or a yardstick using chalk or pins. The markings must be parallel with the floor.

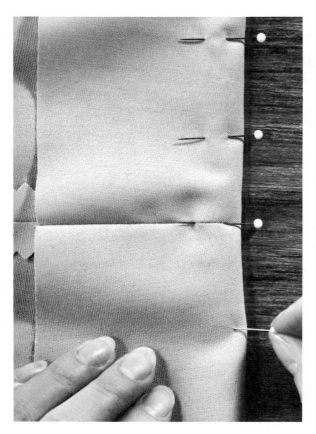

Fold on hemline. Turn hem to wrong side of skirt along marked line, matching the seamlines. Insert pins at right angles to the folded edge, easing them down slightly at seamlines so that the fold follows a smooth, even line. Some fabrics are easier to handle after pinning if you baste about 1/4 inch from the fold. Remove pins as you baste. Press with the lengthwise grain. Never press over pins — and do not press too heavily so a crease forms on the

right side. If fabric is heavy you may use a piece of cardboard or heavy brown wrapping paper between the hem and the garment.

Marking hem depth. Place skirt, turned wrong side out, on a flat surface so that you can work from the hem side. Set the sewing gauge for the desired hem depth plus 1/4 inch for finishing. The recommended depth for an A-line skirt is about 2 inches. Measure and mark hem all around the skirt. Cut away the excess fabric. Trim seam allowances to half their width from hem edge to fold.

Finish the hem. The method for finishing a hem depends on two factors: The fabric used, and the shape of the skirt at the hemline. The finish below is generally used for a slightly flared skirt made of firmly woven cotton, silk or synthetics of light or medium weight.

Clean-finished hem. Staystitch ¼ inch from edge. Turn the top edge of hem under ¼ inch on the stitching line. Set the machine for an ease-stitch and stitch ⅛ inch from fold edge.

On flat surface pin hem edge to skirt, inserting pins at right angles to the hem edge, matching seamlines. If hem does not lie flat, pull up ease thread to adjust the fullness evenly. With a pin, lift up a bobbin stitch and pull it gently; repeat until hem lies flat. Hand-finish with an inside blind-stitch.

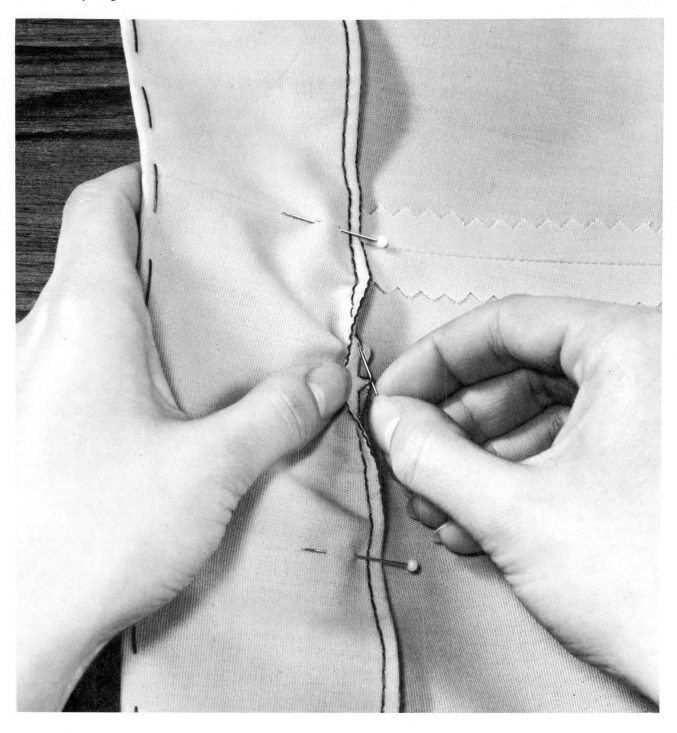

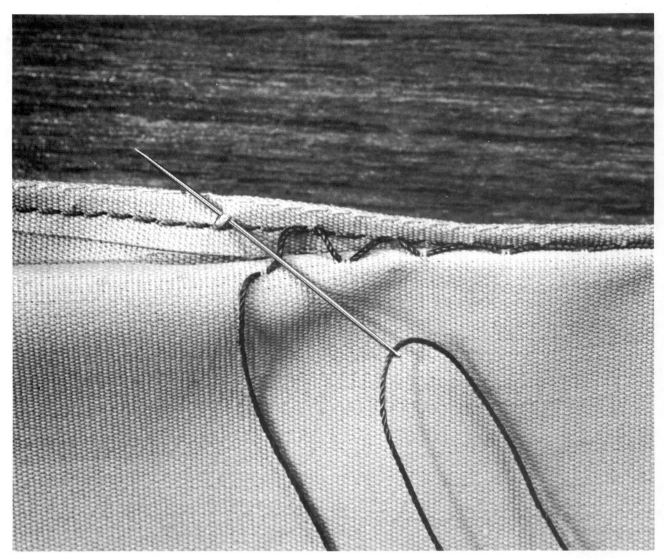

Blind-stitching is used to finish hems because the stitches are made between the wrong sides of skirt and hem. Fold hem back against right side of skirt, the fold in line with the machine-stitching along hem edge. Using a fine needle and single thread work from right to left. Take a stitch in fold at top of hem, then $1/2$ inch to the left take a small stitch in the skirt, picking up only one or two threads. Continue to alternate from fold to hem edge around the skirt. Do not draw stitches too tight. The hem should be inconspicuous on the right side.

finishing steps

Your garment is now complete. Press the skirt following the tips for final pressing in Chapter 15.

To maintain the shape of your skirt while it is hanging, sew a snap at the inside center front and back waistband. Keep this snap closed when the skirt is hanging, and always use a sturdy skirt hanger.

basic blouse

Learning to sew has a happy advantage. When you've finished your lessons, you wear them! You are also the one who gives passing or failing grades on the final examination of your garment, so let's go for that "A" on your homework.

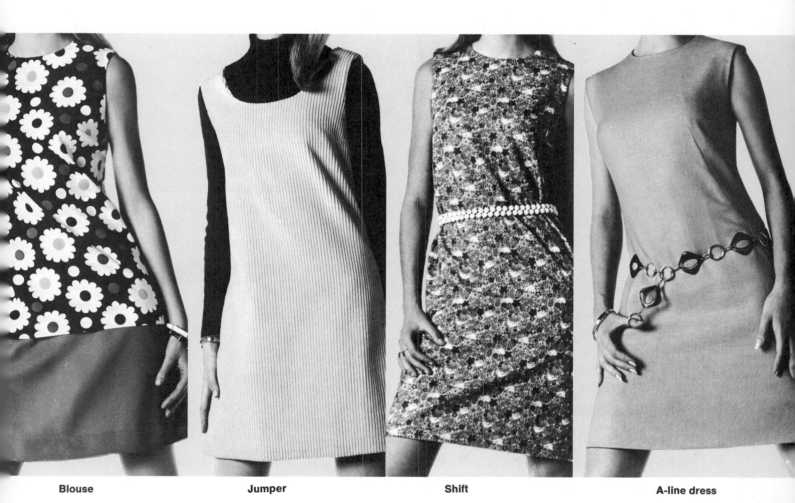

| Blouse | Jumper | Shift | A-line dress |

For your second sewing project pick a pattern that has no collar, sleeves or buttonholes, and requires little fitting. All of the construction and finishing know-how learned while making the blouse above can be applied to the shift, A-line dress or jumper shown here, so you are really learning how to make four things while sewing one.

Again, choose a firm fabric that does not require a lining or underlining. Cottons and blends are good choices for a blouse or dress; for the blouse select a fabric that goes well with the skirt you've just made. Corduroy, wool flannel, medium weight synthetics and bonded wool are suitable for a jumper.

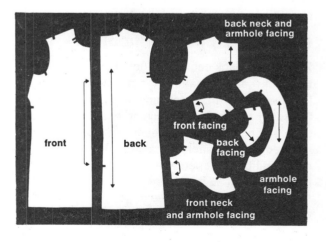

back neck and armhole facing

front facing

back facing

front

back

armhole facing

front neck and armhole facing

blouse front unit

Staystitch the neckline ⅝ inch from the edge. Staystitch the shoulder lines ½ inch from the edge in the direction shown. Staystitch the bottom ¼ inch from the edge; this can be done in either direction because it is on the straight grain. Make the darts (see page 62), and press them down.

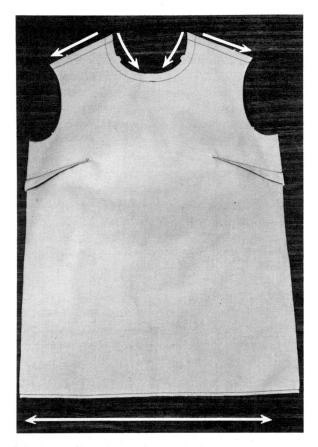

blouse back unit

On both back sections staystitch the neckline ⅝ inch from the edge and the shoulder ½ inch from the edge in the directions shown. Staystitch the bottom ¼ inch from the edge. Make the darts and press them toward the center back.

centered zipper application

Pin the two back sections together along the center back seams, matching notches. Stitch from lower edge to the notch and back-stitch. Adjust the stitch regulator for machine-basting and continue stitching along the seam line from notch to neck edge. The machine-basted edges above the notch will be the opening for the zipper. It should measure about ½ inch longer than the zipper from the notch to the neckline seam to allow for a hook and thread loop closing at the finished neck edge.

Press seam open from lower edge to neck edge. Remove machine basting. This has automatically pressed under the edges to cover the zipper.

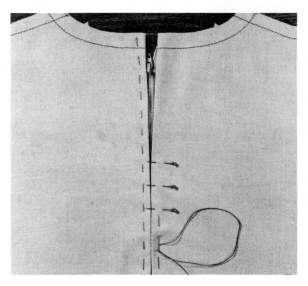

Turn blouse to right side. Place closed zipper right side up under the turned edges of the back opening with the tab end of the zipper ½ inch below neckline. Pin one turned edge to the tape along one side of zipper with the edge of the fold at center of zipper teeth or coil. Pin-baste second side, easing edge of fold up to other edge at the center of the zipper. From the right side hand-baste both back opening edges to the zipper tape, ¼ inch from the center edges. Baste down one side, across lower end of zipper and up the other side. Use basting as a guide for stitching.

Replace the presser foot with the zipper foot.
Starting at neckline edge, stitch down to bottom
of zipper, pivot and stitch slowly across bottom,
making the same number of stitches on each side
of the seamline. Pivot again, and continue to stitch
up the other side as basted. Keep the stitching
an even distance from center on both sides. This
stitching does not have to be directional as centered zippers are usually placed in seams that are
on straight grain. Remove hand basting.

When a centered zipper is used in a garment made
of a plaid or a loosely woven fabric, or if the seam
is slightly curved, the stitching should be done
from the top to bottom on both sides of the zipper.
Pivot at one corner, and stitch across bottom.
Draw thread ends to underside and tie.

Shoulder seams. Place the back unit over the front unit of blouse, right sides together, matching shoulder notches. Pin and stitch the shoulder seams, stitching from the neckline to the armhole.

Pink, zigzag or clean-finish the seam edges. To clean-finish seams, turn under $1/8$ inch and stitch close to the fold edge. Press seams open in the same direction as they were stitched.

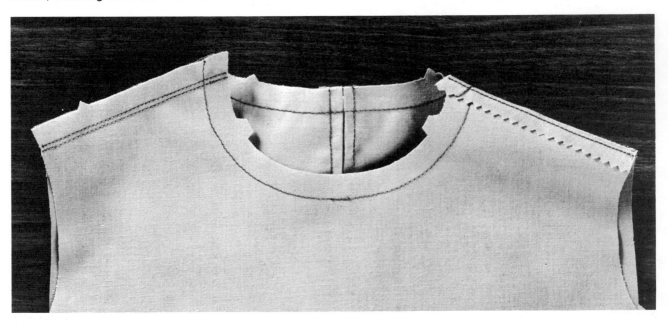

neckline facing unit

Staystitch the neckline edges of the front and back facings $5/8$ inch from the edge in the same directions that the blouse neckline was staystitched. With right sides together stitch both shoulder seams in the neckline facing. Trim the seams to $1/4$ inch, and press them open. Staystitch $1/4$ inch from the outer edge of facing.

Depending upon the fabric used, pink, zigzag or clean-finish the outer edge. To clean-finish a curved edge, turn under on $1/4$ inch staystitching line, and stitch close to the folded edge.

With right sides together pin the facing to the blouse at neck edge, matching center fronts,

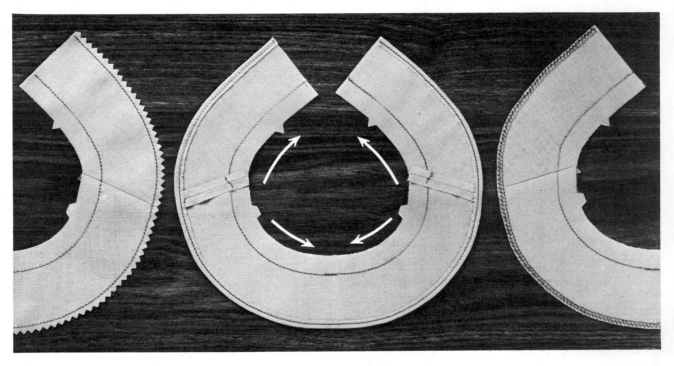

shoulder seams and notches. Ends of the facing extend ⅝ inch beyond back edges of blouse.

Stitch the facing to the blouse on the seamline, using shorter stitches. Trim the seam to ¼ inch. Beginning ⅝ inch from the edges of the facing, make several clips, about 1 inch apart, to the stitching line to release the curve so it will lie flat. Be careful not to clip through the stitching.

seam, stitching through all three thicknesses close to the seamline. Press as stitched, then turn facing to underside of neckline. For hand-understitching see page 182.

Press facing and seam allowance away from garment. Turn facing to underside, and ease seamline under slightly. Press again.

Understitching is a row of regulation machine-stitching parallel to the seamline done on the right side of the facing, to prevent the edge of a facing from rolling to the right side of the garment.

Open out facing and seam allowances away from the garment. Beginning approximately 1 inch from the ends of the facing understitch the neckline

Facing Finish. Turn center back edges of facing diagonally over top ends of zipper tape and hand-stitch in place.

Side seams. Pin the front unit to the back unit at the side seams, matching notches. Stitch the seams from the lower edge of the blouse to the armhole edge. Finish seams and press them open in direction they were stitched.

armhole facings unit

Stitch ¼ inch from the outer edge of both armhole facings. Finish the outer edges with the same
finish used on the neckline facing. Match notches
on ends and stitch underarm seam.

With right sides together pin the facing to the
armhole of the blouse, matching notches. Stitch
the facing to the blouse, using very short stitches.
Trim the seam to a ¼ inch and clip. Understitch
through the facing and the seam allowances, along
the armhole seamline.

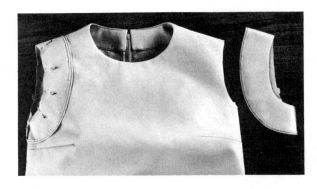

all-in-one facing unit

This facing combines the armhole facings with the
neckline facing. This facing can be used on any
sleeveless garment that has a center back opening and no collar. If the garment is constructed
with an all-in-one facing, apply the facing before
the center back and side seams are stitched.

Staystitch the front and back facings at the neckline ⅝ inch from the edge. With right sides together pin and stitch both shoulder seams, match-

ing notches. Trim the seam allowances to ¼ inch,
and press them open. Staystitch ¼ inch from the
lower edge and pink, zigzag or clean-finish.

Pin the facing to the blouse, right sides together,
matching center fronts and notches on neckline
and armhole edges. Center back edges of the facing are even with the blouse back edges. Stitch
the facing to the blouse at the neckline and armholes, using shorter stitches. Back-stitch at ends

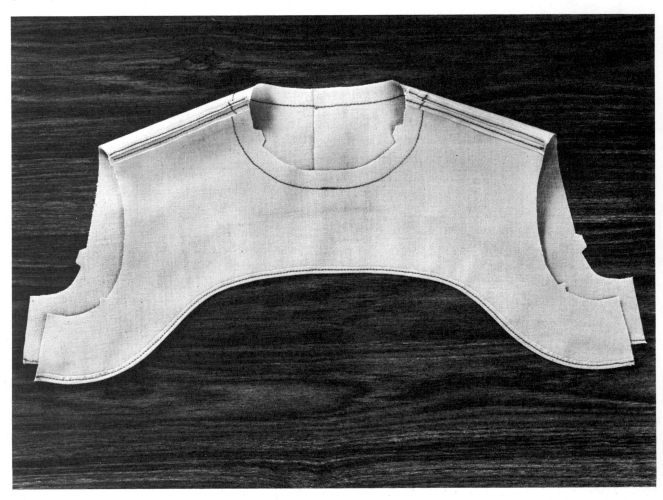

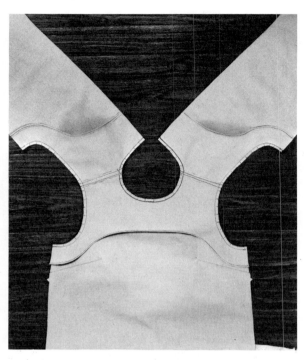

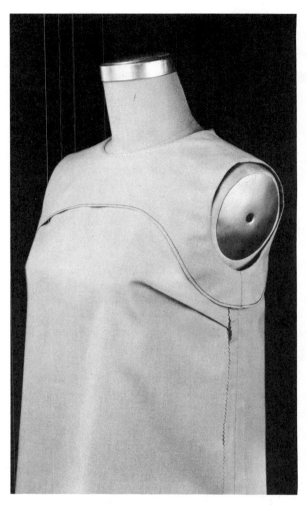

of stitching line. Trim the seam allowance to ¼ inch and clip at intervals on curves. From the front, insert your hand between facing and blouse. Turn facing to the inside by pulling each back section through shoulder opening. To understitch the facing at the neckline and armholes, begin 1

inch from the end of the facing, stitch up to the shoulder as far as possible, and repeat stitching on the other half. Press the facing.

Center back seam and zipper. Machine-baste the center back seam from the top down, checking that the neckline seam matches perfectly and that the neckline seam allowances are turned down. At notch at bottom of zipper opening, change to regulation stitch, backstitch and stitch the remainder of the seam. Insert zipper and finish facings following method on page 74.

Side seams with facings. Pin the front to the back at the side seams and make sure that the armhole seams match. To match seams perfectly, insert a pin through a stitch on the facing seam, ⅝ inch from edge. Bring the pin over and under one stitch in the blouse seam and again through the facing seam close to the first stitch. Stitch the seams from the lower edge of the blouse over the armhole seams to the edge of the facing. Finish seams and press them open in direction they were stitched.

finishing steps

Facing finish. Sew a hook to the right hand top corner and a metal eye or thread loop on left side; see page 201. For hanging snap, see page 201.

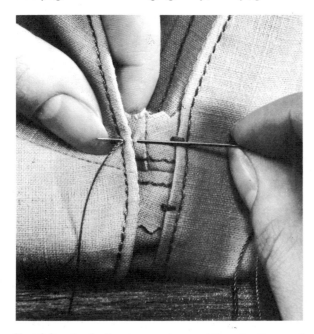

Hand bar-tack the separate neckline facing and the armhole facings at the shoulder seams. Hold the facing and the shoulder seam allowance together while you make 4 or 5 short (¼ inch or less) stitches in one place through the two thicknesses.

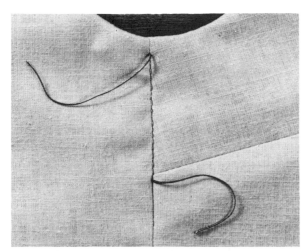

To machine-tack the armhole facing or the one-piece facing at the side seam, match the seam of the facing to the underarm seam of the blouse. Work from the right side, and keep the seamlines together as you stitch slowly in the groove of the seam from the top down for about 2 inches. Secure threads at each end of stitching with backstitching or tie threads on inside.

the hem

When you are making an overblouse, dress or jumper, prepare and finish the hem as shown for the skirt on page 70 or the dress on page 92.

If the blouse is to be tucked inside a skirt waistband, use one of the following finishes. Turn under the raw edge along the line of staystitching, turn a narrow hem, and machine-stitch along the top edge of hem.

Another method is to stitch a second time, around the bottom of the blouse, ⅝ inch from the raw edge and pink the edge.

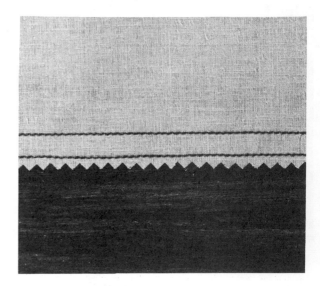

Final press the blouse. Press lightly in the area of the neck and armhole facings to prevent facing edges from leaving an impression on the outside of the garment. Refer to Chapter 15 for more detailed information on this technique.

a shirtdress, no less

The Shirtdress you are about to make introduces you to interfacing, buttons and button-holes, gathers, a collar and sleeves with cuffs — so finish this project first before you drop the word "beginner" from your sewing vocabulary.

The fabric you choose will affect the silhouette of your dress. For a soft look use a fabric that falls into graceful folds; for a bouffant look use a crisper fabric. Medium weight cottons, such as pique, chambray, lenos and gingham, synthetics and silks, plain or in small prints are all good choices for this dress. Remember, if you're using a one-way or napped fabric to follow the nap layout on your Cutting and Sewing Direction Sheet.

This dress used interfacing in two ways: It reinforces areas subjected to extra strain, such as under the buttons and buttonholes of the front closure; and, it gives permanent shaping to collar and cuffs. Refer to the chart on page 104 for detailed information on interfacings and their use.

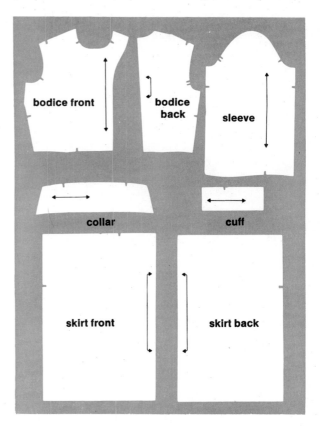

bodice front unit

Staystitch the shoulder and side edges ½ inch from the edge in the direction shown. Staystitch neckline on seamline from shoulder to center and from end of front extension to center. Mark the fold line with hand basting on both bodice fronts using contrasting thread. Transfer the tracing paper markings for buttonholes on the right hand bodice front by machine basting with contrasting thread; mark parallel lines to indicate the exact length of the buttonhole. Extend the ends of each horizontal bastemark ½ inch beyond the vertical measurement markings.

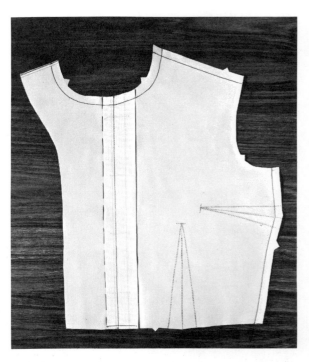

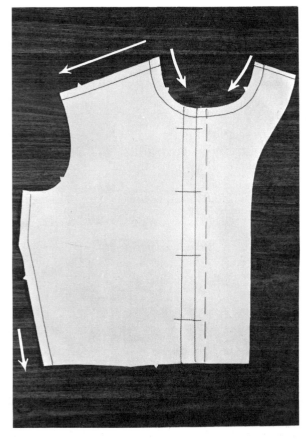

Cut two on-grain strips of interfacing 2 inches wide and 18 inches long to interface the fronts for buttons and buttonholes. On the wrong side of the fabric, pin the interfacing just inside the fold line. Make sure that the two fabric edges are even at the waistline; then trim the upper edge of the interfacing even with the neckline edge. Machine-baste interfacing strips down the center front line on both front sections; then across both ends to secure to garment.

Stitch the underarm darts and press down. Stitch the waistline darts and press toward center front.

Turn under and stitch ¼ inch on upper edge of facing extension. Pink, zigzag or clean finish the unnotched edges of facing; lace can be used on the facing edges for a custom touch. Press facing

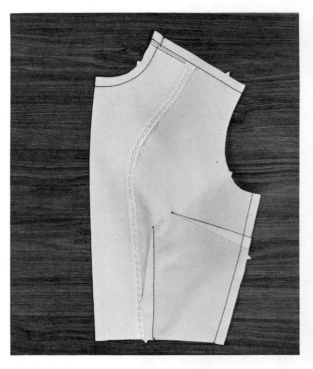

back on fold line. If you are going to use bound buttonholes, make them now. (See page 194.) Machine-made buttonholes can be made when bodice is completed.

bodice back unit

Staystitch neckline, shoulder and side edges, as you did on bodice front. Stitch darts and press toward center back.

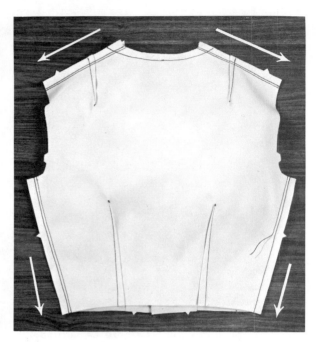

Seams. Pin the back and front units together at shoulder and side seams, matching notches and stitch in direction of arrows. Stitch the left side seam from armhole edge to notch; the edge below the notch is where the zipper will be inserted. Finish seams and press them open.

collar unit

Cut the collar interfacing on the same grain direction as the collar. On the two outside corners of the interfacing trim diagonally 1/4" inside the point where the seamlines meet. This eliminates bulk and makes it easier to turn a sharp point.

You have cut two collar sections. The one that goes on top is referred to as the "collar" and the one that is underneath will be referred to as the "facing". Pin interfacing to wrong side of collar and machine-baste 1/2 inch from the cut edges. Trim interfacing close to stitching. Pin the right

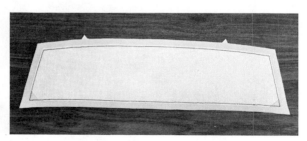

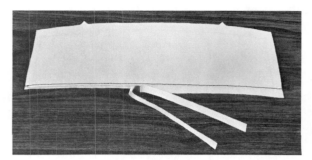

sides of the facing and collar together, matching the markings and notches. Stitch the long un-notched edge of collar from corner to corner, continuing to stitch across seam allowance at each end. Trim the <u>facing</u> seam allowance to a scant 1/8 inch; trim the <u>collar</u> seam allowance to a scant 1/4 inch. This is called "layering" or "grading"

seams to reduce bulk. Press the facing and seam allowance away from the collar, easing the seam-line slightly toward the facing. Understitch the facing, starting and ending 1 inch from each end.

Bring the right sides of the collar and facing together, matching notches at neckline edge, and pin. Stitch across ends continuing to stitch across seam allowances. Trim the seam allowances as described above; trim corners diagonally.

Turn the collar right side out. Gently push corners out with point of closed scissors. To help in work-ing the corners out, use a pin to pull up the stitches to a sharp point.

Attaching the collar. To release the neckline curve in order to attach the straight collar, clip neckline seam allowance at frequent intervals, clipping to the staystitching but not through it. Match mark-ings on collar facing to shoulder seams of bodice. Pin bodice to facing only between shoulder seams, leaving top collar free; place pins crosswise to seam-line. With bodice up, stitch from shoulder seam to shoulder seam, barely inside staystitching line.

Pin both the collar and collar facing to front edges of bodice neckline. Match notches and carefully

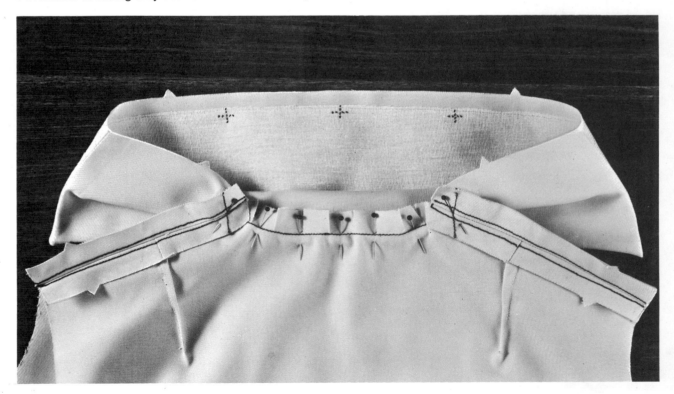

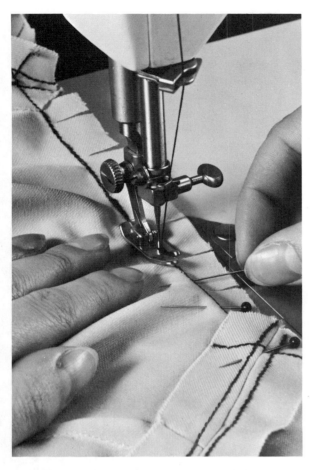

have cut edges even at neckline and waistline. Pin from the front fold to shoulder seam along neckline on both sides. Clip neck edge through all thicknesses at ends of front facings.

Using short stitches, stitch the front edges as basted, from shoulder seam to front edge; start stitching exactly where stitching ended on shoulder. Trim the seam allowance to 1/4 inch; trim the corners. Clip curves at intervals. Press seam allowance toward collar. Turn facings to inside of front, working out corners as on the collar point.

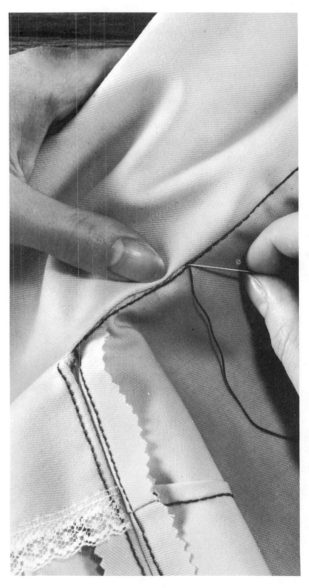

place center front of collar at center front of bodice. Baste through all thicknesses from center front to shoulder seam.

Front facings. Turn bodice front extensions to right side of bodice along fold lines, over the collar. This forms your front facings. Match notches and

Press under 5/8 inch seam allowance on free edge of collar between clips. Pin the turned-under edge of the collar to the neckline stitching line, covering the seam allowance; slipstitch in place. Tack facings to shoulder seams. Press the collar and neckline edge over a tailor's ham.

sleeve unit

Sleeve opening. Machine-stitch along marked slanted lines at lower edge of sleeves, using small reinforcement stitches for 1 inch on each side of

point; take one stitch across point. Slash between lines of stitching. Be sure to clip right up to the stitching line at the point of the slash. Failing to clip close enough creates a bubble at the point and prevents the opening from lying flat and smooth. Spread edges of slash apart, forming an almost straight line. Measure the stitching line from one end to the other. To finish these slashed edges, cut an on-grain strip of fabric 1½ inches wide and as long as the measurement of the slash. Press under ¼ inch on one long edge of strip.

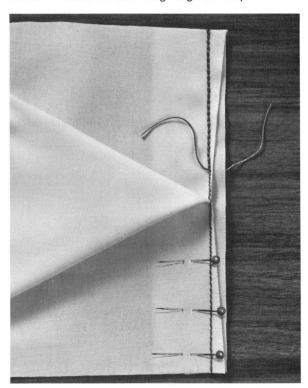

Pin right side of strip to wrong side of slashed edge with the edges of strip and slashed opening even, but the point ¼ inch from strip edge. Sleeve side up, lay in a straight line. Fold extra sleeve fabric out of the way and stitch ¼ inch from edge, using small reinforcement stitches. Press strip away from sleeve; seam toward strip.

Fold and pin the pressed-under edge of strip over seam. Top-stitch close to the turned edge through all thicknesses. Press front edge under; lap over back edge.

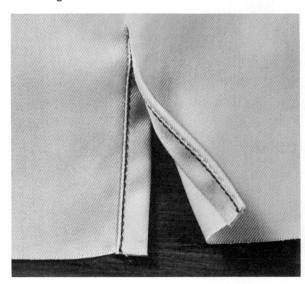

Sleeve. Ease-stitch the sleeve cap between the notches on the seamline. For heavy fabrics, use 6-8 stitches per inch; for lightweight fabrics, use 8-10. Place a second row of ease-stitching ¼ inch from the first, in the seam allowance. Do not clip thread ends.

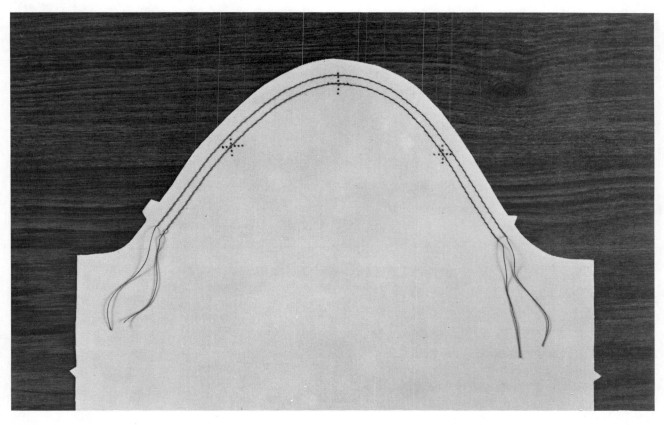

Stitch underarm seams. Finish the seam and press open. Machine-gather (longest stitch on machine) the lower edge of sleeves, placing one row of stitches on the seam line, the second ¼ inch from the first row in the seam allowance. Start and end the two rows of gathering at ends of the opening.

cuff unit

You have four cuff sections which are referred to as "cuff" and "facing" similar to the collar.

Cut the cuff interfacing on the same grain as the cuffs. Mark buttonhole markings on the interfacing.

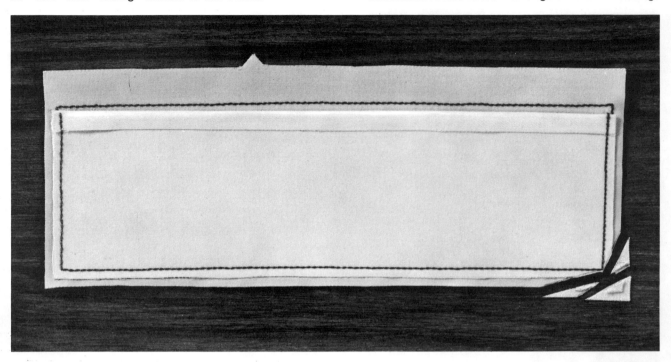

Trim the two outside corners of interfacing diagonally as instructed for collar interfacing on page 83. Pin interfacing to wrong side of cuff and machine baste 1/2 inch from cut edges. Trim interfacing close to stitching. Baste-mark buttonhole marking as you did for the bodice front. If you are making bound buttonholes, make them now.

Press notched edge of cuff facing to wrong side along the seamline; trim this seam allowance to 1/4 inch. With right sides together stitch facing to cuff on unnotched edges; use reinforcement stitching for one inch on each side of corners. To make it easier to trim and turn corners, you may also take one or two small stitches diagonally across the corners.

Layer the seams the same as you did for the collar, trimming diagonally across the corners; taper by trimming seam allowance close to stitching on both sides of points as shown.

Turn cuffs right side out, working out corners as for collar; press.

Attaching cuff. With right sides together, pin the sleeve to the cuff matching notches and underarm seam to marking on cuff. Place sleeve opening edges at ends of cuff as shown. Carefully pull up bobbin thread of gathering stitches so that the

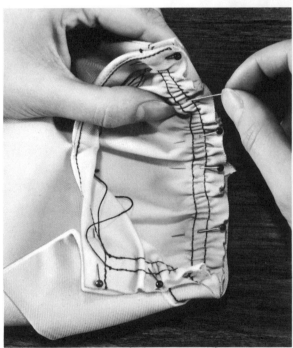

sleeve fits the cuff; tie ends of thread and baste seam. With sleeve on top, stitch in place. Trim seam allowance to 1/4 inch and press toward the cuff. Pin the turned-under edge of cuff facing over the seam and slip-stitch. Turn sleeves right side out, lap the front end of cuff over the back end; pin.

Joining sleeve unit to bodice unit. Hold the bodice wrong side up and with armhole toward you. Pin sleeve to armhole with sleeve inside bodice, right sides together. Place pins at underarm seams, shoulder seam, notches and markings; also

½ inch on each side of shoulder seam. Because the sleeve cap is on the straight grain at this point, no ease is needed. The markings are placed to distribute the fullness evenly in the proper places around the cap.

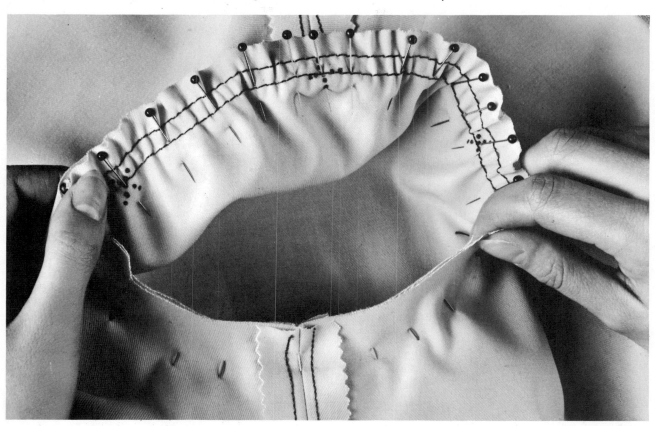

From notches on both sides pull up bobbin thread. Distribute the ease evenly between the pins. To hold ease, wind the thread ends around a pin placed at each end of stitching. There should be no tucks or gathers on the seam line.

Hand-baste on the stitching line. Then, machine-stitch with the sleeve side up so you can see that no puckers are caught in the seam. Start stitching at the underarm seam and make a complete circle. The line of stitching should be barely inside the line of ease-stitching. Make a second row of stitching ⅛ inch from the first row in the seam allowance. Trim close to stitching at underarm between notches. Do not trim sleeve cap. Press the armhole as instructed on page 158.

Finishing bodice. If you are using machine-worked buttonholes, make them now on the right front and cuffs. Lap bodice front, right over left, matching centers and with waistline edges even. Baste across the waistline edge through all thicknesses.

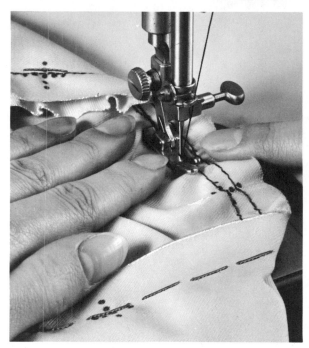

skirt unit

Pin the skirt sections with right sides together, matching notches. Stitch side seams, leaving left side open above the notch for the zipper.

Machine-gather waistline edge, starting and end-ing stitching 1 inch from the left side opening edges; it will be easier to pull up the gathering thread if you break the stitching at the right side seam as shown.

Joining skirt unit to bodice unit. Place the bodice inside the skirt with right sides together. Pin the edges together at waistline, matching centers, notches, side seam and left side edges. Pull up bobbin thread at ends of gathering rows so that skirt fits the bodice the same way as you did for the sleeve to cuff. Pin and baste. With the skirt toward you, stitch the waistline seam in one con-tinuous stitching starting at one edge of side open-ing. Then stitch one edge of straight seam binding just along seam stitching to within 1 inch of open-ing edges. This is to prevent seam from stretching during wear. Trim seam and press the edges up. Do not trim seam binding.

dress zipper

For an underarm application use a dress zipper, or convert a neckline zipper to this by sewing together the edges of the zipper tape above the slide.

The length of the opening should equal the length of the coil plus $\frac{1}{4}$ inch. Turn dress to wrong side. Clip waistline seam 1 inch on each side of opening. Press this section of the seam open. Pin edges of opening together, matching waistline seam. Machine-baste carefully on seamline.

Insert the zipper using the same procedure as given for a skirt zipper in a lapped application on page 64, except when doing final stitching, continue stitching across the top in the same way as for the bottom of the zipper.

Hand-finished zipper. Hand finishing a zipper is a designer touch that gives a professional appearance to any garment. It is also called a "hand-picked" or "hand sewn" zipper. Follow directions for lapped zipper, except before doing the final stitching, baste the zipper on the left side, keeping stitches an even distance from seam. For hand-finishing, use a single strand of regular or heavy-

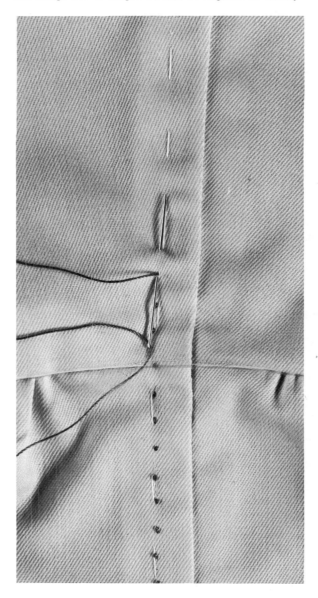

duty thread, silk or buttonhole twist. Start working at bottom end of opening, securing end of thread in zipper tape on underside. Bring needle up through all thicknesses just inside the seamline. Insert needle behind point where thread comes out, taking a stitch over only two or three fabric threads; then bring needle out again about $\frac{1}{8}$ inch ahead of stitching. Continue the stitches across bottom end, up the side, parallel with the seamline, and back to seamline across top of zipper. Fasten thread securely on underside.

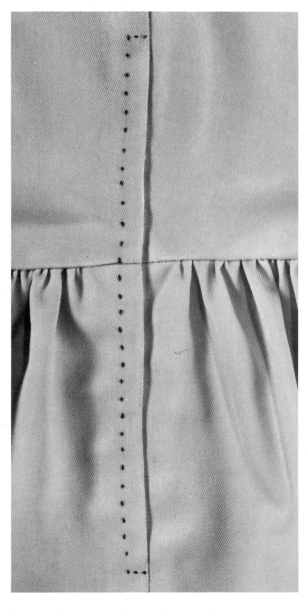

Remove hand-basting stitches. Press; remove machine-basting. For reinforcement turn garment wrong side out, and machine-stitch zipper tape only to the seam allowance.

the hem

Follow the first three steps for making a hem given on page 70. The top edge of hem can be finished

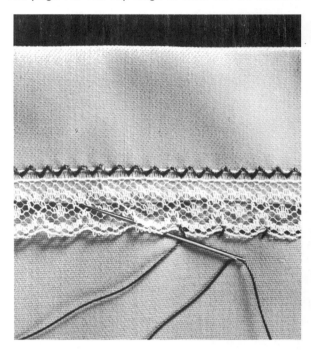

with lace or bias seam binding lapped $\frac{1}{4}$ inch over raw edge and machine-stitched. Secure hem with slip-stitching.

finishing steps

Buttons. Why just button-up your new shirtdress when you can accessorize it with buttons that add an eye-appealing accent? Be imaginative in your selection. Choose a color to harmonize or contrast with the garment fabric; or choose a style to emphasize the fashion mood you want to create.

Place pins through buttonholes at the center front line. Lap cuffs to pin marks, and place a pin in the end of buttonhole closest to end of cuff.

Sewing on buttons. Each button is sewn in position on the center front line, exactly where marked. See instructions on page 193.

Make a small thread loop at the top corner of right front neckline edge. Sew a small button on left front, opposite the loop and under the collar.

Remove basting threads. Final press the dress using techniques given in Chapter 15.

A belt or a ribbon tied around the waistline will add an attractive, finishing touch to the dress when you wear it. You may make a belt using one of the belt ideas found in Chapter 19.

10 to line or underline

At the rate you're expanding your wardrobe this might be a good time to plan some extra closet space before you run out entirely!

Now that you've come through the shirtdress project with flying colors and are no longer a novice, it's time to tackle a more advanced assignment, a dress using either an underlining or a lining, not to mention an invisible zipper.

Underlinings and linings play important and individual roles in fashion-sewing. Each performs a specific function inside the garment to enhance its finished appearance and also protect it from stresses of wear.

Underlining is a layer of lightweight fabric used for a variety of purposes. Cut from the same pattern pieces as the garment, it is joined to the outer fabric pieces before seams are stitched; thus the two layers are handled as one during construction. Underlining may give support to major design lines, add body to a fabric which is too flexible to be shaped alone, or add strength to a loosely woven fabric. Choose an underlining fabric that complements your garment fabric and does not change its natural characteristics.

Lining gives a beautiful, professional finish to the inside of a fashion and may be used in addition to an underlining. Constructed separately, a lining is made by following the same sewing steps as for the garment, omitting collars, cuffs, facings, zippers, etc. A lining protects a fashion from shape changes during wear and helps reduce wrinkling. A seam finish for the garment is seldom required (unless the fabric ravels badly) because the wrong side of the lining is placed against the wrong side of the garment, thereby concealing all seam allowances. Knit and bonded fabrics are not underlined, but may be lined.

Instructions for when and how to line a dress begin on page 94. If you are planning to use a lining in this way, read these important steps before you begin construction. Lining a dress or skirt is different from lining a tailored jacket or coat which is explained in Chapter 11.

The decision to use underlining and/or lining is made when you are planning your garment and selecting a pattern. The type selected (see chart on page 104) is determined by the outer fashion-fabric and the over-all effect desired. Linings and underlinings should be chosen with the same care as the garment fabric.

underlining a dress

Cut garment fabric and underlining separately, from the main pattern pieces and on the same grain. Since they are worked as one fabric during sewing, pattern markings need only to be transferred to underlining but it's wise to mark centers on garment fabric and to cut notches on both.

Place underlining pieces against wrong side of corresponding garment pieces, with marked side of underlining toward you. Smooth together to be sure raw edges are even. Match centers and notches. Pin along center line first, then waistline and side seams, placing pins inside stitching line.

Secure the underlining to the fabric by staystitching as shown in each of the following units. Staystitching is usually done in the correct direction of the grain. When underlining is being used with a fabric that is loosely woven, slippery, thick or napped, to prevent slippage staystitch with the underlining on top even if it necessitates stitching against the grain.

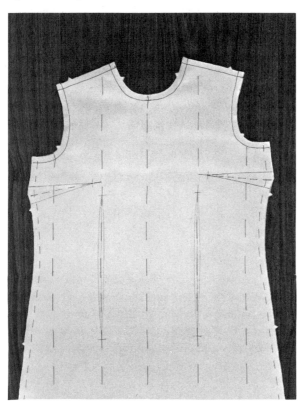

Staystitching an underlining to fabrics such as lightweight silks could result in a puckered look. Test staystitching on fabric scraps. If fabric draws, machine staystitch on the neckline, shoulder and armhole edges. Then hand-baste ½ inch from remaining edges. Hand-baste through center lines of

the darts, going 1 inch beyond termination points. This will hold the fabric layers together and insure a smooth point when the dart is stitched. With some slippery or very loosely woven fabrics, use several rows of long basting stitches about 4 inches apart to hold the two layers together. Do not remove this basting until garment is completed.

dress front unit

Secure the underlining; staystitch the neckline, shoulder and armhole edges. Baste stitch through center lines of darts. Stitch the underarm darts and press them down. Stitch the body (double pointed) darts, clip at waistline and press them toward the center. Remove basting from center of darts.

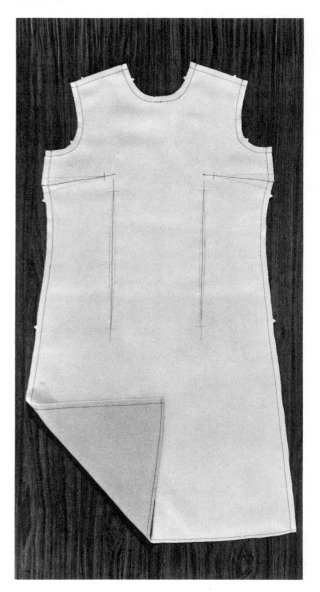

dress back unit

Secure the underlining; staystitch the neckline, shoulder and armhole edges. Stitch the darts, and clip the body darts as done for the front. Press darts toward center.

When using an invisible zipper in a neckline opening, leave the center back seam in the garment open and the neckline unfinished.

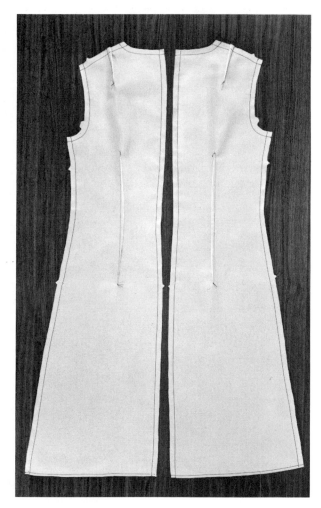

invisible zipper— neckline opening

Remove the regular presser foot; attach the special grooved foot used for inserting invisible zippers. Press the zipper tape before application.

Work with the neckline of dress and top of zipper turned away from you. Open the zipper and place it face down on the right side of the fabric with the zipper teeth along the seamline and the edge of the zipper tape toward the outer edge of the seam allowance. Place the top stop $1/4$ inch below seamline. Lower the right hand groove of zipper

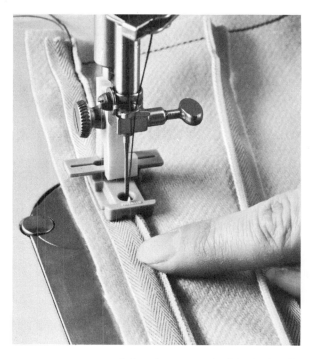

foot over the top of the zipper teeth. Stitch slowly, feeding the zipper teeth through the groove and stitching until the zipper foot touches the pull tab.

Place the other side of the zipper face down on the right side of the opposite edge of the zipper opening, lining up top edges of the zipper. Lower the left hand groove of the zipper foot over the zipper teeth. Stitch slowly down to the pull tab.

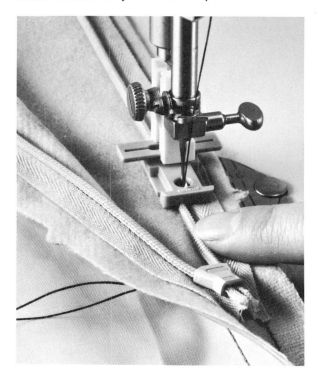

Close the zipper. Replace the special zipper foot with the regular zipper foot or if the invisible zipper foot is adjustable, slide it to the side so you can get the needle into the seamline to stitch the seam below the zipper for about 2 inches. With bulky fabrics this step should be done by hand-stitching.

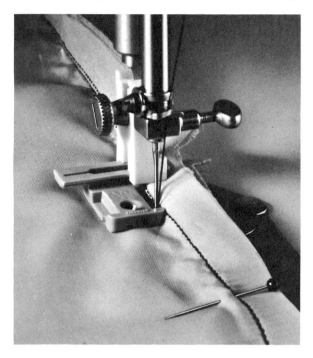

Replace zipper foot with regular presser foot and complete the center back seam, stitching from the

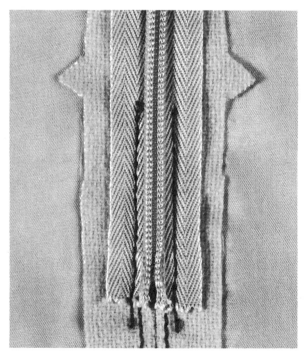

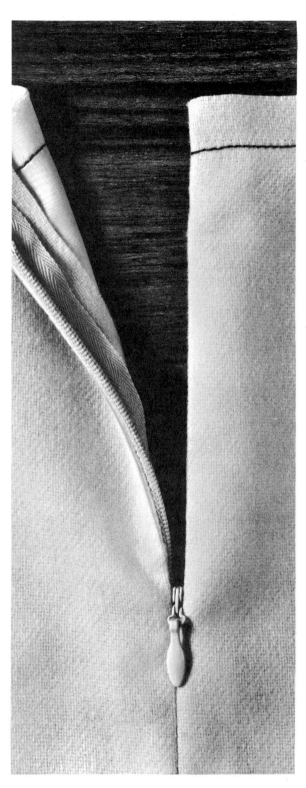

end of the zipper opening to the hem edge. Stitch the lower end of each zipper tape to the seam allowances. Press the seam open.

If you choose to use a regular zipper instead of the invisible zipper, refer to the methods for inserting lapped, slot or hand-sewn zippers as given in Chapters 7, 8 and 9 respectively.

Shoulder seams. Lay the front and back sections right sides together, matching notches. Pin and stitch the seams.

collar unit

Use a firm interfacing fabric, cut in the same grain direction as the collar. Machine-baste interfacing to wrong side of collar, ½ inch from raw edges. Trim interfacing close to stitching. Sew interfacing to collar along center fold line with long running stitches that do not show on the right side.

On one long edge of collar press under the ⅝ inch seam allowance, and trim edge to ¼ inch. Fold right sides of collar together along fold line. Stitch across collar at both ends. Trim seam allowances and corners at each end of fold. Turn collar to the right side and work out corners. Press.

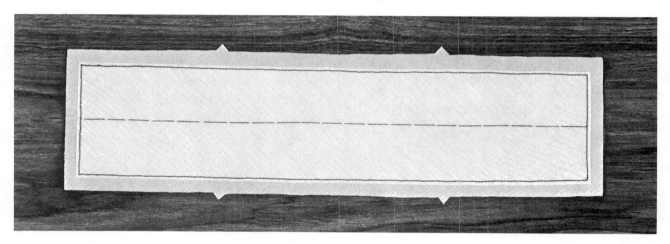

Alternate method. If you prefer a collar with a soft, padded look, use lambswool interfacing, but only interface one half of the collar.

Fold the collar pattern along the center fold line, and use it as a pattern for cutting the lambswool. Cut the interfacing on the same grain direction as the collar. Trim ¾ inch from the lower edge. Use a chalk pencil and ruler to mark a stitching pattern of parallel lines about one inch apart on the lengthwise threads of the lambswool. These lines will be on a diagonal (as illustrated) because of the bias grain. Clip the two lower corners of the interfacing diagonally, ¼ inch inside the stitching lines to eliminate seam bulk.

Staystitch the notched edges of the collar on seamline and the ends ½ inch from the edge. Mark the center fold line with hand-basting. Place the upper edge of the lambswool just below the center fold basting, keeping the ends even on both sides. Pin carefully. Because the collar is cut on the bias, the stitching pattern on the lambswool should be sewn by hand; with long running stitches, catch the lambswool to the collar on the marked lines.

On the interfaced half of the collar press the ⅝ inch seam allowance over the edge of the lambswool. Trim seam allowance to ¼ inch. Fold right sides together along the fold line, and pin. Stitch across each end, backstitching on the upper cor-

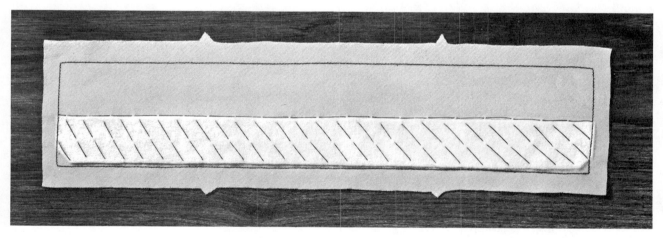

ners. Trim the seam allowance to a scant ¼ inch; trim corners. Turn the collar right side out and work corners out at each end. Press lightly.

When lambswool is applied to a collar cut on

straight grain, the stitching or quilting can be done by hand or machine. Quilting holds the two fabrics together and makes a firmer collar. Use a running stitch ⅛ inch from the edge to secure upper and lower edges of the lambswool interfacing.

Attaching the collar. Clip the seam allowance to the neckline staystitching on each side of the shoulder seam of the dress. With right sides together pin and baste notched edge of the collar to the dress, matching notches, center fronts and shoulder markings. Be sure that center back edges of the collar and dress are even. Stitch collar to neckline edge with the dress side up. Trim seam allowance on the dress to $1/4$ inch and on the collar to $3/8$ inch. Press seam toward collar.

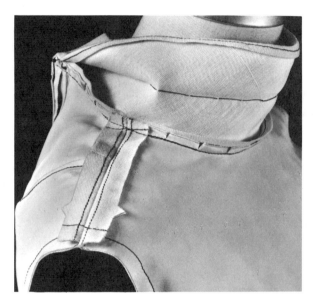

Turn the folded edge of the collar over the neckline seam allowances and slip-stitch it to the dress.

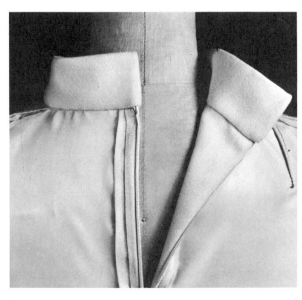

Side seams. Right sides together, pin the front to the back at the side seams and pin or hand-baste. Stitch from bottom edge up to the armhole.

sleeve unit

Underlining sleeves is optional, unless the garment fabric requires underlining to shape well and wear longer, such as fabric that is loosely woven.

Secure the underlining as done previously. Stay-stitch $1/4$ inch from the lower edge. Ease-stitch (10 stitches per inch) the sleeve cap on the seamline between the notches. Place a second row of stitches $1/4$ inch outside the first row in the seam allowance. Pin and stitch elbow dart. Press down.

Lap one edge of bias seam binding over lower edge of sleeve on right side and stitch. Or, you can finish the hem edge by using the bias bound hem on the next page. Press the sleeve hem to the wrong side.

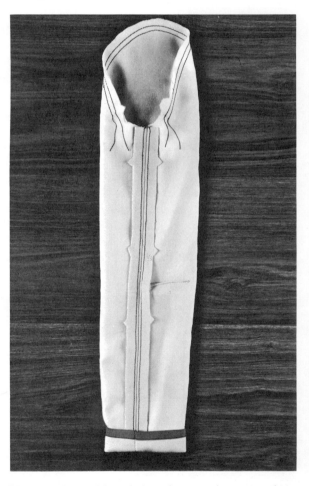

Pin the right side of the sleeve edges together, matching notches. Stitch from the armhole to the lower edge, and finish the seam if necessary. Press the seam open. Press the hem again to reestablish the hemline. Hand-stitch the hem.

Ease the sleeve caps, and attach the sleeves to the dress using the methods on page 89.

the hem

Measure, mark and turn the hem following the steps on page 70. After marking the length, you may stitch 1/4 inch below marking and trim underlining below the stitching to eliminate bulk. Use one of the hem finishes in Chapter 17, or for a fine, custom finish use the bias bound finish given below.

Bias bound hem finish. Cut bias strips of the underlining fabric 1 inch in width. See Making Bias Strips on page 214. With right sides together pin bias strip to hem, keeping edges even. Stitch the strip to the hem in a 1/4 inch seam. Trim seam edges to 1/8 inch. Fold the strip over the raw edges and

press to wrong side of hem. On the right side insert the needle in the well of the seamline (close to turned edge of bias); stitch so the stitching is lost in the seam. Press and turn hem to position. Blind-stitch hem edge to underlining only so that stitches will not show on right side.

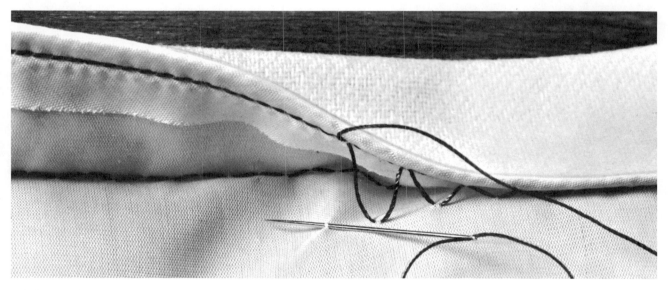

Double-stitched hem. Use this hem for extra support and to prevent the hem from rolling to the right side. Pin along bottom fold; then hand-baste center of hem around skirt. Fold back the top of hem along the basting, and blind-stitch hem to the underlining. Do not draw the stitches tightly. Turn top of hem up, and make the second row of

blind-stitches between the bound edge and underlining. Remove basting.

finishing steps

Sew on hooks and make thread loops at the center back edges of collar. Make sure that all basting has been removed. Final press the dress.

lining a dress

Cut and mark the lining fabric with the same pattern pieces that you used for the garment. Staystitch neckline, shoulder and armhole edges, stitching directionally. Then stitch and press the darts as instructed in the dress front and dress back units. Stitch the shoulder and side seams; stitch center back seam from the hem to 1 inch from zipper opening. Finish seam edges, if desired, and press seams open. Press the edges of the center back opening to the wrong side, along the seamlines.

The lining is attached after the zipper has been inserted in the dress, but before the neckline is finished and the sleeves stitched.

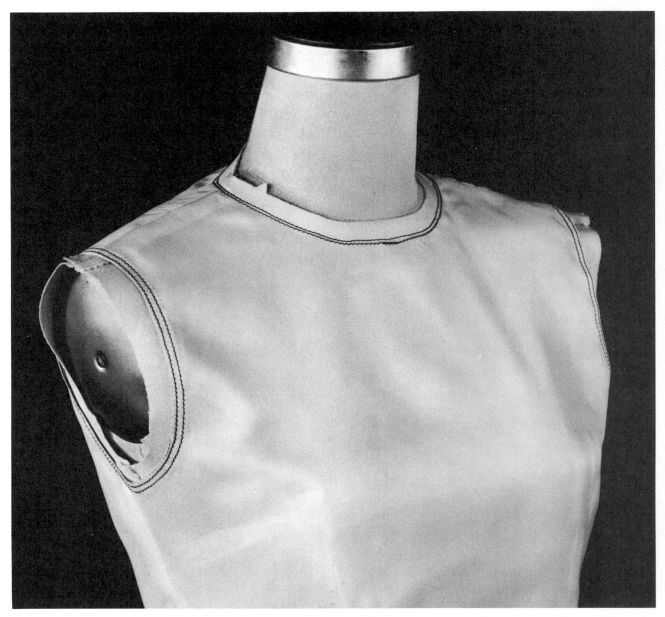

Neckline and armholes. Place the lining inside the garment so that the wrong sides are together, matching all seams. Pin the lining to the dress around the neckline, and stitch $1/2$ inch from the edge. Clip to stitching line and attach and finish the collar as instructed previously. If you are making a sleeveless lined dress, also stitch at armholes the same as at neckline before attaching facings.

Lining sleeves is a matter of preference. If you do not line them, finish armholes of lining this way: clip to staystitching, turn under on staystitching line and stitch close to the fold. Make another row of stitching $1/4$ inch in from the first. If you line the sleeves, refer to the following steps.

Long sleeves. If you are going to use a long, lined sleeve, attach the lining at the armhole seam by hand. Finish the sleeve lining as for a jacket on page 109, allowing $\frac{1}{2}$ inch ease at hem.

Short sleeves. The lining in a short sleeve is handled in a different manner. Cut the lining using the sleeve pattern piece. Ease-stitch the cap of the sleeve and the lining separately as described in

sleeve unit. Trim the hem allowance to $\frac{5}{8}$ inch on both the sleeve and the lining.

With right sides together stitch the sleeve to the lining along the lower edge, using a $\frac{5}{8}$ inch seam. Trim the seam allowance to $\frac{1}{4}$ inch, and press it toward the lining. Understitch through the lining and seam allowance, beginning and ending 1 inch from each end.

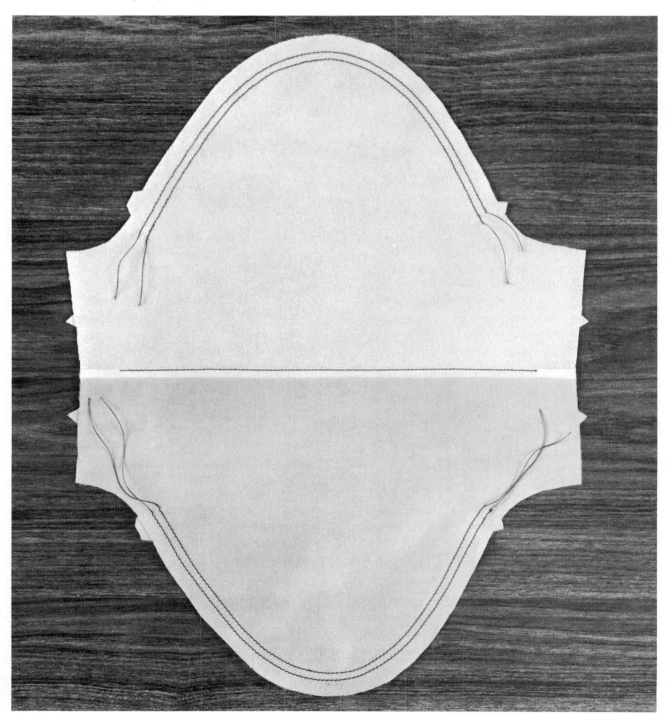

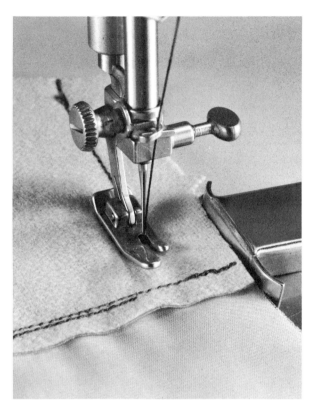

With right sides together and the sleeve and lining spread flat, stitch the underarm seam of the sleeve and lining in a continuous line. Press the seam open, and turn the lining inside the sleeve. Ease only the sleevecap of the dress. Set in sleeve to dress, leaving lining free. Stitch and press.

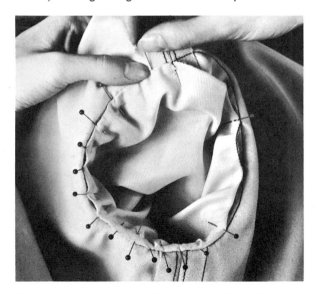

Ease sleeve lining to fit armhole. Turn the raw edge to the inside on the staystitching line and lap it over the armhole seam allowance. Hand-sew to armhole seam with very small slip-stitches.

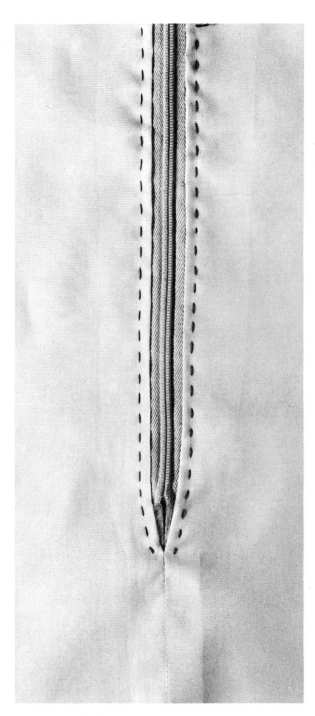

Zipper finish. Pin folded edge of the lining to zipper tape ¹⁄₄ inch from the zipper teeth and slip-stitch. Place a second row of hand-stitching (a short running stitch) ¹⁄₄ inch from the first row to prevent the lining from rolling and catching in the zipper teeth.

The hem of the lining should be one inch shorter than the dress. For a finishing touch, lace or a decorative ribbon may be sewn on the right side of the lining along the stitching line.

flip lining

A flip lining can be inserted in any sleeveless garment that has two side seams, a center back seam and shoulders at least two inches wide. This lining is attached to the neckline and armholes before the side seams and center back seam of the dress and lining are completed. Stitch the lining to the dress and pull it through the shoulders exactly as it was done in the all-in-one facing in Chapter 8. See photographs on pages 78 and 79.

Spread the dress and lining flat. Pin or baste the side seams of the dress and the side seams of the lining. Stitch the side seams of the dress from the lower edge up to lining; then stitch the lining from lower edge up, meeting the point where the dress seam ended. Stitch the center back seams of the dress and lining separately. Tack the lining to the dress at the underarm seams.

Continue construction of the dress. Finish the zipper placket and hem of the lining as described for the lining in the previous paragraphs.

choosing interfacing, underlining and lining

Interfacing, underlining and lining are the three types of fabrics used inside the garment to help you give a professional finish to the outside. The chart on the next page lists general types and gives suggestions for their use. The differences between underlining and lining were explained on the first pages of this chapter.

Interfacing is a third layer of fabric, woven or nonwoven, used between the garment fabric and a facing to give the area support or shape and crispness. Necklines, collars and cuffs use interfacing cut to their shapes. Interfacing strips may be used to reinforce buttonhole areas and to add body and crispness at hemlines.

The nonwoven interfacings are similar to lightweight felt, and do not have grain. Pattern pieces can be placed on them in any direction for cutting. Most nonwovens have a crisp feeling, but in areas where soft shaping is needed a special all-bias nonwoven can be used.

The iron-on type of interfacing can be either woven or nonwoven. Its heat-sensitive backing is fused to the garment fabric with an iron. Iron-ons will usually make a garment fabric stiffer, so they should only be used in small detail areas.

Special interfacing, underlining and lining fabrics are available for each of these important sewing steps. Each comes in a variety of types and you may choose underlinings and linings in fashion colors to harmonize or contrast with the garment fabrics. A print, such as shown in the flip lining on this page is a distinctive personal touch.

Before making your final selection of each inner fabric, place the garment fabric over it, draping both over your hand to see how the two fabrics combine. None of the three types should ever be heavier in weight than the garment fabric. You must decide which type is needed and the following chart offers suggestions to help you. Be sure they have the same care characteristics (either washable or dry cleanable) as the garment fabric and if not preshrunk when purchased, be sure to shrink before cutting.

Your pattern envelope tells how much interfacing is needed as well as lining requirements for a jacket or coat. For underlining and lining when no yardage is given, such as for a dress or skirt, use the same yardage given for the outer fabric.

the inside story of inner fabrics

garment fabric	interfacing	underlining	lining
very light to light weight cottons, silks and blends (voile, lawn, pure silk, lace, sheer crepe, challis)	light weight interfacing with a soft or crisp finish **soft shaping:** bias non-woven **crisp:** organdy, organza (for silk), light weight non-woven	light weight rayon underlining with a soft or crisp finish **soft:** cotton sheath lining **crisp:** organdy, organza (for silk), light weight non-woven	silk-like rayon or polyester lining china silk acetate sheath lining light weight crepe
medium weight cottons blends synthetics silks wools linens (denim, homespun, poplin, silk linen, flannel)	medium weight rayon interfacing with a soft or crisp finish **soft:** bias non-woven **crisp:** medium weight non-woven, light weight hair canvas, canvas interfacing, iron-on woven or non-woven	medium weight rayon underlining with a soft or crisp finish **soft:** bias non-woven **crisp:** medium weight taffeta or non-woven	acetate sheath lining medium weight crepe silk surah polished cotton (for cottons and linens) taffeta
heavy weight cottons linens wools blends (corduroy, brocade, tweed, worsted)	medium or heavy weight rayon or rayon and cotton interfacing with a soft or crisp finish **soft:** soft hair canvas **crisp:** heavy weight non-woven, medium or heavy weight crisp hair canvas or canvas interfacing, worsted interfacing, iron-on woven or non-woven	medium or heavy weight rayon and cotton underlining with a soft or crisp finish **crisp:** medium or heavy weight non-woven	heavy weight taffeta satin crepe-back satin medium weight crepe silk shantung rayon twill
knits jerseys	select one of the woven or non-woven types listed above of appropriate weight and finish	bonded knits are not underlined double knits and jerseys may be underlined with feather-weight polyester non-woven underlinings	linings above of the appropriate weight
leather suede	rayon interfacing, hair canvas or canvas, non-woven, iron-on woven or non-woven	rayon or rayon/cotton underlining of appropriate weight	satin taffeta rayon twill
permanent press	permanent press woven or non-woven interfacing	usually not needed	cotton/polyester or all-polyester sheath lining if permanent press fabric

lining a jacket or coat

Hold it! Don't start turning the pages to see if you skipped a chapter about making a jacket or coat!

Right now you are expert enough to make a simple jacket or coat by following the instructions in the pattern envelope; we're going to show you additional tips on how to line it after you've made it.

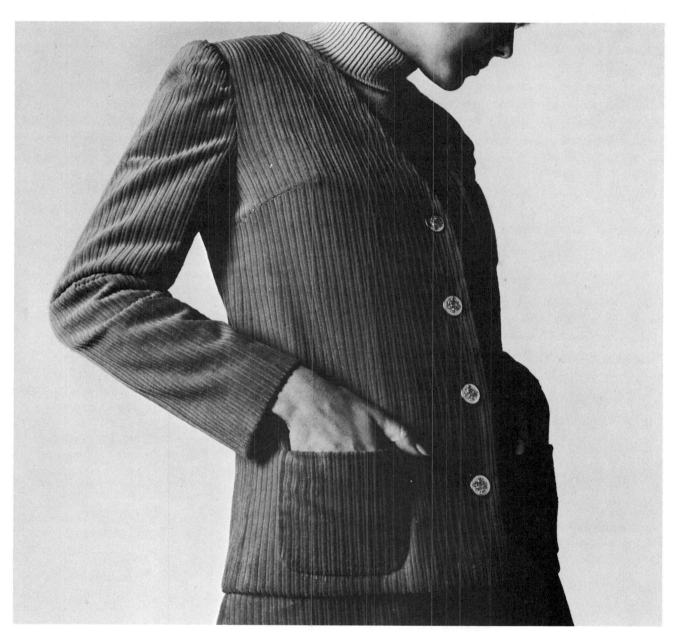

The jacket shown is a style that can be successfully coordinated with a skirt, dress or pants.

A jacket lining can be fashion-wise as well as an inside finish; line a jacket with the same fabric that you used to make a blouse that you'll wear with the jacket, or use a contrasting color or coordinated print. Refer to page 104 for the appropriate linings for various fabric weights.

Jacket and coat linings can be inserted by using the same method except that the coat hem and the lining hem are usually finished separately as shown at the end of this chapter.

cutting the lining

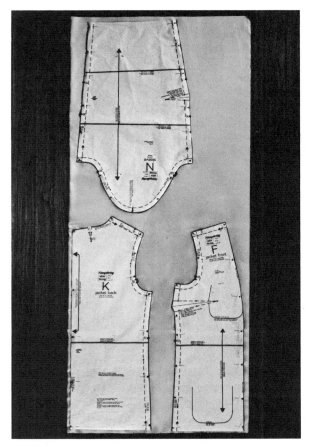

A jacket or coat pattern may not include separate pattern pieces for a lining; follow the cutting layout and special "cutting notes" for instructions for cutting the lining from the garment front, back and sleeve patterns. The front and back are usually marked with "cut-off" lines to convert the pattern pieces for the garment into a lining pattern.

Pleat allowance. There is a release pleat at the center back of the lining for ease. Place the center back edge of the pattern an even ¹/₂ inch from fabric fold. Baste the two thicknesses together, placing the line of basting along the edge of the pattern as shown in the layout above.

making the lining

There are a few differences between making a garment and making a lining for it:

1. The jacket has facings on the fronts and neckline, so the lining is finished by sewing it over the raw edges of the facings.
2. The hem of the lining overlaps the top of the lower edge and sleeve hems.
3. The lining has a release pleat down the center back that is not in the jacket.

Front lining. Staystitch the shoulder and armholes ¹/₂ inch from the edges in the same way that the jacket was done; staystitch neckline and front

edges ⁵/₈ inch from the edge. If there are shoulder darts, they should be stitched from the shoulder to the second small dot, or to about 4 inches from the shoulder. This dart should not be trimmed; press it toward center. Stitch and press other darts the same as jacket.

Back lining. Staystitch back neckline, shoulders and armholes as for jacket; stitch darts and press toward sides.

Center back pleat. Smooth back out flat, and press center back fold to one side along the basting to form a pleat. Working from the right side of lining, catch-stitch the back pleat for about 1¹/₂ inches at neckline, waistline and hemline. Make stitches about ¹/₄ inch apart through the three thicknesses, not over the edge of the fold.

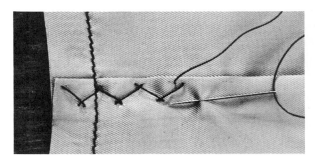

With right sides together pin and stitch the fronts to the back at the shoulder and side seams. Press seams open in the direction they were stitched.

Sleeves. Make sleeves in the same way as the garment sleeves except for the hem; press under ¹/₂ inch on lower edge.

lining put in by hand

The lining may be joined to the jacket either by hand or by machine. When the lining is put in by hand there are two methods that can be used; sleeves may be joined to lining by hand or machine.

Method 1 — Sleeves put in by machine. Pin sleeves in the armholes as instructed for garment and stitch. Trim seam allowance between notches at underarm. Press seam open around the armhole above the notches.

On the front and back neckline edges clip seam allowance to staystitching on curves. Press seam allowance to wrong side on staystitching line. Roll the staystitching under so that it will not show. Press under ½ inch hem at lower edge of lining.

With the wrong sides together match the center back pleat of lining to the center back of neckline facing and pin. Match the side seams of the lining to garment seams at the armholes and pin.

Slip the sleeve lining over the jacket sleeves with wrong sides together. Match and pin shoulder seams together at armhole and neckline. Lap and pin the turned edge of lining over the front facings and the back neckline facing.

Sew the lining to facings with small hemming or slip-stitches (about $1/8$ inch), easing the lining slightly over the bust. Slip-stitch to within 3 inches of the hemline on both sides.

Turn the lining front away from the garment. Pin the side seam allowance of the lining to the side seam allowance of the jacket. Tack loosely with long running stitches, starting 2 inches below the armhole and ending 3 inches above the hem.

With lining right side up, smooth the lining over the jacket at the lower edge. About 3 inches above the hem baste the lining and jacket together all the way across. Pin the bottom fold of lining over the edge of jacket hem, matching the raw edges.

Baste and slip-stitch lining in place. There is some extra length in the lining, so press this fullness down over the hem. This ease in the lining prevents it from drawing and to allow for some shifting in the lining when the jacket is being worn.

Sew the loose lower front edges of the lining to the facings. Remove the basting, and lightly press the entire lining.

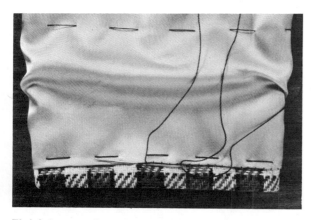

Finish lower edge of sleeves. About 3 inches above the hem baste the lining and jacket together. Lap the pressed edge of lining over sleeve hem ½ inch. Pin and baste. Slip-stitch. The extra length prevents the lining from pulling.

Method 2 — Sleeves put in by hand. Prepare the front and back lining as previously instructed, stitching all seams except the shoulder seams.

The sleeve lining is prepared in the same way as the garment sleeve, but it is not stitched into the lining. Follow the instructions in Method 1 for pinning lining to jacket.

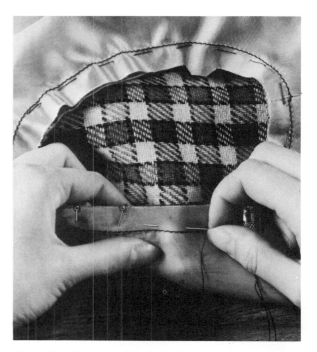

Baste the lining to the armhole edges of the jacket, starting at the underarm seam and working up to 1 inch on each side of the shoulder seam, first on the front, then on the back.

Pin and sew shoulder edge on lining front to jacket shoulder seam.

Turn under the back shoulder edges of lining along the seamline, and pin it over the front edges at the shoulder. Pin back lining over back neckline facing between the shoulder seams, and slip-stitch in position.

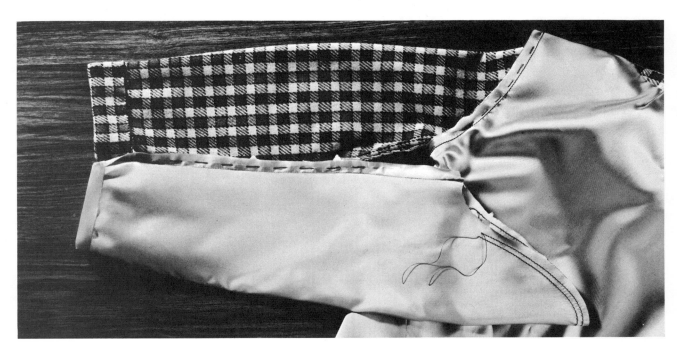

Turn the jacket sleeves and linings wrong side out. Match the pressed-open underarm seams, keeping the top edges even. Pin one seam allowance of the lining to the matching seam allowance in the sleeve. Sew seams together with a long running stitch, starting and ending about 3 inches from the top and bottom of sleeve.

Slip your hand down inside the sleeve lining from the armhole. Grasp the lower edges of the jacket sleeve and lining, and draw them through the lining thereby turning the lining right side out over the jacket sleeve.

Pin lining to armhole at the notches and dots; place top of sleeve mark at the shoulder seam. Draw up the ease threads in top of lining from both ends. Distribute ease evenly, fitting the lining over sleeve. See page 102.

Turn under the edge of lining on the seamline, and pin; sew to the armhole with very small hemming stitches. As the jacket is worn there is strain on the armhole, so be sure that these stitches are very firm. Finish the lower edge of jacket and sleeves the same way as in Method 1.

lining put in by machine

Simple sport jackets or coats or children's clothing can have linings put in by machine

Finish the jacket or coat completely, but do not sew the front and back facings to the interfacing. Complete the lining, stitching sleeves by machine but do not press the front and back neckline edges to the wrong side. Press the hem edges of the lining and the sleeves to the wrong side.

If the lining is to be loose at the lower edge, finish hem on lining before pinning it to the garment. With right sides together pin the front edges and back neckline edge of lining to the front and back facings, matching center backs and shoulder seams. Baste, starting at lower edge of one front facing, and continue around the back neckline to lower edge on the opposite side of garment. Machine-stitch edges together, backstitching at both ends. Clip seam allowance on curved edges; then press seam allowance toward the lining.

Turn the lining right side out. Insert sleeve linings into sleeves. Match underarm seams of lining to garment seams and hem or slip-stitch turned edge to top of hem in the garment as in Method 1. Finish lower edge of sleeves. Press lining lightly.

lining in coat — separate bottom hems

The lining in a coat is usually left loose at the lower edge. When this is done, the lining is hemmed separately, and it should be at least 1 inch shorter than the finished hem of the coat.

The ends of the lining at the lower edge are sewn to the front facings, and the hem is held to the coat at the seamlines with chain tacks. See page 213 for making tacks.

special touches

Embroidered ribbon or lace can be used as a decorative finish on the inside of a jacket. Hand sew the ribbon or lace over the seam where facing and lining meet. Use a narrow width that will go around curves more easily.

Lace edging or rickrack braid can also be used as an inside jacket trim. The edging or braid is stitched to the front and back neckline facings on the seamline before the lining is attached.

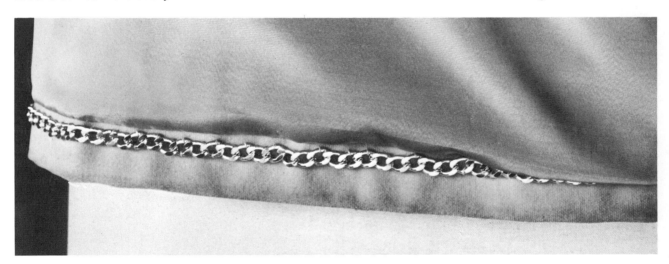

Chain weight. To preserve the hang of the suit jacket and hold it in position, a gold chain weight is both decorative and practical. These chains are available in several weights and lengths. They are constructed of flattened links, made expressly for use along lower hem edges.

The chain should be long enough to extend across the back and beyond the side seams. Lay the chain below the lining, along the top of the hem on the inside of jacket. Overcast by taking a stitch in alternate links along the upper and lower edges of the chain. Take care that the stitches do not go through to the outside of jacket. It's a good idea to remove chain before dry-cleaning the garment since pressing may cause the impression of the chain to show on the outside of the jacket.

chapter 12 the shape of pants to come

Women may not be wearing the pants in the family these days, but they are most certainly wearing pants! Pants have become one of the most popular modes in fashion, ranging all the way from a backyard barbecue to a white tie party. They come in all lengths and widths — bell bottoms, hip huggers, Bermudas, jumpsuits and trim-tailored. They can be elegant, casual, slim-fitted or widely handsome.

Suitable fabrics for pants come in a wide range; for sports — denims, duck, terry cloth, stretch and pique; for elegance — plain or print, linen, bonded lace and silk shantung; for a tailored look—flannel, corduroy and bonded jersey. Knit fabric is an excellent choice for closely fitted pants because its stretchability permits the pants to give when you are in motion and yet retain its shape.

If you are going to underline your pants, pull can be avoided by constructing the underlining and the fabric separately at the side seams.

Four steps are involved in pants-making:
1. Measure—Determine your pants measurements. See page 150 for Pants Measurements.

2. Alter—Adjust the pattern to correspond with your measurements. Refer to Chapter 14.

3. Fit—Adjust a trial pair of pants to solve any figure problems not corrected by measuring and altering. Refer to Chapter 14.

4. Construction—The step-by-step techniques of pants-making are given on the following pages.

Select your pants pattern size by your waist measurement. If your hip measurement is much larger in proportion to your waist, select your pattern according to hip measurement, and adjust waistline by taking deeper darts.

Construction details are given here for two styles of pants. The first has a grosgrain ribbon waistband finish, side zipper and stitched creases. The second are hip huggers with faced waistline, modified fly-front closure and cuffed bottoms.

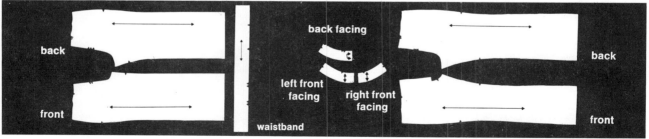

back

front

back facing

left front facing

right front facing

waistband

back

front

pants front unit

Staystitch ⁵/₈ inch from the waistline edges and ¹/₂ inch from the side edges above the notches, as indicated by arrows. Staystitch ¹/₄ inch from the lower edges. Stitch the darts, and press them toward the center front.

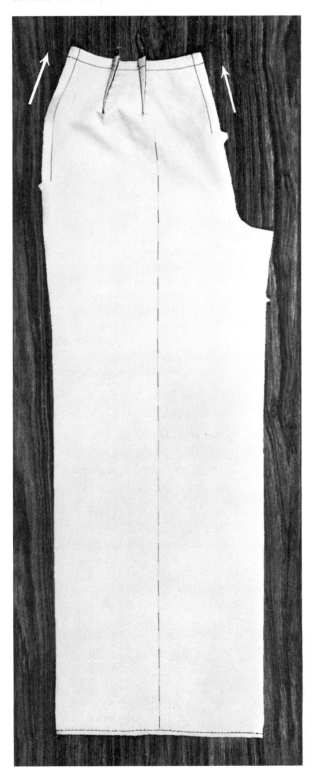

pants back unit

Staystitch ⁵/₈ inch from the waistline edges and ¹/₂ inch from the side seams above the notches. Staystitch ¹/₄ inch from the lower edges. Stitch the darts, and press them toward the center back.

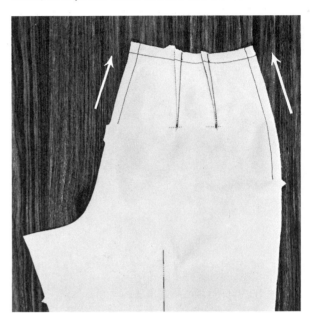

Set the creases before the pants fronts and backs are seamed together. If your pattern does not show a crease line and you want to add it, it should be at the center of each front and back section, stopping just below the waist darts in front and just below crotch level in back. Transfer crease marking to right side of fabric with hand basting. Fold each section on the crease line. Apply steam; then pound the steam into the fabric with the pounding block to set the crease lines.

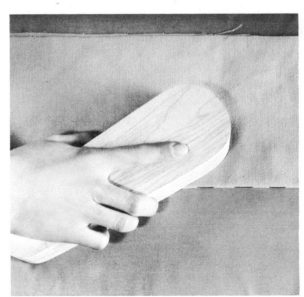

Seams. With right sides together stitch the side seams, leaving an opening for the zipper on the left hand side. Finish lower edges of the pants; in light or medium weight fabric, turn under 1/4 inch and stitch. Bulky and heavy weight fabrics should be finished with seam binding. Lap seam binding 1/4 inch over edge and stitch. Press hem up the desired depth.

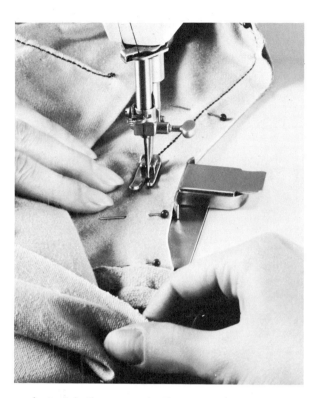

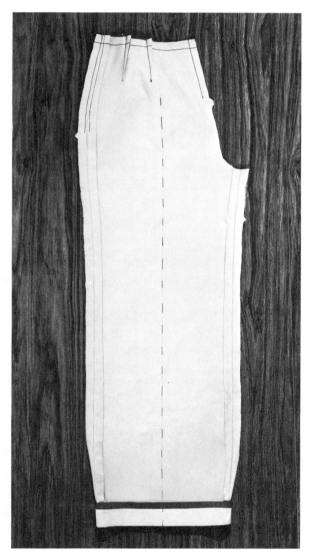

Stitch the inseams (inner leg seams). Finish the seams if necessary. Press seams open, and press the hem again to restore the hemline.

Place one pants leg inside the other, with right sides together and stitch the crotch seam with a continuous line of stitching. If your sewing machine has a stretch stitch use it for the crotch seam. On knits use a narrow zig-zag. On regular machines, use a setting of 20 stitches per inch for this seam,

and stretch the seam in the curved area as you stitch. To reinforce, make a second row of stitching over the first stitching line between notches. Trim seam along curve and clip seam allowance. Press as stitched; press seam open.

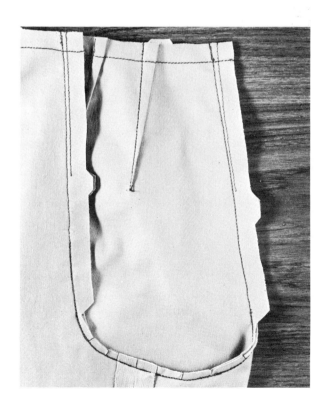

Hems. Now that the hem edges have been finished and pressed, hand sew the hems with a lockstitch. This stitch is recommended for pants because it is strong and helps to prevent the hem from pulling out when the foot is inserted.

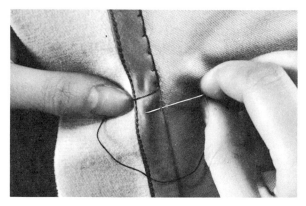

Lockstitch. Lay pants away from you with the hem edge toward you. Fasten the thread in the hem. Lay the thread to the left, and place left thumb over it. Take a small stitch in the garment (1 thread) and then a stitch in the top edge of hem directly opposite of where the thread was fastened; draw needle through over the thread held by the thumb. Draw thread all the way through, and lay it to the left of where stitch was made at top of hem. Hold thread with the left thumb, and take another stitch about $1/4$ inch to the right of the first; continue around the entire hem.

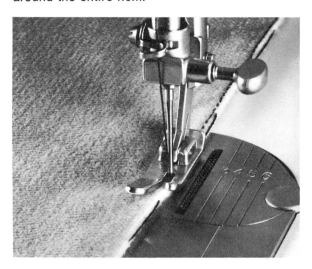

Stitched crease-lines. After the hem of each pants leg is completed, you can set your crease lines permanently by stitching narrow tucks. Fold on the crease line, wrong sides together, and stitch very close to the folded edge only as far up toward the waistline as originally creased and pounded.

waistband unit

Insert the zipper using the lapped method in Chapter 7. Bulk can be eliminated by backing the waistband with grosgrain ribbon. The ribbon should be the same width as the finished waistband and the same length as the waistband pattern.

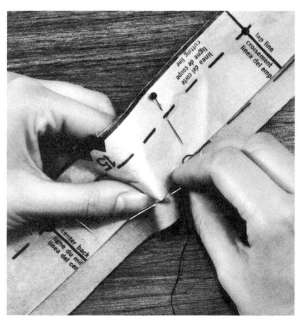

For a grosgrain backed waistband fold the pattern in half, lengthwise. Cut the waistband, adding $1/2$ inch along the folded edge. Before you remove the pattern, baste along the edge of the pattern to mark the fold line, which will be the top of the waistband.

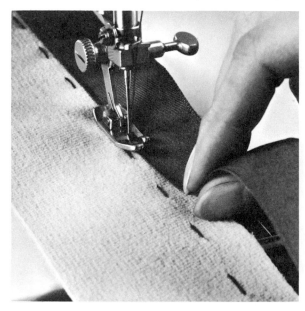

On the right side of the fabric, lap the ribbon over the unnotched edge of the waistband, along the basting. Stitch close to the edge of the ribbon.

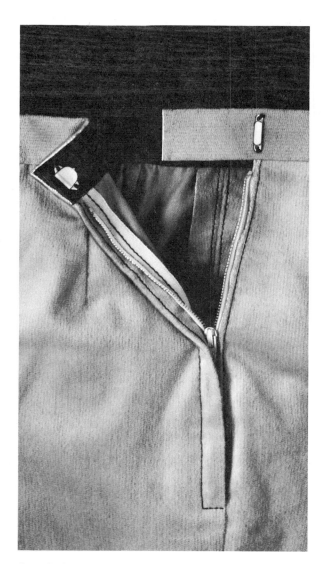

Attach the waistband to the pants, stitch the ends, and finish the band exactly as you did in Chapter 7. Finish ends with large metal hook and eye.

pants with waistline facing

Because these pants have a zipper in the center front seam, rather than in the side seam, the construction of the units is different from those described previously.

front unit

Staystitch waistline edges, side edges above the notches, and lower edges; stitch the darts, and press them as for pants at beginning of chapter.

Reinforce inner corner at bottom of center front opening, using short stitches. Stitch along seamline curve on center fronts starting about 1 inch from the dot; pivot at dot, and stitch to edge.

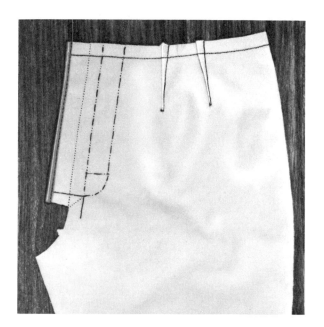

Bind the straight edges of center front extensions from waistline down. Fold a strip of bias seam binding in half, lengthwise, and pin over each edge. Machine-stitch.

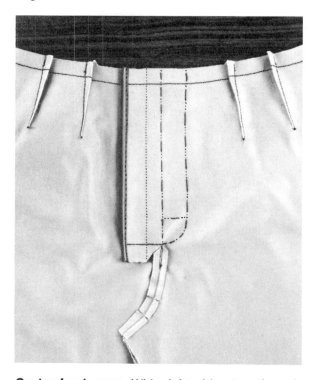

Center front seam. With right sides together pin and stitch center front seam from inner leg edges to dot. Stitch over first stitching line to reinforce. Clip seam allowance diagonally toward corner, and trim curve. Press the seam as stitched; then press seam open.

front waistline facings unit

Staystitch the waistline edges of front facings in same direction as the pants were stitched. Clean-finish unnotched edges of facings by making a $1/4$ inch turn to the wrong side, and stitch close to fold. Bulky fabrics may be finished with double-fold bias seam binding stitched over the raw edges. When seam binding is used, $1/4$ inch should be trimmed off edges before binding.

Apply facings. With right sides together pin facings to front, matching small dots and notches. Baste, easing edge of pants to fit between dot and notch.

Turn the front extensions to the right side (over ends of waistline facings) along the fold lines to form a facing on each side of opening. The left facing is narrower because the fold extends beyond the center front line. Hand or machine-baste facings to waistline edge.

Taped seam. Cotton twill tape or rayon seam binding can be used to prevent the waistline edge from stretching. Pin tape along seamline, and stitch through tape, facings and pants. Trim seam allowance. Clip curves, but do not clip edge of tape.

Open out facings and press seam allowance toward facing. Understitch through facing and seam allowance. Hand-stitch ends of waistline facings to the front facings.

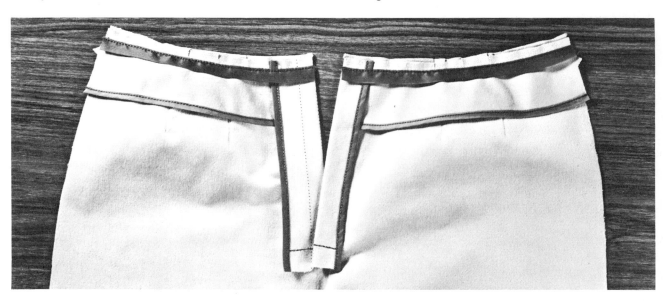

fly-front zipper

Turn top ends of zipper tape to right side. Keep both the zipper and pants front right side up, and pin edge of left hand front to zipper tape with the fold close to zipper teeth, placing the top stop $1/4$ inch below waistline edge. Baste along fold. Machine-stitch, using the zipper foot.

Continue to work with the right side up. Lap right hand front over left hand front. Match center front lines and baste. Pin stitching line on right hand front to zipper tape. Baste along stitching line.

Top-stitch fly front, following the direction of arrows. At the bottom of zipper, starting at the medium dot on stitching line, stitch across to the opening edge. Pivot, and stitch along edge to small dot; pivot again, and stitch along basted line up to the waistline edge.

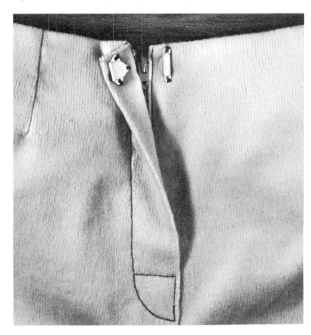

back unit

Staystitch waistline edges, side edges and lower edges as instructed previously; stitch the darts, and press toward center back.

With right sides together stitch center back seam directionally. Stitch a second time over the seam. Trim seam allowance on curve; clip curve. Press seam; then press seam open.

back facing unit

Staystitch ⁵/₈ inch from notched edge of waistline facing. Finish the unnotched edges the same way as front facings were done.

With right sides together pin facing to back waistline, matching small dots and notches. Baste, easing the back to facing. Pin and stitch tape along the seamline as instructed for taped seam under front unit. Trim seam allowance; clip curved seam allowance, press and understitch.

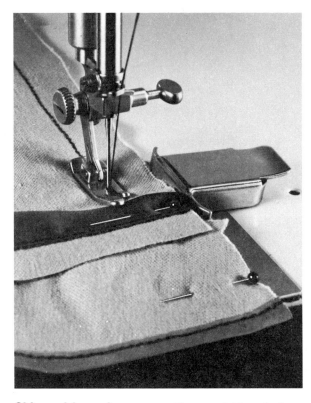

Side and inner leg seams. Turn waistline facings away from pants at the side edges. With right sides together stitch the front and back sections together at side seams, continuing the stitching across the taped seams to the facing edges. Backstitch at each end of seam. Press facings to wrong side, and tack the free edge to seam allowances and darts. Stitch the inner leg seams.

Hems and cuffs. Finish lower edges of pants. Turn up hem depth and press. Because these pants have cuffs the hem is a double width. Hand sew the hems with a lockstitch.

Turn lower edge to right side of pants leg, along fold line, forming the cuff. Press.

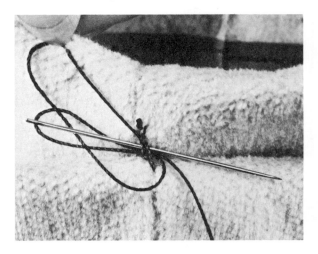

French-tack cuff to pants at the seamlines. To make a French tack, take 2-3 loose stitches between cuff and pants. Work a blanket stitch over the threads. See thread loops, page 199.

It's a fact! You feel and look your best when your clothes fit comfortably and attractively. Perfect figure or not, custom fit is the great advantage you have when you sew your own clothes. If you fit as you sew you're sure to have perfect fit in any fashion.

Your moment of truth comes with the first try-on of your basted garment. This is where fitting comes in. If it doesn't look quite like the illustration on the pattern envelope, remember that you have yet to custom-fit your garment to your figure. This means that you may make minor adjustments in a garment before you do your final stitching and finishing.

A pattern of the right type and size for your figure helps to minimize fitting changes, but because perfect figures are rare, some changes usually are necessary. Fitting is done on fabric; alterations are made on the paper pattern before cutting the fabric. Refer to Chapter 14 for pattern alterations.

Garments which require little fitting, such as an A-line skirt or an easy-fitting shift, will help you to develop sewing "know-how" without encountering difficult fitting problems.

fitting standards

Beautiful fabric and quality construction cannot compensate for a poor fit. A poorly fitted garment will detract from the appearance of its wearer.

Fitting standards are based on the structural lines of the body, and remain the same from year to year. Changes in the fashion picture, however, do affect the amount of "ease" or tolerance in garments and therefore the accepted appearance.

You will become more aware of this as you develop a "feel" for good fit and fashion trends. Figures may vary, but all garments should be made to meet the same fitting standards.

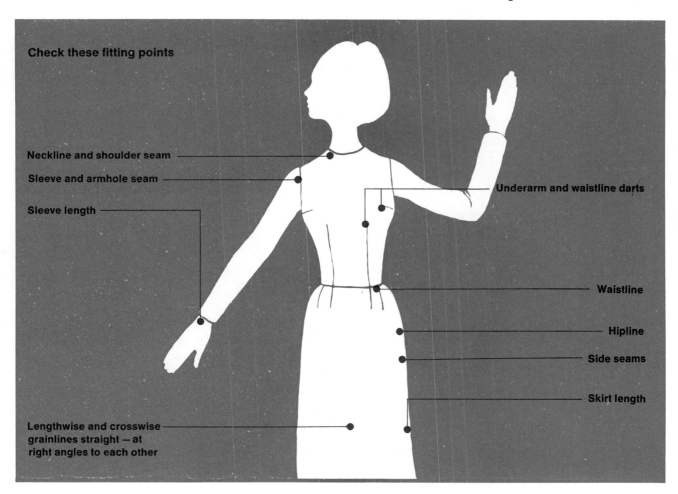

Check these fitting points

Neckline and shoulder seam

Sleeve and armhole seam

Sleeve length

Underarm and waistline darts

Waistline

Hipline

Side seams

Skirt length

Lengthwise and crosswise grainlines straight — at right angles to each other

Some General Fitting Standards

The fashion suits the wearer because it accentuates good features, and plays down poor ones.

The garment looks balanced regardless of any figure irregularities.

Sufficient ease allows the wearer to move freely. The garment looks smooth — no wrinkling, pulling, bagging or drooping.

Seamlines follow the structural lines of the body: straight vertical seams fall perpendicular to the floor; horizontal seams run smoothly over the body curves, parallel to the floor; center front and back seams are in the middle of the figure; side seams fall straight, dividing the figure.

Blouses and Dress Bodices

A well-fitted neckline lies at the base of the neck with no pulls or wrinkles in the bodice. If a collar is to fit well, the neckline must fit correctly.

Low necklines should fit close to the body without gaping. Choose a shape and depth that is flattering to you.

Bodice darts should point to the fullest part of the bust, and end 1 or 2 inches from it. The underarm dart should be on a level with the fullest part of the bust. If two or three darts are used to accommodate a large bust, they should be balanced in relation to the fullest part.

The underarm seam extends in a straight line from the center of the armpit down toward the floor.

Sleeves

Sleeve caps should look round and smooth with no puckers. A gathered sleeve has its fullness evenly distributed so that the arm does not touch the sleeve at any point.

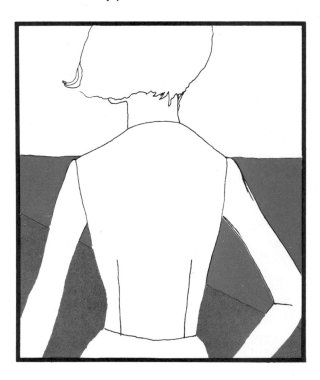

The armhole seam for a regular set-in sleeve forms a smooth curve over the end of the shoulder to a point about halfway down the front and back where the arm joins the body. The lowest point of the seam should be 1 inch below the armpit. The armhole seam should not droop down at the shoulder except in shirt armholes which are so designed.

The shoulder seam should be a straight line on top of the shoulder 1 inch behind the ear lobe, unless it is designed to come further forward.

The positioning of elbow darts depends on the number of darts to be used. A single dart is placed at the middle of the elbow. If there are two darts, the elbow is centered between them. If there are three darts, the center one is placed at the middle of the elbow and the other two are placed equidistant from the center dart.

Sleeves are designed in many lengths so choose lengths that are flattering to you. A long sleeve should end at the beginning of the wristbone.

Skirt

The waistband fits the natural waistline, and is snug enough to hold the skirt in position.

Hip darts point toward the fullest part of the body, and they come to an end above the hipline. The size and number of darts depend on the amount of fabric which has to be distributed smoothly.

On skirt fronts the fullness created by tucks or gathers should be distributed smoothly and directed toward the fullest part of the body.

Hemlines should run parallel to the floor unless they are designed to do otherwise. Choose a skirt length which flatters your legs and proportions.

Pleats are perfect when they lie smooth, are not pulled out of line and fall perpendicular to the floor.

Dresses

Evaluate dresses by following the standards for the bodice and skirt because a dress is a combination of the two. If the dress has a waistline seam, it should encircle the natural waistline snugly unless it has been designed to fall elsewhere. Princess or one-piece dresses should have sufficient ease at the waistline to allow the fabric to lie smoothly.

Coat or Jacket

Apply the standards for a dress to a coat or jacket. These garments should be fitted over the heaviest garment with which they will be worn to insure sufficient ease.

making a basic dress

Why make a basic fitting dress? If your figure deviates from the average, fitting a basic dress is the best way to solve figure problems; for severe problems it may be the only way.

Because fitting changes and pattern alterations are similar, the information gained from fitting the basic can be applied to future pattern alterations. The changes can then be made before cutting the fabric for the garment instead of fitting as you sew. The information learned from the basic applies only to patterns of the same size and type. The basic should never be taken apart and its pieces laid over other patterns for the purpose of altering them. Differences in design and style ease will only create confusion.

Before you cut out the dress, compare your body measurements with those on the back of the pattern envelope.

The measurement comparison will indicate if alterations should be made in the skirt length, size of hips, bodice length and size of waistline.

If there is a difference between the two sets of measurements, make the necessary alterations by adding or subtracting the amount needed when you are cutting the fabric for the garment.

Fitting Preparation

Use a firmly woven, checked fabric such as gingham for the basic. These checks are woven on grain, and make it easier for you to observe the grain lines while you fit.

Staystitch all curved and bias edges; baste mark the center lines. Machine-baste all darts and seams. If the dress has a waistline seam, join the two sections at the waistline.

Prepare the sleeves in the same way. Press darts and seams lightly.

At the zipper opening turn under one edge on the seamline and baste.

Tips on Fitting

While it is difficult to list every detail about fitting, the following applies to the fitting of all garments. Experience will develop your know-how, and bring a feeling for fitting.

Wear the same type undergarments that you will wear with the style of your garment, and shoes with the proper heel height. Always look your best for fittings — with hair combed and usual make-up.

Always fit with the garment right side out as there are often differences between the measurements of both sides of the body. Changes are transferred to the wrong side after fitting.

Analyze the garment carefully according to the standards of a perfect fit while wearing it before a full-length mirror. Begin to fit at the top of the garment, and work your way down because the fit at the top affects the fit of the lower sections.

Avoid overfitting which is fitting too tightly, taking out too much ease. Generally a large figure looks slimmer in a loose fit while a slender figure looks better in a trim fit.

Sections that are to be joined to an area where there has been a fitting change usually need corresponding changes. For example, if the neckline

has been changed, the neckline facings should also be changed.

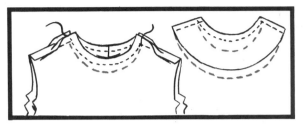

Necklines will fit better if the stitches of the shoulder seam end $5/8$ inch from the neckline edge.

The waistband should be basted on when fitting a skirt. If there is no band, machine-baste seam tape at the skirt waistline to prevent stretching.

Fitting the Basic Dress

A basic dress requires two fittings as a rule, but more may be needed if the problems are many.

To adjust areas where the fabric is strained, open the basted seams or darts, and pin a new seamline where more ease is needed. If the area is loose, pin out the excess fabric.

Neckline: To get a true picture of how a round fitted neckline should look, clip the neckline seam to the staystitching.

Darts: To relocate darts or to make two instead of one, remove basting, pinch in a new dart of the correct width and length in the desired location, and pin as shown. When a dart is made wider, it may also need to be lengthened.

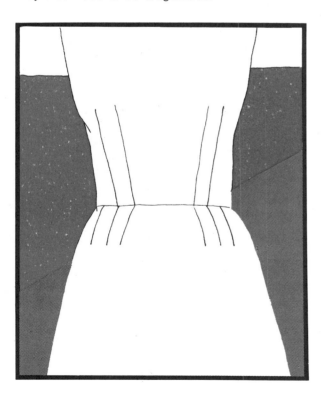

Waistline: To give shape where the figure needs it, seams and darts, both, may need adjusting. For full figures it may be better to make several small darts instead of the usual one or two large ones.

Skirt: Major changes should be made when cutting the fabric, but seams can be pinned in or let out to perfect size. The hips can differ in size, and may require individual fitting. Be sure to check ease for comfort when walking, sitting, etc.

Hems: After all adjustments have been made, turn up the hem to the correct length.

The basic dress does not have design details, but you can use it to visualize certain features that will be on future garments. All details should be of pleasing proportion for the individual figure. Determine the best size and location for pockets, flaps etc. by turning under the seam allowances of these details and pinning them in place.

After you have completed the fitting, transfer the pin-fitted lines to the wrong side of garment by hand-basting or chalk. If the lines need straightening, correct them, and machine-baste changed darts or seams. Again try on the garment to make sure that it is balanced, and that no further fitting adjustments are necessary. Complete all final stitching, and remove the basting. Keep accurate records of this basic fitting for use in altering future patterns.

making a trial garment

A trial garment should be made if the pattern has unfamiliar or complicated details; if the fabric to be sewn is expensive or fragile; or, if you are in doubt about the suitability of the style for you.

Inexpensive fabric can be used, but it should simulate the weight and drape of the final fabric. A coat may be pretested in corduroy, denim or a similar material, and later on you can complete it as a robe. Center front, center back and buttonholes should be marked on the right side of the trial garment. Facings and the top collar section can be eliminated in the cutting.

Alterations of which you are aware should be made when you are cutting the trial fabric. Further adjustments will become evident as you fit the trial garment, and this information should be applied to the cutting of the final fabric.

Study the trial for line, proportion, fullness and design details, all of which should flatter your figure.

steps to a perfect fit

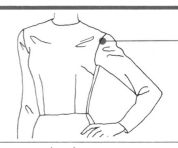

Broad Shoulders

The garment will pull across chest, back and top of sleeves.

Remove sleeve; pin new fitting line out to edge at shoulders, adding up to $^3/_8''$ on shoulder width (taken from seam allowance). Re-set sleeve.

Narrow Shoulders

Sleeve seams will fall off shoulders.

Remove sleeve—make a new fitting line over top at arm taking out excess width at shoulder. Re-set sleeve.

Sloping Shoulders

Fullness will show around the armhole and shoulder. Pick up and pin excess at shoulder, tapering to nothing at neck. Slightly sloping shoulders can be improved by use of shaped shoulder pads.

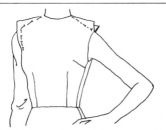

Square Shoulders

Fullness will appear between back, bust and neck. Rip shoulder seams. Add to shoulder edges at armhole, tapering to neck edges.

Round Shoulders

Back bodice will pull above waistline and fullness will appear at back armhole.

Rip shoulders, shoulder darts and waistline seams. Lift excess armhole fabric at back and bring it into shoulder dart, taking up to $^3/_8''$ from armhole seam allowance. Re-pin armhole fitting. Drop back neckline; add up to $^3/_8''$ at waistline for additional length.

Raising or Lowering the Bust Dart

Bust darts will not point to bust; they will be too low or too high.

Rip side seams, re-pin dart higher or lower, parallel to original dart.

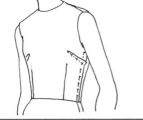

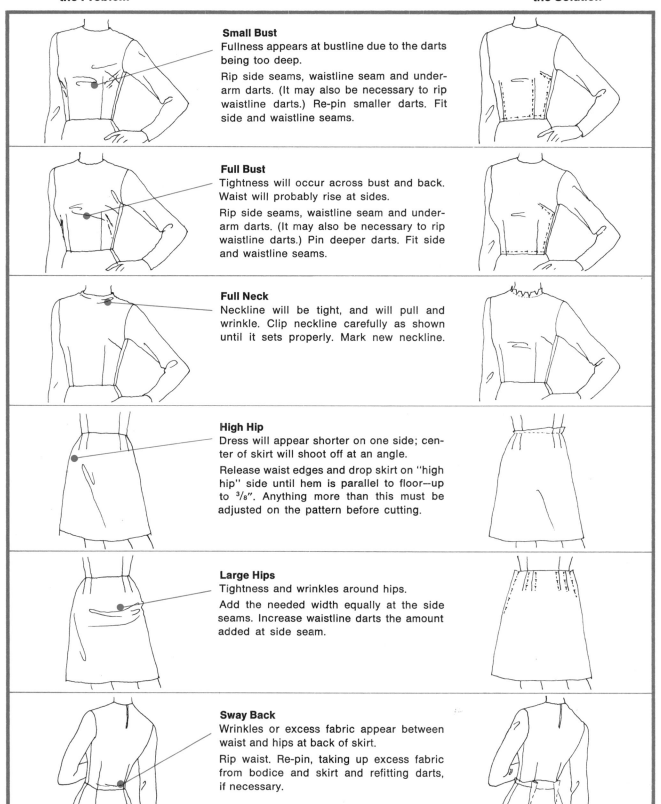

Small Bust

Fullness appears at bustline due to the darts being too deep.

Rip side seams, waistline seam and underarm darts. (It may also be necessary to rip waistline darts.) Re-pin smaller darts. Fit side and waistline seams.

Full Bust

Tightness will occur across bust and back. Waist will probably rise at sides.

Rip side seams, waistline seam and underarm darts. (It may also be necessary to rip waistline darts.) Pin deeper darts. Fit side and waistline seams.

Full Neck

Neckline will be tight, and will pull and wrinkle. Clip neckline carefully as shown until it sets properly. Mark new neckline.

High Hip

Dress will appear shorter on one side; center of skirt will shoot off at an angle.

Release waist edges and drop skirt on "high hip" side until hem is parallel to floor—up to $3/8"$. Anything more than this must be adjusted on the pattern before cutting.

Large Hips

Tightness and wrinkles around hips.

Add the needed width equally at the side seams. Increase waistline darts the amount added at side seam.

Sway Back

Wrinkles or excess fabric appear between waist and hips at back of skirt.

Rip waist. Re-pin, taking up excess fabric from bodice and skirt and refitting darts, if necessary.

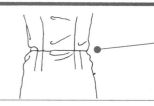

Large Waist

Not enough ease at waistline to fit comfortably. Wrinkles above and below the waist.

Decrease size of darts and let out side seams between bust and hips.

Small Waist

Excess fabric at waistline. Natural waistline is not evident.

Increase size of darts and take in side seams between bust and hips.

Full Upper Arm

Tightness and drawing across upper arm; not enough ease to swing arm freely.

Let out underarm seam allowance up to 3/8″ from armhole edge — tapering to normal seam allowance at elbow.

Large Elbow

Tightness and wrinkles at elbow only.

Pull out back sleeve edge at elbow, holding 5/8″ seam allowance at top and wrist, tapering it up to 1/4″ at elbow.

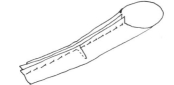

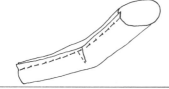

Elbow Dart

The dart should be at the point of the elbow.

Rip dart. Measure up or down from the point of dart the amount needed to make it fit properly and pin in new dart.

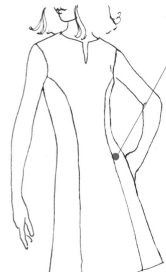

Princess Dress — too large or too small

If too small, there are wrinkles at waist and hips. If dress is too large, you are not aware of natural body line.

Fit on seam allowances, adding or subtracting up to 3/8″ on all seams if necessary. Hold design lines; do not fit the body closely.

customizing your pattern

You're not reading, cutting and stitching your way through this book to make "just a dress". You are out to make a super, custom-fitted, one-of-a-kind fashion creation!

One way to get off to a good start is to adjust the pattern dimensions to your figure dimensions as closely as possible. Patterns are cut to a standard set of measurements in each figure type, and one or more of these measurements may not coincide with yours. However, altering the pattern before you cut the fabric is a simple procedure which will facilitate the fitting of the garment.

Your Body Measurements
Transfer the measurements of your bust, waist, hips and back waist length from page 14 to the chart on page 131. Enter the corresponding pattern measurements from the back of your pattern envelope or from the measurement table on the next page in the spaces indicated by asterisks (*). Do not measure the pattern in these areas because ease is included and varies with each design. See page 16. In addition take the body measurements shown by the tapes on the illustrations below. After each measurement has been taken, enter it on chart.

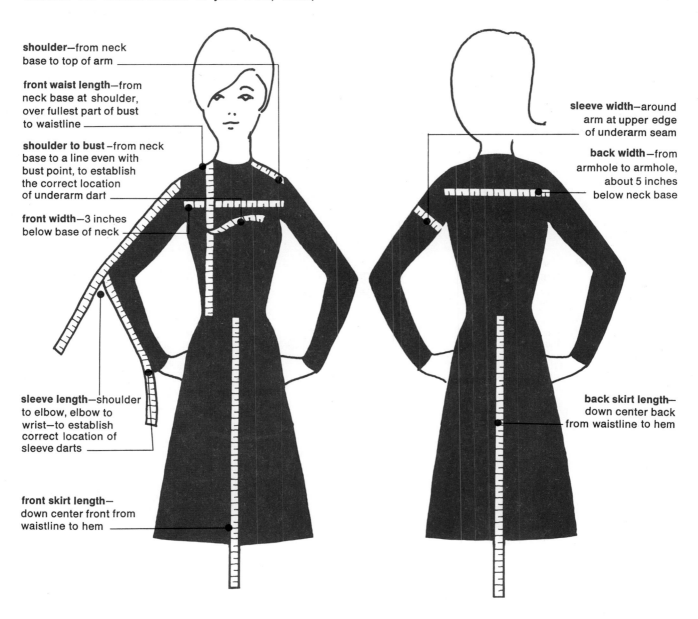

shoulder—from neck base to top of arm

front waist length—from neck base at shoulder, over fullest part of bust to waistline

shoulder to bust—from neck base to a line even with bust point, to establish the correct location of underarm dart

front width—3 inches below base of neck

sleeve length—shoulder to elbow, elbow to wrist—to establish correct location of sleeve darts

front skirt length—down center front from waistline to hem

sleeve width—around arm at upper edge of underarm seam

back width—from armhole to armhole, about 5 inches below neck base

back skirt length—down center back from waistline to hem

Girls

SIZE	7	8	10	12	14
Breast	26	27	28 1/2	30	32
Waist	23	23 1/2	24 1/2	25 1/2	26 1/2
Hip	27	28	30	32	34
Back Waist Length*	11 1/2	12	12 3/4	13 1/4	14 1/4
Front Waist Length	12 3/8	13	13 7/8	14 3/4	15 5/8
Shoulder Length	3 11/16	3 13/16	4	4 3/16	4 3/8
Back Width	11 3/4	12	12 1/2	13	13 1/2
Front Width	10 3/4	11	11 1/2	12	12 1/2
Sleeve Length	17 1/2	18 1/4	19 3/4	21 1/4	22
Sleeve Width	10 3/8	10 5/8	11 1/8	11 5/8	12 1/8
Neck	13 1/4	13 1/2	14	14 1/2	15

Miss Petite

SIZE	6MP	8MP	10MP	12MP	14MP	16MP
Bust	30 1/2	31 1/2	32 1/2	34	36	38
Waist	22 1/2	23 1/2	24 1/2	26	27 1/2	29 1/2
Hip (7" point)	32 1/2	33 1/2	34 1/2	36	38	40
Back Waist Length	14 1/2	14 3/4	15	15 1/4	15 1/2	15 3/4
Front Waist Length	15 5/8	16	16 3/4	17	17 3/8	17 3/4
Shoulder Length	4 3/8	4 1/2	4 5/8	4 3/4	4 7/8	5
Back Width	13 3/4	14	14 1/4	14 5/8	15 1/8	15 5/8
Front Width	13	13 1/4	13 1/2	13 7/8	14 3/8	14 7/8
Sleeve Length	20 1/2	20 11/16	20 7/8	21 1/8	21 3/8	21 5/8
Sleeve Width	11 1/2	12	12 1/2	13	13 1/2	14
Neck	14	14 1/2	15	15 1/2	16	16 1/2

Junior

SIZE	5	7	9	11	13	15
Bust	30	31	32	33 1/2	35	37
Waist	21 1/2	22 1/2	23 1/2	24 1/2	26	28
Hip	32	33	34	35 1/2	37	39
Back Waist Length*	15	15 1/4	15 1/2	15 3/4	16	16 1/4
Front Waist Length	16	16 3/8	16 3/4	17 1/8	17 1/2	17 7/8
Shoulder Length	4 1/2	4 5/8	4 3/4	4 7/8	5	5 1/8
Back Width	13 3/8	13 5/8	13 7/8	14 1/8	14 5/8	15 1/8
Front Width	12 5/8	12 7/8	13 1/8	13 1/2	13 7/8	14 3/8
Sleeve Length	21 15/16	22 1/8	22 5/16	22 1/2	22 3/4	23
Sleeve Width	12	12 1/4	12 1/2	12 3/4	13 1/4	13 3/4
Neck	13 3/4	14 1/4	14 3/4	15 1/4	15 3/4	16 1/4

Junior Petite

SIZE	3JP	5JP	7JP	9JP	11JP	13JP
Bust	30 1/2	31	32	33	34	35
Waist	22	22 1/2	23 1/2	24 1/2	25 1/2	26 1/2
Hip	31 1/2	32	33	34	35	36
Back Waist Length*	14	14 1/4	14 1/2	14 3/4	15	15 1/4
Front Waist Length	15 3/8	15 11/16	16	16 5/16	16 5/8	16 15/16
Shoulder Length	4 3/8	4 7/16	4 1/2	4 9/16	4 5/8	4 11/16
Back Width	13 1/4	13 1/2	13 3/4	14	14 1/4	14 1/2
Front Width	12 5/8	12 7/8	13 1/8	13 3/8	13 5/8	13 7/8
Sleeve Length	20 3/4	20 15/16	21 1/8	21 5/16	21 1/2	21 11/16
Sleeve Width	11	11 7/16	11 7/8	12 5/16	12 3/4	13 3/16
Neck	14	14 1/4	14 1/2	14 3/4	15	15 1/4

Young Junior/Teen

SIZE	5/6	7/8	9/10	11/12	13/14	15/16
Bust	28	29	30 1/2	32	33 1/2	35
Waist	22	23	24	25	26	27
Hip	31	32	33 1/2	35	36 1/2	38
Back Waist Length*	13 1/2	14	14 1/2	15	15 1/2	15 3/4
Front Waist Length	14 3/4	15 5/16	15 7/8	16 7/16	16 7/8	17 5/16
Shoulder Length	4	4 1/8	4 1/4	4 3/8	4 1/2	4 5/8
Back Width	12 3/4	12 5/16	13 1/8	13 5/16	13 1/2	13 11/16
Front Width	12	12 3/16	12 3/8	12 7/16	12 3/4	12 15/16
Sleeve Length	21 3/8	21 3/4	22 1/8	22 1/2	22 7/8	23 1/4
Sleeve Width	10 7/8	11 3/8	11 7/8	12 3/8	12 7/8	13 3/8
Neck	13 5/8	14 1/8	14 5/8	15 1/8	15 5/8	16 1/8

Misses'

SIZE	6	8	10	12	14	16	18	20
Bust	30 1/2	31 1/2	32 1/2	34	36	38	40	42
Waist	22	23	24	25 1/2	27	29	31	33
Hip	32 1/2	33 1/2	34 1/2	36	38	40	42	44
Back Waist Length*	15 1/2	15 3/4	16	16 1/4	16 1/2	16 3/4	17	17 1/4
Front Waist Length	16 5/8	17	17 3/8	17 3/4	18 1/8	18 1/2	18 7/8	19 1/4
Shoulder Length	4 5/8	4 3/4	4 7/8	5	5 1/8	5 1/4	5 3/8	5 1/2
Back Width	13 3/4	14	14 1/4	14 5/8	15 1/8	15 5/8	16 1/8	16 5/8
Front Width	13	13 1/4	13 1/2	13 7/8	14 3/8	14 7/8	15 3/8	15 7/8
Sleeve Length	22 1/2	22 13/16	23	23 1/4	23 1/2	23 3/4	24	24 1/4
Sleeve Width	12	12 1/4	12 1/2	13	13 1/2	14	14 1/4	15
Neck	14 1/4	14 3/4	15 1/4	15 3/4	16 1/4	16 3/4	17 1/4	17 3/4

Half-Size

SIZE	10 1/2	12 1/2	14 1/2	16 1/2	18 1/2	20 1/2	22 1/2	24 1/2
Bust	33	35	37	39	41	43	45	47
Waist	26	28	30	32	34	36 1/2	39	41 1/2
Hip	35	37	39	41	43	45 1/2	48	50 1/2
Back Waist Length*	15	15 1/4	15 1/2	15 3/4	15 7/8	16	16 1/4	16 1/4
Front Waist Length	17	17 3/8	17 3/4	18 1/8	18 3/8	18 5/8	18 7/8	19 1/8
Shoulder Length	4 1/2	4 5/8	4 3/4	4 7/8	5	5 1/16	5 1/8	5 3/16
Back Width	14 1/2	15	15 1/2	16	16 1/2	17	17 1/2	18
Front Width	13 5/8	14	14 1/2	15	15 1/2	16	16 1/2	17
Sleeve Length	22 1/4	22 1/2	22 3/4	23	23 1/4	23 1/2	24	24 1/4
Sleeve Width	13	13 1/2	14	14 1/2	15	15 1/2	16	16 1/2
Neck	15 1/2	16	16 1/2	17	17 1/2	18	18 1/2	19

Women's

SIZE	38	40	42	44	46	48	50
Bust	42	44	46	48	50	52	54
Waist	34	36	38	40 1/2	43	45 1/2	48
Hip	44	46	48	50	52	54	56
Back Waist Length*	17 1/4	17 3/8	17 1/2	17 5/8	17 3/4	17 7/8	18
Front Waist Length	19 5/8	19 7/8	20 1/8	20 3/8	20 5/8	20 7/8	21 1/8
Shoulder Length	4 15/16	5	5 1/16	5 1/8	5 3/16	5 1/4	5 5/16
Back Width	16 1/4	16 3/4	17 1/4	17 3/4	18 1/4	18 3/4	19 1/4
Front Width	16	16 1/2	17	17 1/2	18	18 1/2	19
Sleeve Length	23 3/4	24	24 1/4	24 1/2	24 3/4	25	25 1/4
Sleeve Width	15 1/2	16	16 1/2	17	17 1/2	18	18 1/2
Neck	18 3/8	18 7/8	19 3/8	19 7/8	20 3/8	20 7/8	21 3/8

*Another 1/8" ease is added to all sizes of patterns over the body back waist length.

	your measurements	pattern * measurements	+ adjustment −	
bust		*		
waist		*		
hips		*		
back waist length		*		
back bodice width				
shoulder				
front bodice width				
front waist length				
shoulder to bust				
sleeve width				
front skirt length				
back skirt length				
sleeve, shoulder to elbow				
sleeve, elbow to wrist				

*Enter measurements given on pattern envelope back or from chart on page 130.

Measure the Pattern

Take the corresponding measurements of the pattern, but first pin-in any darts, pleats or gathers over which you will be measuring; then measure from seamline to seamline (except on the long sleeve and bodice front where two measurements are taken as shown in the diagram). Enter these the chart. A comparison of the two sets of measurements will indicate whether any basic alterations are necessary in your pattern. Instructions for making all basic pattern adjustments will be found on the pages that follow.

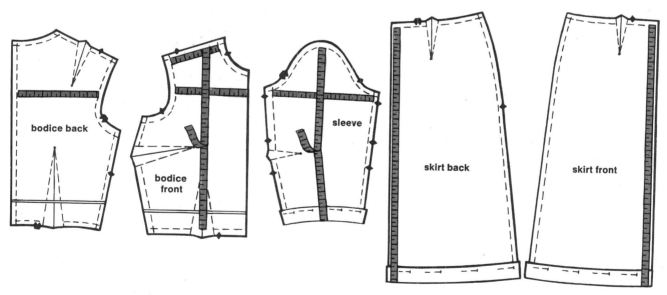

pattern alterations

Because a figure problem usually involves only one area of the body, the instructions are grouped under the following headings: bodice, shoulder, upper back, sleeve, waistline, skirt and pants.

Grainlines. The arrows on the pattern illustrations indicate fabric grainlines which should always be kept straight. Cutting a pattern section may change one end of an arrow, in which case, ignore the direction of the cut off point, and extend the main part of the arrow.

The solid black outline on the illustrations represents the original pattern lines; the lines in solid color are the new cutting lines. Always reposition the notches on the new cutting line. Seam allowances remain ⁵/₈ inch unless otherwise specified.

Lengthening or shortening are the two alterations most often needed, and they are the easiest to make. Most patterns have printed lengthening-shortening lines to show where this adjustment should be made. Remember that lengthening or enlarging alterations cannot be made after the fabric has been cut.

If a pattern piece does not have these lines printed on it, the illustrations in this chapter will show you where to draw lines to use as guides for cutting it apart or shortening it with a tuck.

bodice adjustments

Long-waisted

In this case the waistline of the garment falls above the natural waistline. Make adjustments on the front and back patterns, unless otherwise specified. Refer to your measurement chart to determine the amount to be added.

a) Dress with Waistline Seam

Cut the pattern apart on the lengthening line. Place paper under the two edges and spread pattern the necessary distance.

Keep the center front edges of pattern straight and the cut edges parallel; pin or tape pattern to paper. Complete the dart, seam and cutting lines as indicated by the solid lines in color.

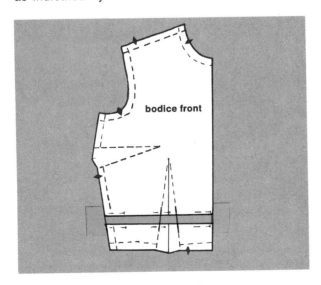

A bodice with kimono sleeves is lengthened just above the waistline as instructed in (a).

b) One-piece Dress

If there is no lengthening line on the pattern, draw a line about 1 inch above the indicated waistline. Follow the instructions given **previously**.

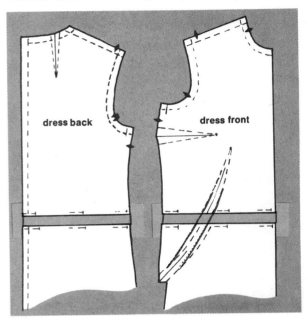

Short-waisted

The bodice of the garment is too long. This may cause wrinkles to form around the bodice, or result in the waistline falling below the natural waistline. Refer to the measurement chart to determine the amount to be shortened. Treat the front and back alike unless otherwise specified.

a) Dress with Waistline Seam

Measure up from the shortening line the amount to be shortened.

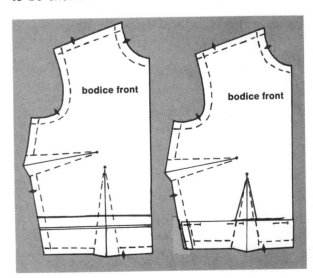

Draw a line across the pattern. Fold pattern on shortening line; bring fold up to the drawn line, keeping center front edge straight. Pin or tape the fold flat.

Place paper under pattern at bottom corner; pin or tape pattern to paper. Draw a new cutting line, and straighten the darts as shown by the solid lines in color.

A bodice with kimono sleeves is shortened just above the waistline as instructed above.

b) One-piece Dress

If there is no shortening line on the pattern, draw a line about 1 inch above the indicated waistline. Measure up from the first drawn line the amount to be shortened, and draw a second line. Fold pattern on the first line, and bring the fold to second line. Pin or tape in place.

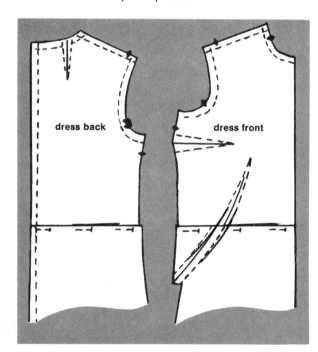

Bust Dart — Raised or Lowered

Adjustment is necessary if the underarm dart does not point to the fullest part of the bust. If a major amount of adjustment is necessary, use the instructions under *High Bust* or *Low Bust*. If the amount of adjustment is slight, use the method which follows.

a) Raise the Dart

On the pattern front measure up from the dart point the amount needed to be raised, and mark it. Draw new dart lines from the underarm seam to the new point on the top and bottom.

Extend the point of the waistline dart the same amount that the underarm dart was raised.

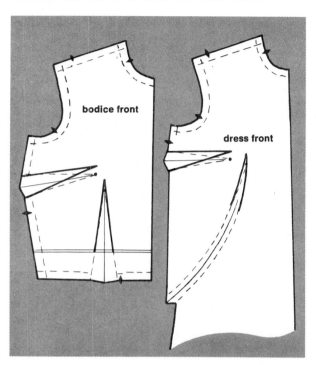

b) Lower the Dart

On the pattern front measure down from the dart point the amount it should be lowered, and mark it. Draw new dart lines on the top and bottom from the underarm seam to the new point.

Lower the point of the waistline dart the same amount that the underarm dart was lowered.

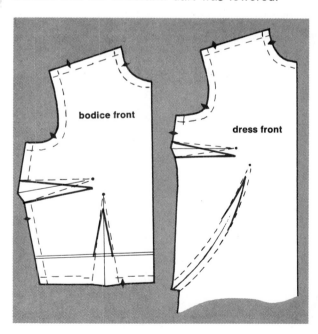

One-piece dress. The darts can be adjusted in the same manner as instructed above.

Very High Bust
The underarm dart needs to be raised.

On the pattern front draw a square around the dart; at a right angle to the center front, 1 inch below armhole, draw a straight line the length of dart. Draw a second line, parallel to the first, ½ inch below the dart. Draw a vertical line at the end of dart.

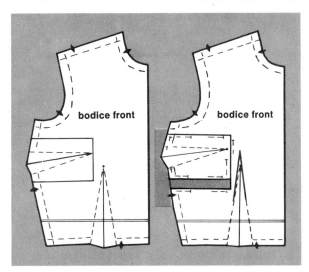

Cut pattern on the lines above and below the dart. Cut line at end of dart. Place paper under pattern; pin or tape the edges.

Slide the dart section <u>up</u> to align the point of dart with the fullest part of bust. Lap edges of pattern evenly, and keep the vertical edges even; pin or tape in place.

Extend the point of waistline dart the same amount that the underarm dart was raised.

Very Low Bust
The underarm dart needs to be lowered.

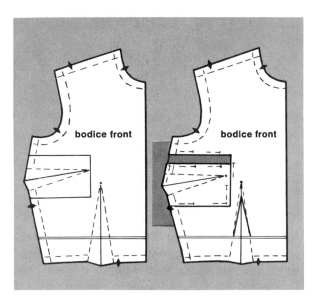

Draw a square around the dart as instructed under *Very High Bust*.

Cut the pattern in the same way. Place paper under pattern, and pin or tape the edges.

Slide the dart section <u>down</u> to align point of dart with the fullest part of the bust. Lap pattern evenly, and keep the straight vertical edges even; pin or tape in place.

Lower point of waistline dart the same amount that the underarm dart was lowered.

shoulder adjustments

Narrow Shoulders
The seamline of armhole falls off at the shoulder.

a) Sleeveless, or with Set-in Sleeves
On both front and back patterns, draw a line about 5 inches long, starting at the middle of the shoulder line. Continue the line horizontally to the armhole seamline above notch. Cut the pattern on this line. Lap the cut edges the needed amount at shoulder; pin or tape to paper.

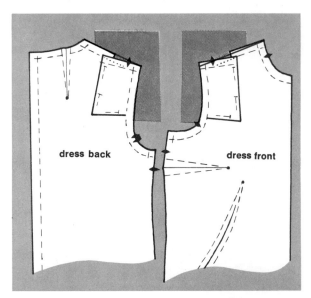

Draw a new shoulder line as indicated by dotted line and a new cutting line indicated by solid line in color. Treat front and back in the same manner.

If the bodice has a seam over the bust, the shoulder can be made narrower by removing the needed amount at the shoulder line and tapering the seam toward the bust.

b) Shoulder of Kimono Sleeve
On both front and back patterns, draw a line from the shoulder notch to waistline, ending at side of waistline dart near the underarm seam. If bodice has no waistline dart, draw the line to the center of the waistline seamline. Measure from the notch

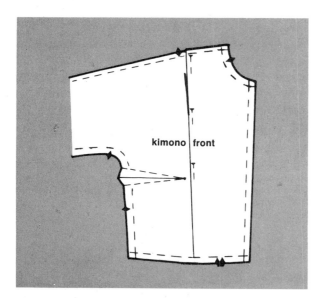

toward the neckline the amount needed to shorten. Draw a second line from this line to waistline dart.

Fold pattern on the second line, and bring crease to the first line, tapering to the dart.

Broad Shoulders

There will be a strain across the shoulders.

a) Sleeveless, or with Set-in Sleeves

On both front and back patterns, draw a line about 5 inches long, starting at the shoulder line. Continue the line horizontally to the armhole seamline above notch. Cut the pattern on this line. Place paper under the cut edges.

Separate edges at shoulder line the needed amount; pin or tape to paper.

Draw a new cutting line between neckline and armhole as indicated by the solid line in color.

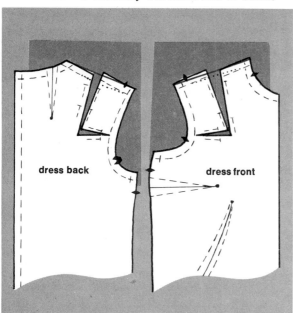

b) Bodice with Kimono Sleeve

On both front and back patterns, draw a line from shoulder notch to waistline, ending at side of waistline dart near the underarm seam. If bodice has no waistline dart, draw the line to the center of the waistline seamline.

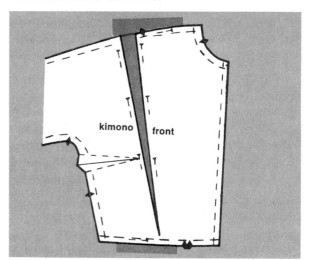

Cut the pattern on this line almost to the waistline seamline.

Place paper under cut edges, and separate edges to the needed amount at shoulder line; taper to waistline. Pin or tape to paper.

Complete cutting lines as indicated by the solid line in color.

Sloping Shoulders

Fullness will show around the armhole and front and back of sleeve.

a) Sleeveless, or with Set-in Sleeves

Measure the excess amount down from the shoulder line at the armhole.

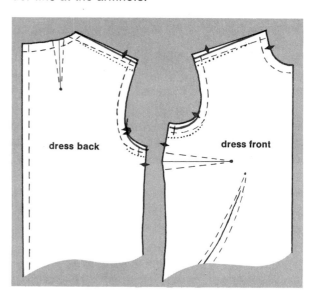

Measure down the same amount at the lower end of armhole.

Draw a new shoulder line, tapering from the neckline to armhole edge, and draw a new armhole curve as indicated by the solid lines in color. Treat the back in the same manner.

b) One-piece Dress

Back and front shoulders and armholes are handled in the same manner as above.

c) Bodice with Kimono Sleeve

Measure, mark and cut pattern in the same way as for kimono sleeves under <u>Square Shoulders</u>.

Place paper under cut edges, and separate at the center front line to the needed amount; pin or tape to paper. Straighten the center line, and draw a new neckline.

Square Shoulders

Fullness appears at the front and back neckline.

a) Sleeveless, or with Set-in Sleeves

Place paper under shoulder and armhole of bodice front. Pin or tape pattern to paper.

Mark the amount needed above the shoulder line at armhole end.

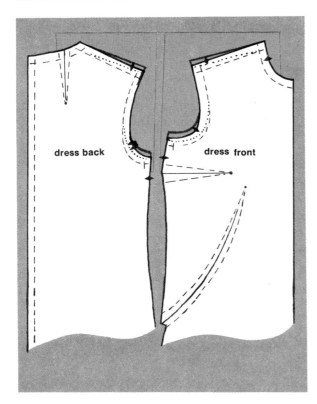

Mark the same amount above the bottom of armhole. Draw a new shoulder line, tapering from neckline to armhole edge, and a new armhole curve as indicated by the lines in color. Treat the back in the same manner.

b) Bodice with Kimono Sleeves

Measure down 3 to 4 inches from neckline seamline, and mark on center front line.

Draw a line from the mark to the shoulder notch. Cut pattern along line from center to shoulder seamline. Place paper under the cut edges.

Lap the edges amount needed, tapering to nothing at shoulder line. Straighten center front line. Make the same adjustment on the back.

Fullness at Neck Base

Neckline is tight, and garment pulls and wrinkles.

Mark a new seamline on neckline edge, and cut seam allowance to the proper seam width.

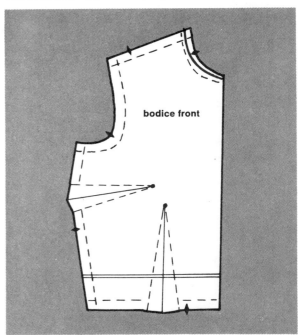

Make the same adjustment on the neckline facing, trimming the neckline edge and adding to the outside edge to restore the original width.

upper back adjustments

Round Shoulders

The back bodice pulls across shoulders, causing fullness at back armholes. The waistline pulls up at the center back. Make adjustments on the back pattern piece only.

a) Bodice with Shoulder Dart

Draw a straight line across pattern below the shoulder dart from the center back to the armhole seamline. Cut pattern on this line; place paper under cut edges. Separate edges the amount needed. Pin or tape to paper.

Draw new cutting line from lower cut edge to the neckline. Straighten neckline curve.

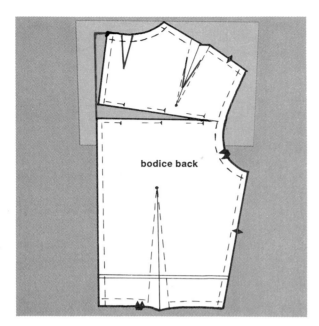

Make a neckline dart to take up the amount added to the outside edge.

Make the shoulder dart slightly shorter.

b) Bodice with Neckline Dart

Draw a line straight across below neckline dart from center back to the armhole seamline. Cut pattern on this line; place paper under cut edges.

Separate cut edges the amount needed; pin or tape to paper.

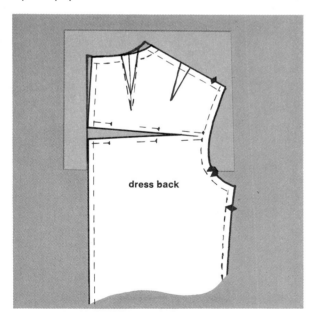

Draw a straight line from the lower cut edge to the neckline.

Add the same amount to the neck edge of the shoulder seam that was added at the center back.

Draw a new cutting line at the neckline as indicated by the line in color.

Re-draw neckline dart of the same width, but a little shorter.

Make a shoulder dart, taking up the amount added to the shoulder seam.

Very Erect Back

There is extra length between the neckline and waistline so the back will not hang smoothly. The chart will show how much the back waist length has to be shortened. Make the adjustments only on the back pattern.

a) Sleeveless, or with Set-in Sleeves

Draw a line straight across pattern below neckline or shoulder dart, from center back edge.

Cut pattern on the line just to the armhole seamline. Lap the cut edges the amount needed to shorten; pin or tape in place.

Straighten center back line as shown by the line in color.

The neckline dart will be smaller, or may be omitted entirely.

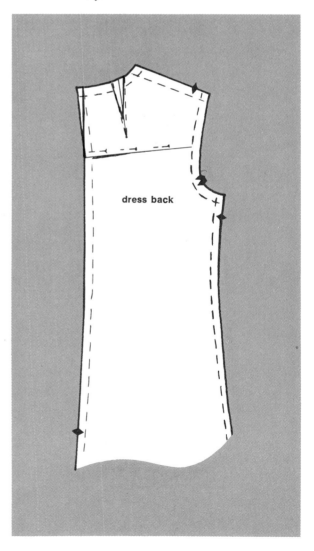

b) Bodice with Kimono Sleeves

Measure about $3\frac{1}{2}$ inches from the neckline down center back, and mark it. Draw a line from the mark to shoulder notch.

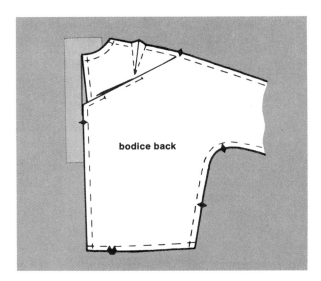

Cut pattern on line from center line almost to the shoulder line. Lap the cut edges the amount needed to shorten; pin or tape in place.

Straighten center back line as shown by color.

Narrow Back

The garment appears too wide across back bodice.

Starting at the center of shoulder line, draw a line to the bottom, parallel to the center back line. Draw a second line parallel to the first with the distance between the lines equal to $\frac{1}{2}$ the amount to be removed.

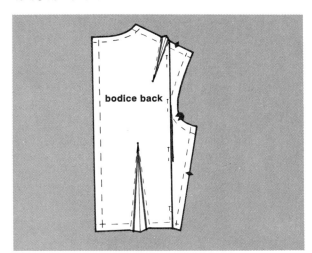

Fold the pattern on the first line, and bring the fold to the second line; pin a tuck.

To match the shoulder seams to bodice front and the waistline seams to the skirt back, redraw the darts, decreasing them by the amount removed.

Wide Back

The garment appears strained across back.

Starting at the center of shoulder line, draw a line to the bottom, parallel to the center back line. Cut pattern apart. Place paper under cut edges.

Spread pattern apart to $\frac{1}{2}$ the amount to be added; pin or tape the edges to paper.

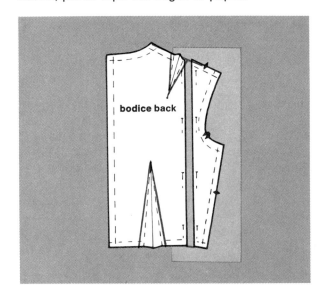

To match the shoulder seams to bodice front and the waistline seams to skirt back, increase the depth of the darts.

bust adjustments

Small Bust

There is extra fullness at the bustline because the darts are too deep and the waistline is too long.

Decrease the width of the underarm and waistline darts the amount necessary to fit properly.

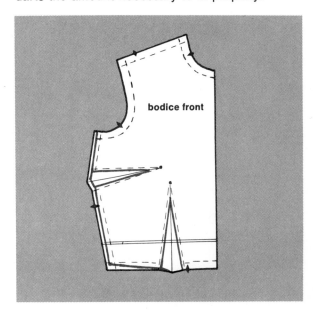

Mark a new waistline seam from the waistline dart out to the underarm seam. Draw a new underarm cutting line.

Full Bust

When in motion, tightness will occur across the bust and at the back of bodice; the waistline may rise at the sides.

Make the underarm and waistline darts deeper.

Move the underarm seamline out slightly from bottom of dart to waistline.

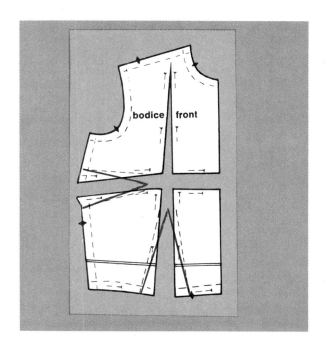

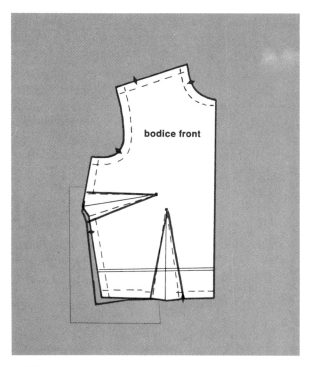

Slant the waistline seam downward from the dart to edge of pattern.

Very Full Bust

The waistline of bodice is drawn up out of line across the front; movement is restricted across the bust and back.

Draw a vertical line through center of waistline dart up to the shoulder line.

Draw a horizontal line through center of underarm dart straight across to the center front.

Cut on the horizontal line from center front to the underarm seam; place paper under pattern. Separate pattern at center front $1/2$ the amount needed to enlarge. Pin along the center front edge, keeping the edges in a straight line. Cut on the vertical line from waistline to shoulder seam. At bottom edge of upper side section, separate the pattern edges $1/2$ the amount needed to enlarge. Pin or tape these edges to paper. Where the

vertical and horizontal slashes meet, separate the lower side from the upper section the same amount as at center front. The vertical slash will taper. Redraw dart lines. If amount added is great, make two darts instead of one at waistline.

Flat or Hollow Chest

Wrinkles form above the bustline because the bodice is too long from the neckline to the bust.

a) Sleeveless, or with Set-in Sleeves

Measure 3 inches below neckline at center front. Draw a straight line from this point to the shoulder seamline at the armhole.

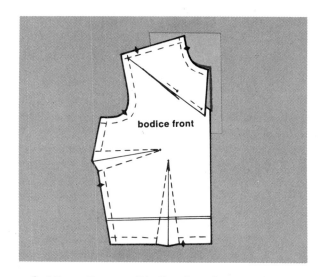

Cut the pattern on this line. Lap the cut edges the amount necessary at center front; pin or tape together. Straighten center front line, and straighten front neckline curve slightly in the pattern margin.

sleeve adjustments

When you are making adjustments in a sleeve pattern, it is important to keep the original shape of the sleeve cap; if the original shape cannot be retained, ease the extra fabric evenly. Many sleeve alterations are made in conjunction with bodice alterations. Refer to both sections when necessary.

Adjusting Sleeve Length

Long sleeves may need alterations above and below the elbow so two lengthening and shortening lines will be found on patterns with elbow darts.

a) Shortening Set-in Sleeve

If the sleeve is to be shortened in two places, draw a line above the printed shortening lines ¹/₂ the amount needed to shorten.

Fold pattern on the printed line, and bring crease to the drawn line, keeping the grainline straight; pin. Draw new cutting and seam lines.

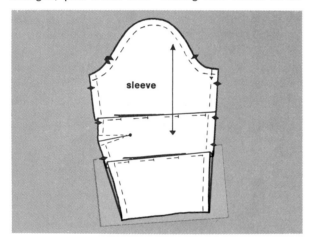

b) Lengthening Set-in Sleeve

Cut the pattern apart on both lengthening lines. Place paper under the cut edges; spread the edges apart ¹/₂ the amount needed to lengthen at each point. Pin or tape edges to paper.

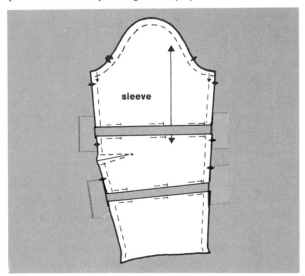

c) Shortening or Lengthening Kimono Sleeve

If it is a long sleeve, it should be shortened above and below the elbow, dividing the amount needed to shorten as instructed in (a).

If the sleeve needs to be lengthened above and below the elbow, divide the amount as instructed in (b). If this adjustment is made only at one point, separate the edges the full amount needed to lengthen.

Elbow Dart

The dart should be at the point of the elbow. If it needs to be raised or lowered, follow the instructions below. Color shows new placement of dart.

a) Lower Elbow Dart

On the pattern, measure down from point of dart the needed amount, and mark it.

Draw a new line from this mark parallel to the original upper line of dart.

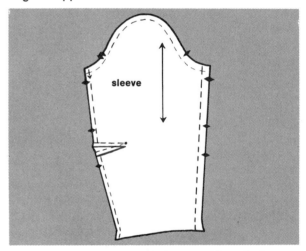

Draw in lower line of dart, making dart same width as originally.

b) Raise Elbow Dart

On the pattern, measure up from point of dart the needed amount, and mark it.

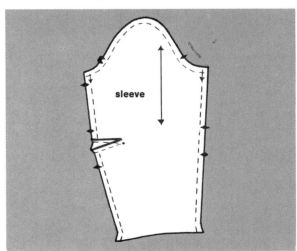

Draw a new line from this mark parallel to the original lower line of dart.

Draw in the upper line of dart, making the dart the same width as originally.

Large Arm

From the dot at the top of sleeve cap, draw a line to the wrist, keeping it parallel to the grainline. Cut pattern apart on this line.

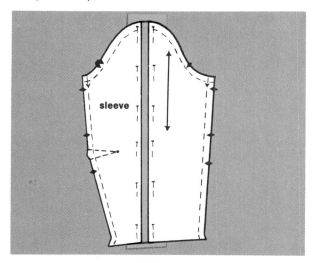

Pin or tape cut edge of sleeve front to paper. Lay cut edge of sleeve back on paper the needed distance from edge of sleeve front, keeping edges parallel; pin or tape to paper.

On front and back bodice increase the armhole at side seam by adding ½ the amount added to the sleeve; then taper the cutting line to waistline.

Thin Arm

From the dot at top of sleeve cap draw a line to the wrist, parallel to the grainline. On this line make a tuck of the needed depth; pin or tape.

At the underarm seam in both the front and back, raise curve ½ amount taken up in pleat.

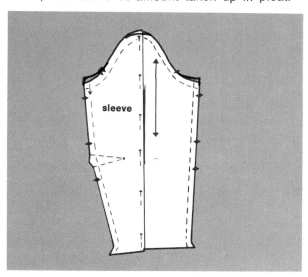

Draw new cutting lines at upper edge and underarm seams as indicated by lines in color.

On the front and back bodice patterns take off from the side seams at the underarm ½ the amount that of the tuck in sleeve, tapering to nothing at waistline. Draw a new line and raise the underarm same as for sleeve.

Large Elbow

Draw a line down center of sleeve from top seamline to elbow, keeping line parallel to the grainline. Lay edge of ruler along solid line of elbow dart, and continue the line until it meets first line. Cut pattern through the solid line of dart and drawn line then up to the seamline at top of sleeve. Place paper under pattern, and pin or tape main section of sleeve to paper.

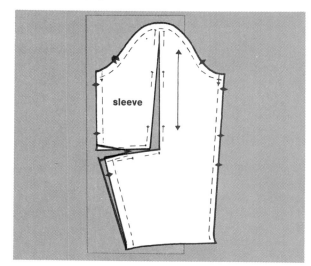

At the corner of slash separate the cut edges the amount needed to enlarge elbow. The cut edges will taper to seamline at top of sleeve.

Draw a new cutting line from upper cut edge of dart, tapering to the original cutting line as indicated by the line in color.

To restore the original length of the underarm seamline make a deeper elbow dart.

Large Upper Arm

Draw a line down the center of sleeve, parallel to the grainline.

Cut pattern on this line, starting at top of sleeve and ending at the wrist line just above bottom edge of pattern.

Draw a straight line through the center of a piece of paper equal in length to the pattern. This line will be used as the grainline.

Place the cut edges of pattern over the paper. With the slash in pattern on the line place a pin on each side of the slash at the bottom edge.

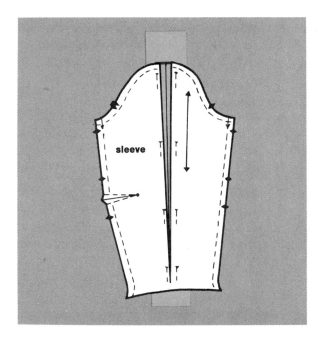

Separate the top edges to the amount needed, keeping cut edges an equal distance on each side of the new grainline, while tapering to nothing at bottom. Pin or tape to paper.

Complete the cutting line at top of sleeve.

On front and back dress patterns at armhole edge of side seam add $1/2$ the amount added to the sleeve, tapering to cutting line at the waistline.

Extra Large Upper Arm

Draw a line from top of sleeve to wrist, parallel to grainline. Cut the pattern on this line.

Draw a straight line on a piece of paper equal

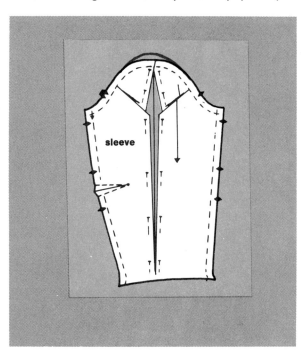

in length to the pattern. This will be the new grainline. Place pattern on paper; about 1 inch below underarm edges spread the cut edges the amount needed; pin. Make diagonal folds in pattern above notch, pleating out the fullness, and tapering to nothing at seamline above notches; pin or tape to paper.

Draw new cutting line at top of sleeve in the amount pleated out.

On front and back dress patterns at the armhole edge of side seam add $1/2$ the amount added to sleeve, tapering to the cutting line at the waistline.

Decreasing Ease in Sleeve Cap

It may be desirable to decrease the amount of ease for fabrics that do not ease well such as permanent press. This may make the sleeve feel tighter.

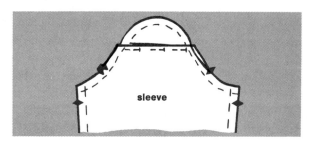

The adjustment is made by pinning out an even fold on the pattern on the crosswise grainline. Divide the amount to be removed into quarters. For example: If you want to remove $1/2$ inch, make $1/8$ inch tuck. Redraw the seamline where folded.

skirt adjustments

Adjusting Skirt Length

In most cases, skirt lengths are altered by adding or subtracting at the lower edge. If a full skirt is to maintain its curve, the amount of alteration must be measured accurately.

On some skirts, such as those having released pleats at the hemline, in order not to change the proportion it is better to lengthen or shorten at the hip line. If the pattern has no line, draw one about 7 inches below the waistline and lengthen or shorten following the instructions for lengthening and shortening bodice on page 132.

Large Hips — Skirt

This figure problem is common. Large hips cause the skirt to pull across the hips so that it will not hang smoothly from the waistline.

At side seams of both front and back add $1/4$ the needed amount from waistline to lower edge. Do not remove excess waistline fullness only at the top of the side seams above the hipline; it will distort the grainline and emphasize large hips. If fullness is concentrated in the back hip area, add to the back side seams only. The reverse is true if fullness is concentrated at the front hips.

Restore the original size of the waistline by increasing the width of the dart nearer the side seam the same amount that was added to the side seams. Increase the dart width by drawing new stitching lines <u>outside</u> the original line. If the front has only one dart make a second one near the side seam as indicated in color, taking up the amount the pattern was increased at side seam.(a)

Large Hips — One-piece Dress
These patterns are purchased to fit the bust measurement, and they are often too small in the hips.

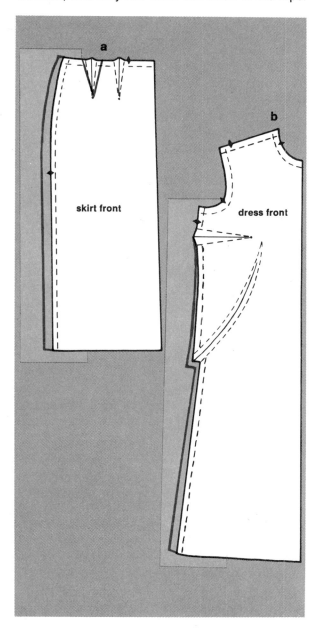

To increase the hipline, add 1/4 the amount needed on the front and back patterns from the hipline to the lower edge. Then taper the allowance to the dart in the front on underarm seam and to same position on back. Side seams can be fitted slightly at waistline in the fitting.(b)

One High Hip
The skirt appears to be shorter on one side, and the center of skirt shoots off at an angle. If there is only a slight difference, the adjustment can be made in the fitting. If hip is noticeably large, alter the pattern as follows.

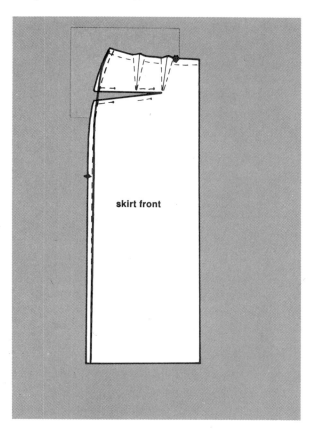

Cut paper duplicates of the back and front skirt patterns. Transfer darts and seamline markings. Make the following adjustment on the front pattern, working on the piece for the side with the high hip. Draw a line from side of pattern at hipline to point of waistline dart nearest to center front line. Cut on this line; place paper under cut edges, and pin or tape lower edge of slash to paper. Separate edges of slash the amount needed, and fasten the top cut edge to paper. Mark new seamline along side edge. Treat the back in the same way. Lay the center front edges together, and tape them to make a complete skirt front. Make a complete skirt back in the same way. Skirt will need to be cut on a single thickness of fabric.

Small Buttocks

Small buttocks cause the back of skirt to have excess fullness below the darts.

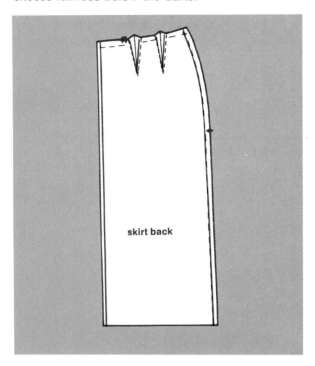

Make each dart in back less deep. Remove equal amount from center back and side seams from waistline to lower edge.

Large Buttocks

Draw a vertical line on skirt back, starting between

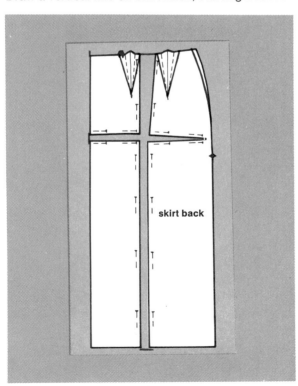

darts at waistline and to the lower edge. Keep line parallel to grainline. Slit on vertical line; place paper under the two cut edges, and spread ½ the amount needed to widen. Tape pattern to paper.

Draw a horizontal line from center back to the side seamline, about 7 inches below waistline.

Cut across pattern on line; place paper under the two cut edges, and spread them so that the center back lines are aligned vertically.

Increase darts proportionately so that waistline will retain its original size. Draw new cutting lines.

Large Waistline

When the waistline is only slightly larger than the pattern, the amount needed can be added to the side seams and front and back of the bodice and skirt. If the waistline is quite a bit larger than the pattern, width should be added at the darts as well as the side seams.

Place paper under bodice and skirt front and back patterns at the waistline.

Divide the amount needed by the number of darts plus the seams. (For instance, if there are two darts in front and four in back and two seams the amount needed is divided by eight.)

To decrease the width of each dart draw new stitching lines <u>inside</u> the original dart lines.

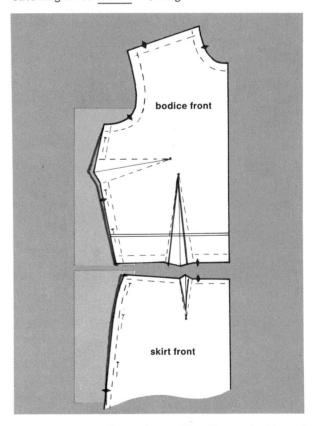

Measure out from the cutting lines at sides of waistline the required amount. From this point draw a line tapering to nothing at the armhole on bodice, and draw another line on the skirt to the hipline. The new cutting lines are indicated in color.

Small Waistline

For a minor adjustment divide the amount to be decreased into quarters and remove from side seams of skirt and bodice tapering seam allowance to armhole and hipline.

If a greater adjustment is necessary, use the method which follows.

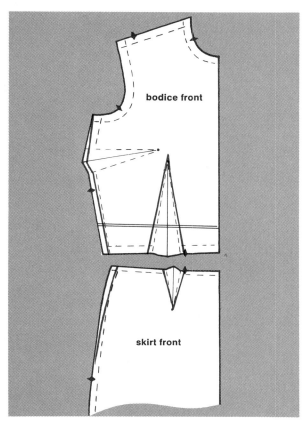

Divide the amount to be removed by the number of darts (front and back) plus the side seams. Increase the width of each dart the required amount by drawing new stitching lines <u>outside</u> the original dart lines.

On the bodice and skirt measure in the same amount from each side seam.

Draw a line tapering to the armhole on the bodice, and draw another line to the hipline on the skirt. The solid lines in color indicate the new stitching and cutting lines.

Large Abdomen

Bodice Adjustment: Draw a vertical line through center of waistline dart to shoulder line. Draw a horizontal line about 3 inches above waistline from the center front to the underarm seamline.

Cut bodice on drawn lines. Spread upper and lower sections $1/2$ the amount needed keeping center front straight. Tape edges of pattern to paper.

Redraw dart and new cutting lines.

Skirt adjustment: Draw vertical line on pattern through center of dart nearest center front to within 1 inch of lower edge.

Draw a horizontal line below ends of darts from center front to side seamline.

Lay the pattern on paper, and cut on drawn lines. Separate the sections and draw new lines the same way as you did the bodice.

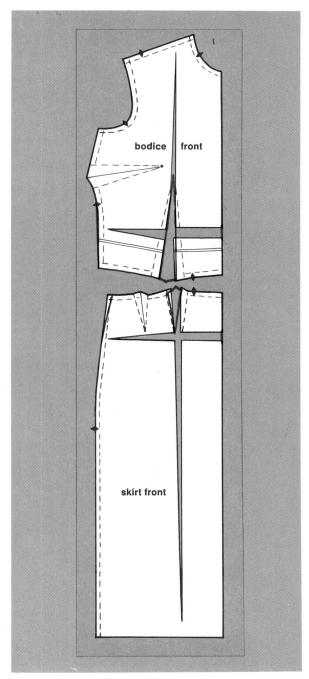

Princess Dress

Adjustments are made differently on a **Princess** style garment because it has no waistline seam, nor does it have underarm darts, as a rule.

Curved Bustline Seam

The fullest part of the curve on the pattern must correspond to the fullest part of the bust.

Raising the Bustline

On front pattern, draw a horizontal line across the pattern just above the upper bust notch; then draw a diagonal line from above the notch on the side front section to underarm seam.

Draw a second line above the first the amount the bust is to be raised. Fold on the first line, bring fold to second line. Pin or tape tuck flat.

On the side front, take a diagonal tuck from the curved seam, tapering to nothing at side seam.

An adjustment is necessary to keep the waistline balanced with the back pattern. To do this, cut both the front and side front sections on the altera-

tion line above waistline. Place a piece of paper under pattern. Spread cut edges same amount as bust was raised. Pin or tape pattern to paper. Straighten cutting lines.

Lowering the Bustline

On front pattern draw a horizontal line across the pattern just above the upper bust notch, then draw a diagonal line from above the notch on side front section to underarm seam.

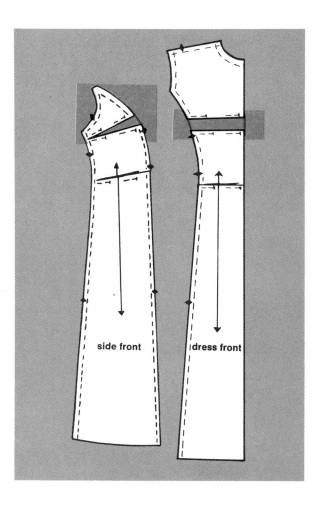

Cut pattern on this line. Place a piece of paper under cut edges. Spread cut edges the amount the bust is to be lowered. On the side front taper from nothing at side seam to full amount on curved seam. Pin or tape to paper.

An adjustment is necessary to keep the waistline balanced with the back pattern. To do this, draw a line both on the front and side front sections above the alteration line above waistline the same amount as bust was lowered. Fold on line, bring fold to drawn line. Pin or tape tuck and straighten cutting lines.

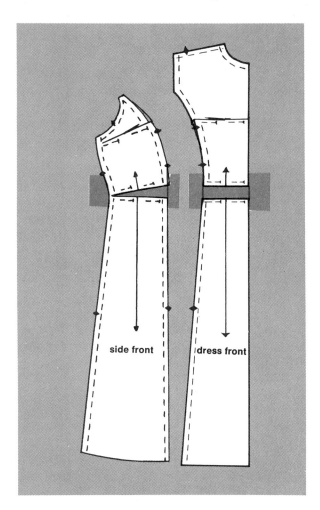

pants adjustments

While the illustrations show plain, full-length pants in every phase of alteration, the following instructions are for pants of all types and lengths. The adjustments in corresponding areas are the same for all styles.

Measurement Chart

Take the measurements indicated by the tapes on the illustrations; measure the pattern as instructed on page 148. Enter both sets of measurements on the chart; the differences between the two sets will show which alterations are necessary.

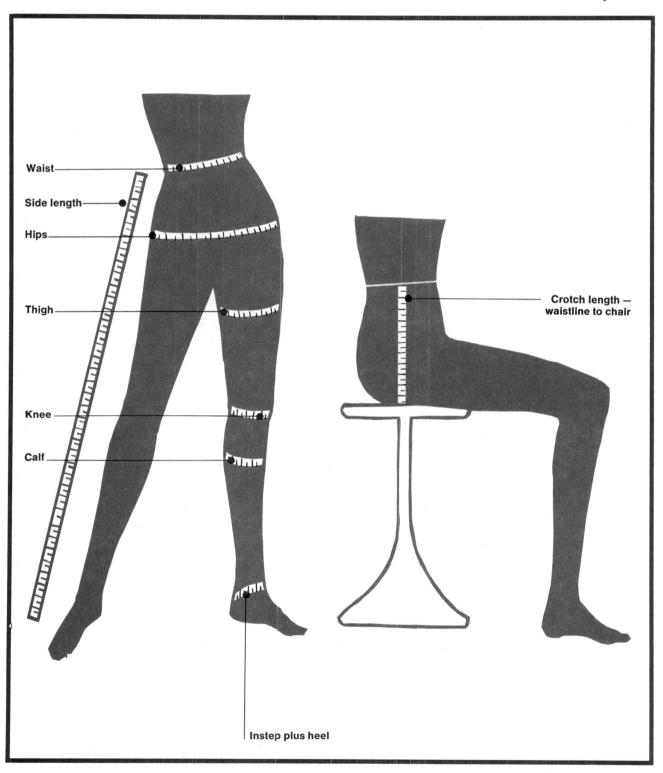

Waist

Side length

Hips

Thigh

Knee

Calf

Crotch length —
waistline to chair

Instep plus heel

Pants Measurements

	Wear the undergarments that you usually wear with pants and with the help of a second person take the measurements indicated on the chart.	Inches	Ease
Waist	(entire); as tight as you wear a waistband		
Hip	(fullest part) Distance from waistline ———inches		2"
Thigh	(fullest part) Distance from waistline ———inches		2½"
Side length	Waistline to ankle (or desired length)		
Crotch depth	(Sit on flat chair or stool with feet on floor) Follow the contour of the body from waistline to hip Hold tape straight from hip to chair		½-1"✻
Knee	(girth)		
Calf	(girth) Distance from calf to knee		
Instep + heel	Girth across heel and over instep Your foot will not go through pants legs if this measurement is less than measurement at hemline.		
✻ ½ inch ease for figures with 35 inch hip or less. ¾ inch ease for figures with 35 to 38 inch hips. 1 inch for figures with hips over 38 inches.			

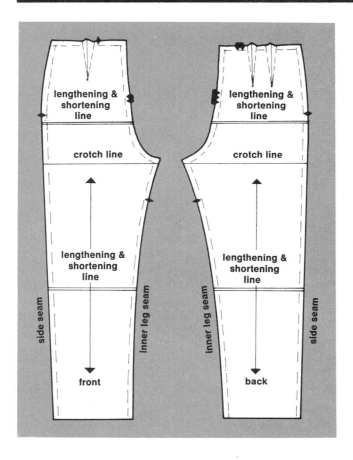

Your pants pattern should look like <u>the illustration at left</u> if accurate measurements are to be taken. If the crotch line is not indicated on your pattern, draw a horizontal line from the crotch to the side seam at a right angle to the grain line.

Waistline and Hip Alterations

To make these adjustments, either larger or smaller, follow the steps as outlined for the skirt on page 145. For problems such as high hip or large abdomen, refer to the previous pages, and use the same methods that solved these problems for you while you were making a skirt or dress.

Thigh Width

Measure across the front and back patterns, from seamline to seamline, at the same point where you measured the fullest part of your upper leg. Add the front and back measurements. If the total is less than your own measurement plus ease, widen the pattern. If the total is more, and you prefer

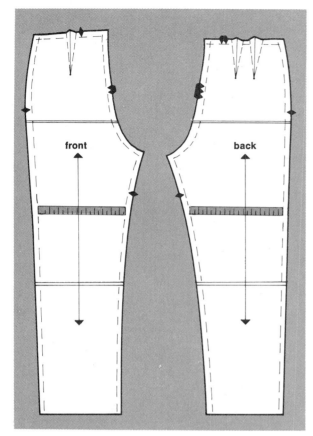

narrow pants, narrow the pattern. Alter both the front and back pattern pieces.

Widening Pants

Mark $1/4$ the amount to be widened at the thigh line on the front and back patterns, marking <u>outside</u> the cutting lines of the side and inner leg seams.

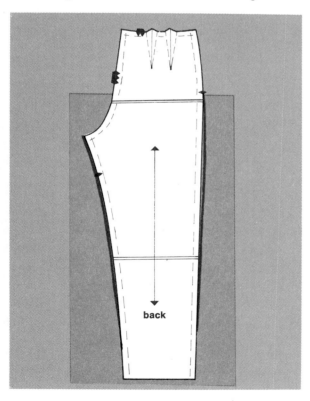

Draw a line along the side seam from the hipline through the thigh line, tapering in to hemline. Draw a line along the inner leg seam, starting at the lower end of the crotch, through the thigh line mark, tapering in to meet hemline. These are new cutting lines.

Narrowing Pants

Mark $1/4$ the amount to be narrowed at the thigh line on the front and back patterns, marking <u>inside</u> the cutting lines on the side and inner leg seams.

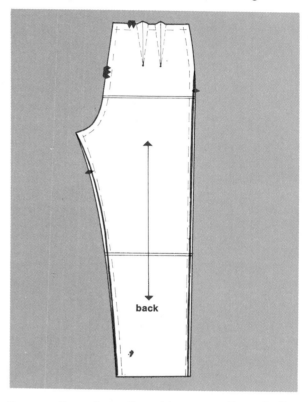

Draw a line along the side seam, through the thigh line mark, slanting outward to hemline. Draw new cutting line along the inner leg seam, starting at the lower end of crotch, through the thigh line mark, slanting outward to hemline.

Adjusting Length

Pants may need lengthening or shortening both above and below the crotch line. Two lengthening-shortening lines generally will be found on full-length pants patterns. The comparison of your measurements and the pattern measurements on the chart will show whether or not the pants need adjusting at both places or only at one.

Crotch Depth

Measure the distance from the waistline seamline to the crotch line. If this measurement is less than your crotch depth plus ease, lengthen the pattern; if it is more, shorten the pattern.

Lengthening Crotch

Cut pattern apart on the alteration line. Place paper under the two cut edges, and spread them the needed amount. Keep the grainlines straight and the cut edges parallel. Pin or tape pattern to paper.

Treat front and back in the same manner.

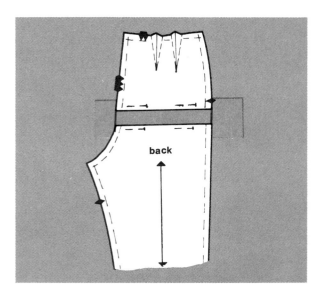

Shortening Crotch

Measure up from the shortening line the amount to be shortened. Draw a line across the pattern. Fold pattern on the printed line; bring fold up to the drawn line, keeping grainline straight. Pin or tape the fold flat.

Treat front and back in the same manner.

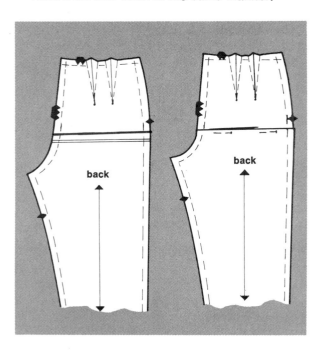

Side Length

Measure at the side seam of pattern from the waistline seamline to lower edge. Compare this measurement with your own measurement plus the hem depth. The difference is the amount to be lengthened or shortened. Lengthen or shorten on the printed line of the pattern between the crotch and lower edge of front and back. Follow the same procedure as given for lengthening and shortening the crotch.

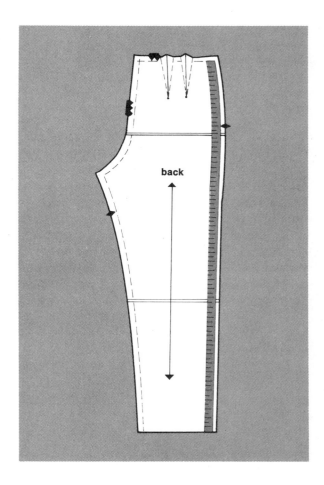

Fitting the Pants

The adjustments made in your pants by measurement will eliminate the major differences between you and your pattern, but there are some problems that are best solved by fitting a pair of trial pants.

Denim or heavyweight cotton are suitable; a checked fabric is a good choice, the checks aiding in the determination of grain perfection. If you use a sport fashion fabric, you will be able to wear the trial pants after you use them for fitting.

Cut and machine-baste the pants and waistband, referring to Chapter 12 for construction details. Baste the zipper in the opening.

Check the fit of your pants. Have the adjustments pinned by another person, and transfer them to your pattern. The altered trial pants can be used as a guide for altering all future pants patterns.

1. Check waist and hip comfort. If too loose or too tight, alter as for the skirt on page 142 to 145.

2. Check the crotch depth, both sitting and standing. If it is too tight, hangs too low or is uncomfortable when sitting, alter as instructed previously under Crotch Depth.

3. Check crotch width. If there is pull across the front and/or back at crotch level, add to the crotch inner leg seams. If there is too much fabric, take in the crotch inner leg seams.

a) To widen, add the needed amount to the front and/or back inner leg seams. Follow the shape of

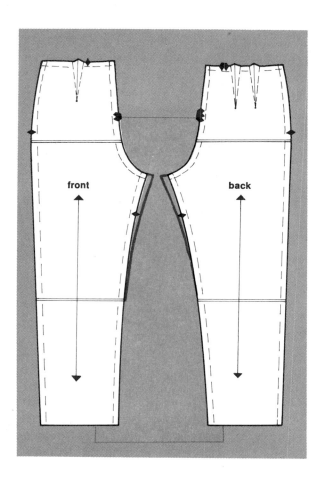

the pattern, and draw a new cutting line, slanting it to meet the original cutting line at the lengthening-shortening line.

b) To narrow, mark the amount needed inside the cutting line. Follow the shape of the trial pants,

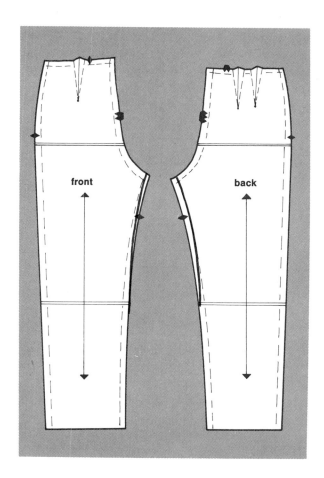

and draw a new cutting line, tapering it to meet the original cutting line at the alteration line.

4. Check the thigh width. If it is too tight or too loose, alter as instructed under Thigh Width.

5. Check the length and shape of darts. Darts should end just above the fullest contours of the figure. Curved darts are better suited to some of the more rounded figures.

6. Check the front of your pants. If the crotch seam pulls forward, or if there are wrinkles below the waistline, it is caused by a large abdomen. Lengthen the front pattern as instructed below.

Large Abdomen

Measure the amount needed (do not exceed $3/4$ inch) upward on the crotch seam. Draw a new cutting line, tapering from crotch seam to the original line at the side seam. See next page.

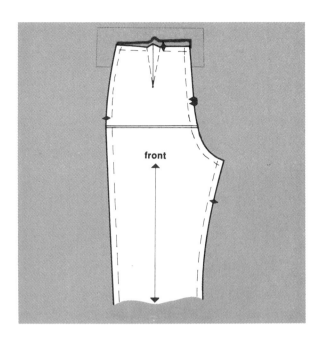

7. Check the back of your pants. If the back crotch is too tight, or the back is too figure-defining, it is caused by large buttocks or a prominent seat. Alter the back section.

Large Buttocks

To determine how much to add, first measure across your buttocks from side seam to side seam. Then divide this measurement by 2. On the side seam of the pattern back, measure down from the waistline the same depth at which you measured yourself. Mark. From this point measure across the pattern to the crotch in a straight line.

The difference between your own half measurement and the measurement of the pattern back is the amount needed to enlarge.

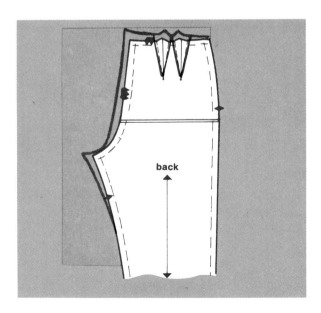

Measure ¹/₂ the needed amount upward on crotch seam above waistline cutting line. At the hipline, measure the same amount out from the crotch cutting line. At the bottom point of crotch seamline, measure out ¹/₂ the necessary amount for the new cutting line. Following the shape of the original crotch seam, draw a new cutting line through these markings, tapering to the original cutting lines at inner leg seam and at waistline near the side seam. The solid line in color indicates the new cutting line. Make darts deeper at the waistline to retain the original waistline size.

Flat Buttocks

If the back seam is too loose, and there are wrinkles across the seat at hip level, flat buttocks are the cause. Alter the back trial pants as instructed below.

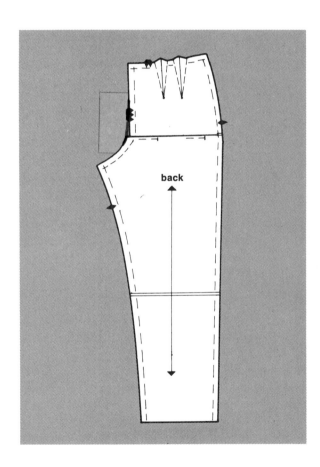

On the upper alteration line of the pants back pattern only, take a diagonal tuck. At the crotch seam make the tuck depth half the amount necessary to remove, and taper to nothing at the outer leg seam. Reestablish the original cutting line above the pleat.

press now—or pay later

If you're visualizing yourself slaving away over a hot iron to get that professional look in your garments, <u>forget it!!</u>

Sewing construction pressing is a far cry from household ironing; the exotic shapes of the implements, alone, should tell you that. You will be amazed at how easy it is to press like a real "pro".

Pressing skill is often the determining factor in whether you achieve a custom-made look. Proper pressing before, during and after construction is essential to the creation of professional looking garments. The right equipment, combined with the knowledge of when and how to use it, is the prerequisite for successful pressing.

"Press as you stitch" and "press directionally" should be your bywords in sewing. Construction pressing smooths seams and shapes areas thereby making the next sewing step easier. "Press as you stitch" does not mean that you have to jump up to press after each line of stitching. It means that a seam should be pressed before it is stitched to another garment section. Usually several darts or seams can be pressed at the same time.

Keep in mind the type of fabric being pressed, remembering to change the variables of pressure, moisture and heat relative to the fiber and/or texture. When working with a new fabric, always trial press a scrap or a hidden area of the garment.

Mastery of the art of pressing requires patience; experience and knowledge will develop with your sewing and fitting skills.

Proper equipment for pressing is described fully in Chapter 1. This equipment is essential, and it should be placed near your sewing machine.

controlling the variable factors

Pressure, moisture and heat are the variable factors that must be controlled to insure professional results and to protect your fabric. It is good procedure always to test press the fabric being used with the following points in mind.

Pressure
While pressing the great majority of fabrics, keep the weight of the iron in your hand, exert light pressure on the fabric and never rest the full weight of the iron on the fabric. A careful lifting and lowering motion is the rule when pressing with the iron. Additional pressure is necessary only for crease-resistant and firmly woven fabrics.

Moisture
Most fabrics require moisture for pressing, but excessive moisture will spot, ruin the texture or give an overpressed look in some cases. To avoid damage to your fabric use a press cloth when it is necessary to press on the right side.

A wet press cloth is not needed for any fabric. When dampening the press cloth, control the amount of moisture by wetting a third of the cloth, and roll and wring it to distribute the moisture.

For fabrics that require additional moisture but will not take it directly, place a dampened cheesecloth over the drill cloth or dampen the drill cloth with a wet sponge.

When additional moisture is needed on small, concentrated areas, use a small brush, such as a pastry brush, and apply moisture to the drill cloth or directly to the fabric if possible.

Heat
Check the heat settings on your iron, and test press the fabric. Some fabrics can deteriorate or become harsh and brittle under excessive iron heat.

Iron shine
Precautions must be taken when pressing fabric on the right side that overpressing with an iron that is too hot or too much moisture do not cause iron shine. The drill cloth and the steam iron cloth are excellent for this purpose. In an emergency, very heavy brown paper, cut from a supermarket bag, makes a satisfactory substitute for a drill cloth.

standard fabrics

Besides the three variable factors related to the iron, there are three additional factors related to the fabric; fiber, texture and thickness or weight. Knowledge of the special requirements for pressing each of the textile fibers is necessary for pressing various fabrics. When a fabric is composed of a blend of fibers, follow the instructions for pressing the fiber which requires the lowest heat.

Cotton is the easiest fabric to press, but it should be handled according to its weight. Lightweight cotton requires a heat setting similar to that used for silk while heavyweight cotton requires a heat setting similar to that used for linen. Moisture is generally used, but the fabric should be pressed completely dry. Press first with steam, then press with the steam off. Smooth, light colored cotton may be pressed on either side. Dark colors, dull finishes and textures require a dry cheesecloth or steam iron cloth when pressed on the right side.

Rayon requires low heat. The steam iron usually supplies sufficient moisture. Press from the wrong side and use a dry cheesecloth, steam iron cloth or a drill cloth.

Linen is treated in a similar way to cotton, but it requires a higher heat setting and usually more moisture. Press until it is dry.

Wool is sensitive to excesses of pressure, moisture and heat. It requires a moist heat, but it should not be pressed when it is very damp or completely dry. When pressing napped surfaces or soft textures on the right side, use wool or wool sewn to a drill cloth as a press cloth. Use a clothes brush to help raise the nap while there is still some moisture left in the fabric.

Silk and man-made fibers require great care in pressing; minimal amounts of pressure, moisture and heat should be used for them. Most fabrics made with these fibers may be pressed without a press cloth, but it is safer to use a thin press cloth to protect the fabric. When moisture is needed, test to see that the fabric doesn't water-spot. A piece of tissue paper, placed between the fabric and the iron will prevent water-spots.

textures

Many fabrics have, as their outstanding characteristic, the texture they receive from various manufacturing and finishing processes. Proper pressing methods will retain these textures.

Glossy fabrics, such as glazed chintz and polished cotton, are pressed on the right side without a pressing cloth and with little or no moisture.

Dull-finished fabrics are pressed on the wrong side or on the right side using the proper press cloth for the specific fabric. This information is very important for fabrics such as acetate from which iron shine cannot be removed.

Napped or pile fabrics such as fleece, deep-pile fake furs, corduroy and velvet, must be steamed rather than pressed to prevent the nap or pile from flattening. When you press a long napped fabric, press in the direction of the nap. You may use one of the following methods:

A piece of self-fabric can be used as a press cloth when pressing on the right side, such as shown on the corduroy above. When you press a seam on the inside, use self-fabric on the underside.

Press the fabric, pile side down, on a needle board (described in Chapter 1). After pressing, softly brush the fabric in the direction of the pile.

Raised surface designs are pressed on a softly padded board from the wrong side. Light pressure is best on woven or embossed fabric, but heavier pressure is used to emphasize the design on embroidered fabric.

Special fabrics. Methods for pressing the special fabrics (leather, lace, knits, etc.) are explained in Chapter 16 along with the other techniques for handling these fabrics.

construction pressing

Construction pressing has a basic aim: to press a specific detail without pressing the entire area. The one exception is the pressing of the first detail in a garment section in which case the entire section is pressed.

To be able to pinpoint a detail for pressing, the garment has to be positioned correctly and the proper equipment used. Use both hands to lift the fabric when moving it to help each section keep its shape. Always press on grain in the same direction that the stitching was done. Do not skip steps because each pressing helps to make the next construction step easier.

Over-all care is also important. When a sewing session is finished, see that all garment sections are laid away smoothly. Unnecessary folds and creases can be prevented if each garment section is hung carefully after it is pressed. Small sections and pieces can be placed over a hanger that has been padded with a turkish towel.

Remove pins and bastings wherever possible before pressing. Pressing over pins can mar the fabric as well as the sole plate of the iron, and bastings leave an imprint. When basting is needed to hold layers of fabric together while pressing, use a fine silk thread.

Seams. For smoother seam lines, make it a habit to press as stitched, that is, press all stitching lines flat before pressing seams open, or to either side. Straight seams are generally pressed open with the exception of topstitched seams or pleats.

After pressing along the stitching line, place the seam, wrong side up, on a seam roll, a tailor's board or on the edge of a sleeve board. Smooth the fabric crosswise, and open the seam with your fingers. Press with the point of the iron in the direction of the grain. If the fabric requires moisture, press the seam open first without moisture, using the iron only on the stitching line.

Final press the seam on the outside of the garment, using a press cloth when necessary.

Areas that are to be shaped are placed over a section of a tailor's ham or a seam roll which properly fits the area to be pressed. The following are garment areas which must be shaped on a cushion.

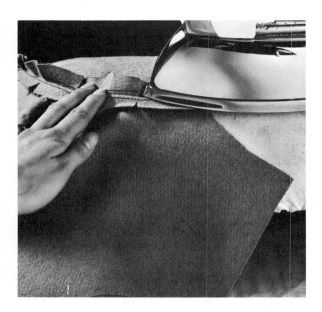

A curved seam, such as a yoke or bodice seam across the bustline, or the bust and waistline curves on a fitted seam, should be molded over the ham to maintain a soft, rounded look.

Waistline seams are pressed toward the bodice over a ham. For smaller sizes and for some styles this seam should be pressed on the sleeve board.

Darts and tucks. With the point of iron toward the point of dart, press flat as stitched; then press in the direction desired. Do not press beyond the point of dart or the stitching line of tuck.

Place the point of the dart at the end of cushion. Press the dart carefully away from the line of stitching, to avoid a pleated effect on the right side. If the imprint will show on the right side of fabric, place a strip of paper under the fold of the dart.

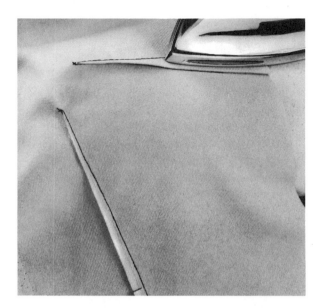

Bodice darts or tucks and back skirt darts are pressed on a cushion. Horizontal darts, such as bust darts, are pressed down toward the hem. Vertical darts, such as waistline and shoulder darts, are pressed toward center front or center back.

Double-pointed darts must be clipped at the widest part to within $1/4$ inch of the stitching line in order to have them lay flat.

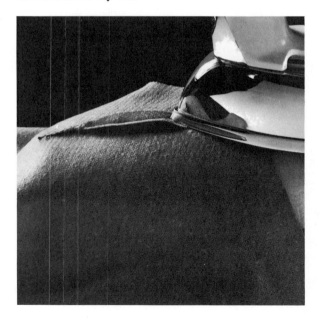

In heavy fabric trim dart away to a $3/8$ inch seam as far down as it is that width; then slash fold to $1/2$ inch from point. Lay dart over ham and press seam open with point of iron. Below the seam use a metal knitting needle to divide dart. Press on each side of the stitching line.

Elbow darts are pressed on the cushion toward the cuff on the lengthwise grain of the sleeve. If there is ease at the elbow instead of darts, press the sleeve seam crosswise to smooth fullness at the elbow roll (the way the fabric curves away from seamline). Press seam open on a sleeve board.

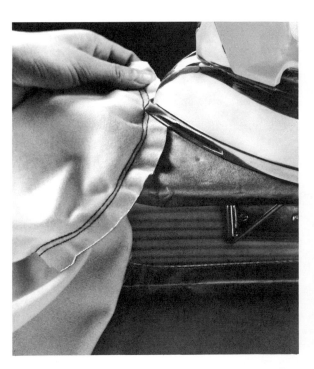

Armhole seam. Lay the top of sleeve seam, (between notches) edges together, over the edge of sleeve board with sleeve side up. Use point of iron and press seam allowance only. The seam allowance will turn into the sleeve without further pressing. The underarm section of seam (between notches) should not be pressed.

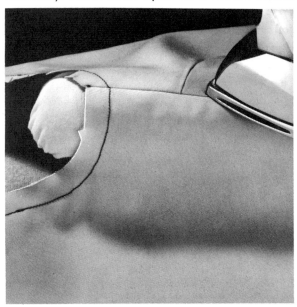

The shoulder roll should be pressed in the same way as the elbow roll. Press the seam open on the underside from the neckline to the armhole. From the right side shape and press the back shoulder line on the lengthwise grain around the edge of the curved cushion.

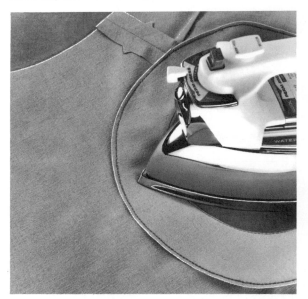

An understitched facing falls into place for pressing almost automatically. Shape this area in your fingers to perfect the line of the faced edges. Always establish the edge of a facing on the underside before pressing on the topside. When pressing on the topside, keep fingers ahead of the iron to maintain a perfect edge.

Hems. Place garment wrong side out on ironing board with the hem on the right hand side. Work on grain of fabric, lifting, rather than gliding, the iron from one section to another. When there is fullness at the top of the hem, use heavy paper between the garment and the hem to shrink out gathers when possible. Otherwise press gathers flat around the hem.

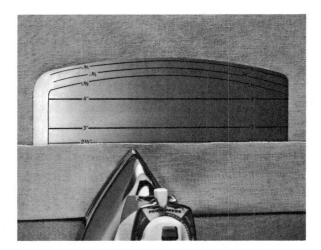

Straight hems can be pressed using the straight edge of the automatic hem gauge. Always press the hem on grain from the hem edge to the folded edge. When the particular style dictates a softer look, do not press a sharp edge at the hemline.

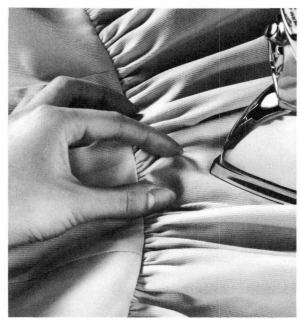

Gathers and shirring are pressed by working point of iron into, never across, the gathers. Press toward the stitching line. Work from the right side, and avoid creases by lifting the folds away from the iron as you progress.

Pleats should be basted before pressing. Press on the wrong side along the line of stitching and along the fold to set the crease. Turn the garment to the right side, remove the basting and press, using a strip of paper under the pleat to prevent an imprint.

The edge and point presser on the tailor's board is used to press seams, collars and facings open before they are trimmed and turned.

The pounding block is used on the outside of the garment to obtain sharp edges without shine on wool and other heavy fabrics. Steam an area the exact length of the block; then quickly remove the iron and pound the area with the block. The pounding block is used mainly in tailoring buttonholes, lapels, collars, facings, hems, pleats and pockets. It is never used on the zipper.

If fabric has nap or pile, use a cloth mitt instead of the pounding block to flatten these areas without damaging the nap or pile.

Use light pressure to prevent impressions of construction details from showing on the right side.

Maintaining the well-pressed look

Here are same additional tips for maintaining a well-pressed look:

To remove shine, raise nap and eliminate an overpressed look effectively, hold the steam iron $1/2$ to 1 inch away from the fabric, allowing the steam to penetrate. This method is particularly helpful when pressing a garment detail, such as a rolled collar or a lapel, because the extra moisture permits the fabric to be manipulated to shape.

Apply white vinegar with a narrow paint brush to remove creases or iron-shine from areas that have been altered. After the white vinegar has been applied, steam-press the altered area. Pretest this method on a scrap or on an inconspicuous area of the garment.

A stiff clothes brush can be substituted for a needle board when you are pressing small areas of a napped fabric.

When pressing a laundered garment, press on the underside first to reopen seams, set darts, smooth the sleeve cap, etc.

Touch-up pressing will be minimized if you hang your garments properly. Choose a strong, contoured hanger to maintain the shape of the garment. Never hang a garment inside out. Fasten some of the buttons and close zippers. Remove any accessories (belt, scarves or jewelry) that might pull a garment out of shape.

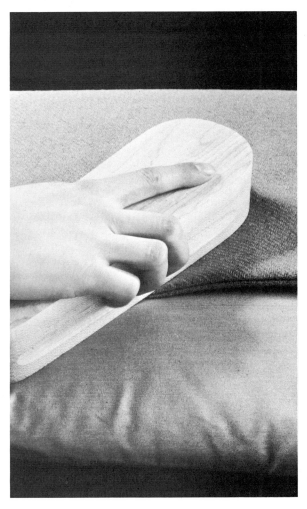

Final pressing

The amount of final pressing can be kept to a minimum touch-up here and there, if each step of construction pressing has been done with care.

Follow the same methods and instructions regarding equipment, grain, pressure, moisture and heat in the final pressing as you did in construction pressing. Press the hem on the grain of the fabric. Use the iron with a lifting and lowering motion while keeping the weight of the iron in your hand.

A kaleidoscope of colorful fabrics to dazzle and tempt the eye . . . versatile, sewable textures and designs, a fabulous variety to take you through four seasons. Most of all, ready to send your personal sewing dream into orbit.

Feminine, flowing sheers, exquisite Chantilly and embroidered laces and the serene mystery of shadow sheers.

Your active life calls for an action fabric,
here's the answer in one vital word; knits,
for super go-power — double knits,
jerseys and bonded fabrics of all types.

On this page — a sheik's ransom of color in stripes, plaids and diagonals , the gentle wools and miraculous synthetic blends.

Step right up to the bright young fakes, the "for reals" and the sumptuous piles, all the up and coming dash you love in patent vinyl, cotton suede, cut velvet, synthetic broadtail, curly lamb and leather.

16 sew a special fabric

Special fabrics range from soft, feminine lace to exciting man-made furs. They are the special effects department of fashion.

Special techniques are required in their sewing and handling, but they open such a vast world of creativity to you that they are well worth the extra effort. Follow the procedures listed for your fabric, but if a special procedure is not listed, follow the standard techniques.

guides to follow

It is impossible to list all fabrics requiring special handling as the list grows almost from day to day. Develop an approach that will help you to sew any fabric. The suggestions that follow will aid you regardless of which fabrics you use.

• Read the fabric labels; follow special instructions for cutting, marking, stitching, etc.
• Experiment with the fabric; test it for suitable procedures for marking, making buttonholes, seams, seam finishes, hems and darts. Pins leave marks on some of these fabrics, so pinning should be done within the seam allowance. Fabrics often suggest their own best techniques. Ready-to-wear garments are good sources of inspiration for style selection and appropriate sewing techniques.
• Make the seam test described in Chapter 6 to learn which is the best needle size, stitch length, tension and pressure for your special fabric. Test-press the seam using the method for your fabric as described later in this chapter.
• Select pattern styles which complement the fabric. Some patterns feature special fabrics which are illustrated on the front of the envelope. These patterns include instructions for their handling on the back of the pattern envelope and in the Cutting and Sewing Directions.

laces and sheers

These fabrics impart a graceful, feminine look to clothes. Because they are transparent, sheers and laces are frequently handled in a similar manner.

Laces are made in all types of fibers, and they are not necessarily as fragile as they look. See page 167 for handling bonded lace. If you buy a lace with a one-way or panel design, see Chapter 5 for one-way fabric cutting instructions.

Transparent or sheer underlinings can be made with tulle, net, organdy and organza; opaque underlinings can be made with peau de soie, linen, cotton, sateen, dull finished taffeta or crepe. Either match the lace, or use a subtle contrasting color.

Cutting. If the fabric slips when you are cutting, anchor the fabric to the cutting board or pin to tissue paper, and cut the paper and fabric as one.

Although lace has no grain, it may have an "up and down" or the design may require matching. Place the pattern to show the design at its best. The right side of lace usually has a cord outlining the design pattern.

Instead of a selvage some lace has a decorative edge which can be used in place of a hem or other finish at the bottom of a skirt, a sleeve or down a front opening, but plan the sleeve or hem length before you cut the fabric. Lace with repeat designs can be hand-clipped to form a decorative edge by clipping away the threads which attach the design motif to the rest of the lace.

Sheers of today are easy to care for, and most are easy to sew. Made of various fibers, they range from soft chiffon to crisp organdy. It is easier to work with crisp sheers than with filmy ones.

Most sheers are used without a lining for a "see-through" effect. A coordinating slip about 1 inch shorter than the garment may be planned as part of the total look.

Patterns should include enough ease for a gentle fit. Gathered skirts and billowy sleeves are good details for sheer garments. Select styles having a minimum of seams and without a center front seam so that a lace design will not be disturbed.

Gathered skirts of sheer fabric can be cut on the crosswise grain to avoid extra seams, or they can be cut double, in which case the lengthwise fold becomes the hemline. If you use the double cut method you will need to purchase extra fabric and plan the hem length before you cut.

Marking methods are given in Chapter 5, but make a test on a scrap of fabric to be sure that it is not marred in the marking. Tailor's tacks are best for most laces and sheers.

Stitching. Baste the seams to prevent slippage when machine-stitching. Lace can be prevented from catching in the feed dog or presser foot if you place strips of tissue paper between the fabric and the machine. Stitch the tissue and fabric as one. Tear the paper away after each line of stitching is finished.

Seams. Inconspicuous seams are important to the appearance of sheer garments, so use narrow French, triple-stitched or double-stitched seams.

Double-stitched seam. Stitch on the seamline; then place a second row of stitching about $1/8$ inch from the first row in the seam allowance. The second row can be either straight stitching or a fine zig-zag stitch. Trim seam allowance close to second line of stitching. Armhole seams for set-in sleeves can be finished in the same way, but the second row of stitching should be placed $1/4$ inch from the first row for extra strength.

Directions for the French and triple-stitched seams are in Chapter 17.

Darts can be double-stitched then trimmed close to the second line of stitching. It is easier to stitch darts in unlined, heavy lace if they are slashed on the fold line to within $5/8$ inch of point. Stitch dart, press seam open and trim edges to $1/4$ inch.

Make facings of tulle or net, or finish the edges with a French binding of self or coordinating fabric.

Tulle facing. Lace edges can be finished with strips of tulle. Cut strips $2^1/_2$ inches wide on crosswise grain. Fold in half lengthwise, and stitch raw edges

to the right side of lace on seamline. Make a second line of stitching $1/8$ inch from the first within the seam allowance. Trim close to second line. Turn strip to wrong side along seamline of garment, and slip-stitch in place.

Flocked, printed or embroidered sheers can be faced or bound with plain sheer fabric that matches the background color.

Buttonholes. Hand-worked buttonholes can be used on sheers; machine-worked can be used on both sheers and laces. For interfacing use lightweight sheer, net or marquisette.

Button loops of coordinated fabric make attractive closures for lace and sheers.

Zippers can be machine-stitched, and finished by hand, or the entire application can be by hand.

Hems in sheer fabrics can be deep or very narrow. A rolled hem is suitable for a circular skirt. Deep hems and double hems help the hang of sheer skirts and give them a high quality look. A hem can be as much as 12 inches deep. Turn desired amount to wrong side; turn under raw edge $1/4$ inch; slip-stitch in place.

A double hem can be used only on a straight edge. Turn hem up to desired depth and press. Make a second turn with raw edge in the fold. Slip-stitch.

A narrow hem is essential for lace. Finish bottom edge with tulle facing as described at left, but make the strip of tulle wider for the hem finish.

Rolled hems or hems finished with horsehair braid are suitable for lace. See page 184 Stiffened Hem.

Pressing. Some sheers pucker when pressed with steam, so be sure to test a scrap. Lace can be pressed with regular steam settings. Lay the lace face down on a wool press cloth or on a turkish towel to avoid flattening the raised design. Cover lace with a thin press cloth to prevent iron from catching in lace.

knits

Because they are comfortable to wear, easy to care for and wrinkle-resistant, knits adapt easily to today's mode of living, and have become popular for all occasions.

Knit fabrics are made of yarn which is looped together like chain stitches instead of being woven. There are two basic types of fabric: the horizontally knitted fabric which stretches mostly in a crosswise direction (most knits are of this type); the vertically knitted fabric, more tightly woven with less give, and does not ravel. Tricot is an example of the vertical knit.

Both types have lengthwise ribs which can be compared to the lengthwise grain of a woven fabric. When you buy knits, be sure that the ribs are not badly twisted out of line.

Knitted fabrics can be bought either in tubular form or in flat lengths. Single knits, which include tricots and jerseys, have a soft feel and a definite right and wrong side. These are suitable for patterns having gathers and draping. Double-knits are made with two sets of yarn in a double stitch so that the fabric looks the same on both sides. They are firm, but flexible, and tailor beautifully.

Patterns. The type of knit will determine the style, but as a general rule, avoid full circular or gored skirts with bias lines.

Preparation. Shrink all knit fabrics, except those that are bonded, before cutting. See Chapter 4 for shrinking instructions. To open a tubular knit cut along a rib close to the fold line but not on the fold. Press the center fold to remove it. If it does not press out completely, place pattern so that crease will not be prominent.

A lengthwise rib can be used as a guide when folding knits by marking with hand-basting near, not on, the center fold. Chalk-mark crosswise ends with a yardstick at right angles to the basting.

Cutting. Lay fabric flat without tension; avoid stretching while pinning and cutting.

Stitching. Staystitch shoulders, necklines and armholes. Reinforce shoulders and waistline seams with straight seam tape.

Use a stitch length of 12 to 15 per inch and fine (11) to medium (14) needles. The thread used will depend on the fiber content of the fabric, but cotton covered polyester thread is good for knits because it stretches with the fabric.

Seams. Refer to Guiding Fabric in Chapter 6. A welt seam or top-stitching are good for double knits. As knits do not ravel, no seam finish is needed on plain seams.

Faced edges should be interfaced to prevent stretching. A binding of self-fabric makes an attractive finish for neckline, sleeves and outside edges of a jacket.

Buttonholes, either bound or machine-worked, and button-loops are suitable. Interface with firm muslin or lawn.

Hems. The catch-stitch hem is good because it gives with the fabric. Follow instructions for a Catch-stitch Hem in Chapter 17.

Press lengthwise, lifting and lowering the iron to avoid stretching the fabric. Always use a press cloth. When you press seams, place strips of brown paper under the seam allowances to prevent seam impressions from showing through to the right side of the garment.

bondeds

A bonded fabric consists of an outer or face fabric of almost any fiber fused to a lining fabric such as tricot or taffeta. The permanent backing gives stability to the face fabrics and prevents stretching. It adds comfort and "instant" lining to such favorites as jerseys, flannels, laces and crepes. Before you make the purchase, check the grain of the face fabric. Do not buy it if it is badly off grain because it cannot be straightened.

Patterns that are simple and without intricate seams or details should be selected for bondeds.

Cutting. Place pattern on right side so grainline can be seen. With some bonded fabrics, it is best to cut single thicknesses. For pieces cut on the fold, cut the first half, flip pattern over on fold line and cut the other half. On bulky fabrics, cut facing as one with the garment to eliminate seams. Mark with tailor's tacks.

Stitching. Use thread suitable to face fabric, and make a test seam to determine correct tension, pressure, needle and stitch length. Use a top-stitched or flat fell seam if suitable to design.

Darts should be pressed flat like a pleat, and centered over the stitching line.

plaids and stripes

To work successfully with plaids learn to recognize the variations. If a plaid is even, it is exactly the same on both sides of the prominent bar in both

even

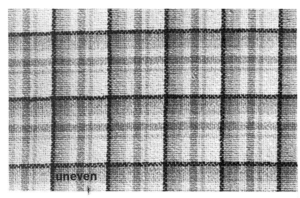

uneven

directions, crosswise and lengthwise. An uneven plaid varies on both sides of the bar either on the crosswise, the lengthwise or both and makes matching at the seams more difficult. Stripes can also be even or uneven, but only in one direction, either lengthwise or crosswise.

Before you purchase your fabric, study its effect on your figure by holding it up in front of a mirror. Plaids and stripes should be kept in scale with your figure. Do not buy from small samples which do not show the repeat of the design.

Plaids require extra yardage for matching in both directions. If yardage is not given, add $1/8$ yard for small plaids, $1/4$ to $1/2$ yard for medium plaids, and up to 1 yard for very large plaids. Stripes require slightly less extra yardage because they are matched in only one direction.

Pattern. Choose patterns having few pieces and seams and with simple, unbroken lines. Those which feature plaids or stripes are your best choice. Avoid circular yokes, most gored skirts, and for uneven plaids or stripes, kimono sleeves.

Cutting. Match plaids and stripes at these points: On a bodice, blouse or one-piece dress match crosswise bars at side seam notches, along center front and center back seams. If there is an under-arm dart, side seams will only match from the dart down. Match the front notch of a set-in sleeve to the notch on the bodice. Usually the sleeve and armhole cannot be matched at both the front and back notches. On kimono sleeves match front and back below notch on the shoulder seam. Match raglan sleeves at the notch on the armhole seam. Match collars at center back seam to the center back of garment.

How to match. Using a soft lead pencil, trace the stripe or plaid design of the fabric onto the tissue pattern along the seam line. Colors may be indicated by using colored crayons or by writing the color in the space. Place the pattern piece to be joined over the first piece, matching the notches having the same numbers and with seam lines matching. Trace the design from the first pattern piece to the second along the seam line. This piece can then be placed on a second area of fabric to correspond with the lines of the first piece.

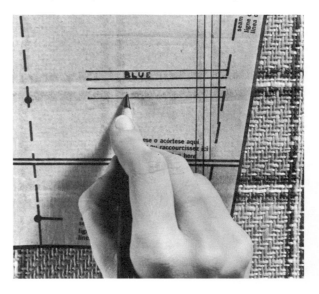

All skir seams should match although the vertical bars may not match toward the top of the seams. Plaids and vertical stripes will not match down the entire length of any seam unless the seamlines of the two sections to be joined are equal in slant.

Experiment with the pattern layout to determine a pleasing effect. If possible, the dominant lengthwise bar should fall at center front and center back and at the center of the sleeve. Dominant crosswise bars are unattractive over the crown of the bust or across the abdomen.

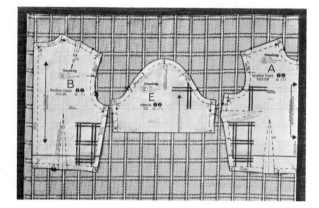

Lay out the bodice front section first, then the bodice back followed by the sleeves or skirt and the remaining pieces. Illustrated is a bodice placed on an even plaid with center front line and center back seam on a dominant lengthwise bar and notches on matching crosswise bars. The front sleeve notch is placed on the same bar as the armhole notch of the front bodice.

Even plaids and stripes can be cut on double layers of fabric; uneven ones may be cut on single or double layers depending on the design. It is more accurate to cut all plaids on a single layer of fabric. When you cut a single layer, cut one section at a time, place it on the fabric again, matching all bars,

and then cut another section. Be sure to reverse the pattern piece for the second cutting. For double layers pin fabric together, crosswise and/or lengthwise bars matching, to prevent slippage. For the uneven types lay pattern pieces with all their tops facing in the same direction.

It is often difficult to achieve a balanced appearance in the front of a garment with uneven designs. It may be necessary to create a seam at the center front and back if the pattern does not have them. If you create a seam, be sure to add $5/8$ inch seam allowance to pattern.

Lay the pattern pieces on a single thickness of fabric with the center front seamline on the center of a lengthwise bar and with a balanced arrangement of the crosswise bars. Cut the first piece adding $5/8$ inch seam allowance at center, but do not unpin the pattern. Lay the fabric and its pinned-on pattern on a second area of the fabric with the bars matching in both directions. This method of cutting can only be used on a fabric without a definite right or wrong side because one of the fabric pieces will be turned over when seamed.

Chevrons at the seamlines are made by cutting plaids and stripes on the bias. Fold the fabric back on itself to see how it will chevron. Whenever possible, select a pattern illustrated with chevrons because the pattern pieces will have special grain lines and layout to follow. To get a chevron effect with a balanced plaid there must be a bias seam where the chevron is to appear. For a chevron in an unbalanced plaid the fabric must be reversible.

Cut collars, cuffs and pockets on the bias to create a subtle, interesting contrast.

Stitching. Match seamlines by placing fabric layers together with all stripes matching. Pin exactly on the bars. The top seam allowance can be turned back to make sure that the stripes are perfectly matched. Baste; then stitch a test seam to determine how often to pin. Stitch at a moderate pace.

Match bias seamlines perfectly by pressing under one seam allowance and lapping it over the other. Slip-baste from right side. Machine-stitch from wrong side on basted line.

Match thread, zipper and seam tape to the dominant color in the fabric.

diagonals

Special sewing techniques are not required for a fabric with a diagonal weave, but it is important to select the right pattern and to cut the fabric in such a way that the prominent lines will create an attractive effect in the final garment.

In a twill weave the filling yarns pass over one or more warp yarns thereby forming a diagonal line or "twill" which runs either from the upper right to the lower left or from the upper left to the right.

In some fabrics the diagonal is almost invisible. In others such as gabardine (B), denim (C) and silk surah the weave is so fine that the diagonal is not the problem, but the shading is. The fabric may show a color difference when garment pieces are joined on the bias. The prominent diagonal shown here in a tweed (A) requires careful planning before it is cut.

Patterns. Before you buy a pattern, read the back of the envelope. The styles which are marked "not suitable" for diagonal fabrics actually refer to the prominent diagonals. The best patterns are those with slim skirts, few seams, set-in sleeves and straight underarm darts. Avoid patterns with bias seams, long bias darts, wide A-line or gored skirts, long kimono sleeves and V-necklines.

If the pattern has been carefully selected, you can follow the regular cutting layout. If your fabric has a napped surface, use a nap layout. Experiment with the placement of details, collars, pockets, waistbands and trimmings to see which way you would like the diagonals to run.

A straight or slightly shaped notched collar is best, you can try cutting the collar on a bias either along the rib or across the rib.

Chevrons can be formed where seams join if the fabric is reversible. Open fabric to its full width. Measure length of pattern pieces being used for chevrons, and cut two lengths of fabric. Pin right side of one length to wrong side of the other. Lay on pattern, and cut the two layers together as one.

permanent press

Permanent press is the last word in easy-care, wash-and-wear fabrics. If properly sewn and laundered, permanent press garments should require little or no ironing. They come in a variety of textures and weights, and are usually a blend of polyester and cotton fibers.

This fabric cannot be straightened so if it is badly off grain, do not buy it. Make sure that plaids and checks run at right angles to the selvages.

Patterns with simple lines and uncomplicated details should be selected. If the fabric is the least bit off grain, lay the pattern pieces to follow the pattern, not the grain. Press a section of the center fold. If it does not press out, avoid it when laying out the pattern.

Mark smooth fabrics in solid colors with only the tracing wheel. See Chapter 5.

Stitching. Because of its finish, this fabric may pucker when it is stitched. Avoid long seams and zippers set in long seams on the straight grain, as they pucker more than seams slightly off grain or on the bias. Sleeve caps tend to pucker with this fabric which is difficult to ease, so remove some of the ease from the cap on the pattern.

Stitch with a cotton covered polyester-core thread with a stitch length of 10 to 14 per inch. Tension should be loose. Use a fine needle with the regular, not zig-zag, throat plate.

Choose washable interfacings, underlinings and linings which do not require ironing. Laces, trims, tapes and bindings must be shrunk before use if they are not labeled for wash-and-wear.

For zippers the lapped application is preferred as there is less puckering. It is important to pre-shrink the closed zipper. Immerse in hot water for a few minutes and allow to air dry. Repeat and press zipper lightly before applying it.

After basting the seam closed clip stitches at 2 inch intervals before pressing open. Use a stitch length of 10 to 12 per inch for all steps. As you stitch, pin or baste the zipper in position, easing tape to seams. Touch-up ironing will give a smoother look to the application.

Press during construction at a low heat setting. For the final pressing use a high heat setting for synthetic or cotton with steam or a damp press cloth. Some of these fabrics are sensitive to heat so test press them first.

deep pile or fur-like fabrics

The newest "frankly fakes" come in amazingly long and plush textures, and the fur fabrics, especially, can give enjoyment as well as a feeling of luxury without the cost and care of the "real" thing.

The pile is usually synthetic with either a knitted or woven backing of cotton or synthetic fiber.

These fabrics should be bought using yardages for fabrics with nap. If not given, add $3/8$ to $3/4$ of a yard for cutting one-way and matching designs. Read the labels to see whether the fabric is washable or dry-cleanable.

Patterns. Select simple designs with few seams for coats, jackets, jumpers, skirts, sleeveless vests and accessories.

Cutting. When fabric is very wide, eliminate as many seams as possible. Cut straight facings in one with the garment. Taffeta or satin may also be used for facings to eliminate bulk at edges.

Place pattern on backing side of fabric with tops of all pattern pieces facing in same direction. Cut so that pile runs down. Do not fold very deep pile, but cut it on single thickness. It may be better to use a razor blade, and cut only the backing from the wrong side to prevent the pile from being cut.

Stitching. Use a coarse needle and heavy duty thread. Set stitch length for about 10 per inch. Hand-baste to prevent creeping and puckering while machine-stitching.

Seams. Stitch in the direction of the pile wherever possible. Use seam tape to reinforce points of strain. Use a needle to lift pile caught in stitched seam on right side.

Shear pile from the seam allowances to eliminate bulk of the very deep pile fabrics. Curved seams should not be clipped too deeply.

Darts. Split down the center and shear pile as you did on the seams. Press them open.

Closures. On very deep pile fabrics, buttonholes are difficult to make so use metal hooks, decorative metal frogs or leather closures. On low pile fabrics machine-made buttonholes are appropriate.

Pressing. Place fabric, pile side down, on velvet board with a press cloth over backing. Steam press without touching the fabric. Test press on a sample seam. If pile side must be pressed, place on velvet board and cover with a terry cloth towel.

leathers and leather-likes

Leather is sold by the individual skin. Even though you select skins of uniform weight and color, many skins will have thin spots. Therefore, buy the pattern first as it will help you to determine how many skins are needed by placing the pattern pieces on the skins. You may have to cut the pattern pieces apart, adding design lines such as a yoke, gores in a skirt or center seams. Be sure to add seam allowances at these points.

Interface and line all leathers. Extend front interfacing to armhole for support. Cut facings from skins, or line leather to the edge. Firmly woven synthetic fabric makes a good lining. Very soft leathers may have to be underlined.

Leather-like fabrics are sold by the yard. Interface these fabrics, and line all coats and vests. For a washable leather-like (check manufacturer's label) use a wash-and-wear lining.

Patterns with simple, unbroken lines are best. Avoid eased seams, especially in real leather. It is possible to use set-in sleeves on the leather-likes if ease is removed from the sleeve cap. Raglan sleeves are easier to use on all these fabrics.

Your pattern must fit before cutting so make the necessary alterations. The garment, itself, should not be altered because needles and pins leave permanent holes in these fabrics.

Cutting. Bulk can be avoided by trimming the pattern seam allowances to $3/8$ inch before laying it out. Cut a complete paper pattern for front and back pieces. Do not fold skins: lay the pattern on a single thickness.

Leather does not have a grain, but all pattern pieces must be placed on the skins facing in one direction, either all on the crosswise or all on the lengthwise. Lay all pieces on suede so that the nap runs down.

Prevent marring by pinning only in the seam allowance, or use cellophane tape to hold the pattern in place. Mark construction details on the wrong side with chalk, using a ruler for straight lines. Dressmakers' carbon with a smooth edged tracing wheel can also be used on leather-likes.

Stitching. Seams may be pinned or basted within the seam allowance, or you can use paper clips to hold the edges together.

Silk or heavy-duty mercerized thread may be used on leathers, but use only heavy-duty mercerized on the leather-likes. Use hand and machine needles that are sharp. The wedge-pointed needles, made especially for stitching leather, are very good. Use machine needles from sizes 11 to 16, depending on the weight of the leather. Use a stitch length from 8 to 12 stitches per inch.

Tie the thread ends; never backstitch because it can cut the leather. Reinforce points of strain by stitching preshrunk, straight seam tape into the seam. Clip the tape at intervals to prevent it from pulling. Handle leather gently. Stitch slowly, and do not pull the leather under the presser foot while stitching or it will stretch.

Finger-press seams open, and top-stitch an even distance on both sides of the seamline. Seam allowances can be glued to hold them in place.

To glue: Spread a thin line of rubber cement or fabric glue over the stitches on the underside of the seam allowance. Finger-press seam allowance against the garment. If more pressure is needed on the leather, use the pounding block to flatten the seams.

If you use a welt or lapped seam, no gluing is necessary. Cut out tiny "Vs" to flatten curved seams. Round all the corners when stitching because with leather, corners that are pointed do not turn well.

Taper darts to a fine point, and tie threads. Slash open and trim; press open and glue in place.

Bound buttonholes look handsome on soft leather. Instead of basting, hold ends of strips with cellophane tape. It is practical to use a bound buttonhole maker on these "fabrics." Machine-worked or hand-worked buttonholes may be used, or you can double-stitch around the marking and slash along the line. Reinforce all buttons by placing a small button on the underside.

Zippers. Do not baste garment opening closed. Use cellophane tape to hold zipper in place, and do the final stitching from right side by hand or by machine.

Make **hems** less than 2 inches wide. Chalk-mark hemline on wrong side of leather. Glue and hammer lightly in place for an invisible finish, or top-stitch $1/2$ to 1 inch from the hem turn.

Pressing. Use a dry iron (no steam) on a warm setting, and press over brown paper or a press cloth. Check the manufacturer's label for instructions on pressing leather-likes as their surfaces can be harmed by excess heat.

In one way or another these sewing "basics" are used in every garment you sew, and the final look of quality in your fashion will depend largely on how well you have applied them. A perfect hand stitch is still basic to the finest couture sewing.

Basic hand-stitches are used in a number of ways: for temporary stitches, hemming, seams, finishing and decoration.

While plain seams shape the garment, and decorative seams are used to emphasize the design, special seams are required for many of the special fashion fabrics.

Facings add the necessary body and finish to edges of necklines, armhole openings and, in some instances, to waistlines.

The hem is the final step in the completion of a garment; it should be even, hang smoothly and not look obvious.

hand stitches

Cut the thread diagonally, using the just-cut end to thread the needle. Pull thread slowly through eye of needle, and knot the same just-cut end before you begin to sew.

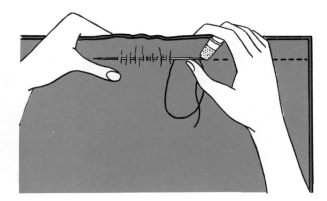

Running stitch. The length of the stitch depends upon its usage (seams in hand-made garments, hand-gathering, hand-run tucks, mending, etc.). Take several stitches on a long, fine needle by weaving the point in and out of the fabric. Slide the stitches back onto the thread without taking the needle out of the fabric. Repeat, taking groups of stitches on the needle several times before you draw the thread through the fabric.

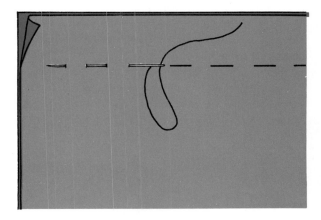

Hand basting. Make regular stitches about $1/4$ inch long, spaced about $1/4$ inch apart. Machine basting is shown in Chapter 6.

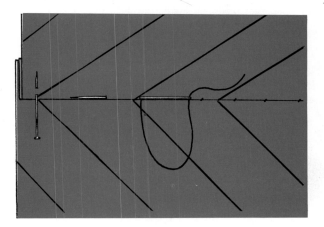

Slip basting is used when matching seams in striped or plaid fabrics, lapping curved seams, and for altering garments on the right side. With the fabric right side up, turn under one seam allowance, and lap it over the right side of adjoining seam allowance. Pin, placing pins at right angles to the seam. Bring needle to right side at edge of fold. Insert needle into fold directly above, and bring it out of fold about $3/8$ inch to the left. Insert needle directly below fold in lower layer, and take a stitch of the same length. Continue to alternate the stitches in fold and below fold.

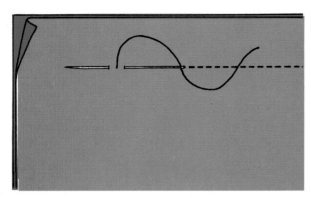

Back stitch is a stitch that is used wherever a strong hand stitch is needed or where machine stitches may be too obvious. Work from right to left: Fasten the thread, take 1/8 inch stitch. Insert needle back at the start of the first stitch and bring point of needle out 1/8 inch to the left of where thread came out. Reinsert the needle at the end of stitch and continue in the manner described.

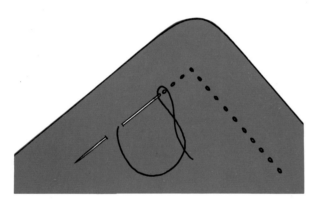

Hand-picking is a stitch used as a final detail in many areas of a garment (collars, cuffs, pockets, etc.). This is a half backstitch, and it is made in the same way as a backstitch except that instead of going back 1/8 inch, take the stitch over only two or three fabric threads. For detailed instructions on its use in the last step of a zipper application, see page 91.

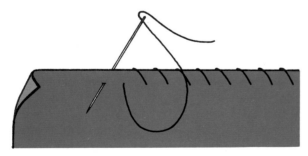

Overcasting is used on raw edges to help prevent the fabric from raveling. The stitch is usually worked from right to left. Make slanted stitches about 1/8 inch deep and 1/4 inch apart.

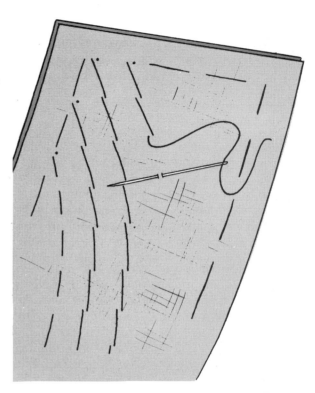

Padding stitch. This stitch is used in tailoring to hold interfacing or underlining to the garment fabric. Work from the wrong side, holding the fabric in the left hand. With the needle pointing to the left, take a stitch about 3/8 long through the interfacing, but pick up only one or two threads of the fabric. Take a second stitch about 1/2 inch below the first. Continuing in this way will form long diagonal stitches on the wrong side, but only barely visible crosswise stitches on the right side.

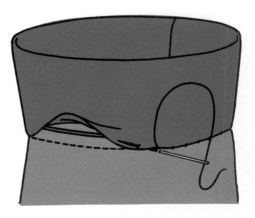

Slipstitch. This stitch is used for a turned edge or wherever it is desirable to use a stitch that is invisible from both sides. Pick up a single thread below the fold edge. Slip the needle in the fold for about 1/4 inch. Bring out needle and pick up a single thread below the fold. Again, slip needle in fold edge and continue in this manner.

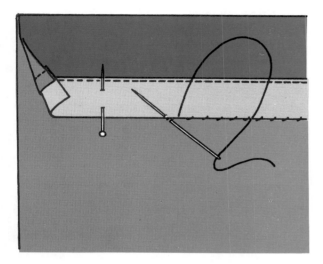

Hemming stitch (also called blind-stitch). This stitch can be used over the edge of a hem or between the hem and the garment. You can clean-finish the hem, or finish it with seam binding or bias binding. Work from right to left or toward you. Begin at a seam by starting with a couple of small backstitches or with a knot caught under the seam allowance. Pick up a single fabric thread in the garment, and insert the needle under hem edge about 1/4 inch beyond the point where you brought the needle up. The stitches slant on the wrong side, and should not be visible on the right side.

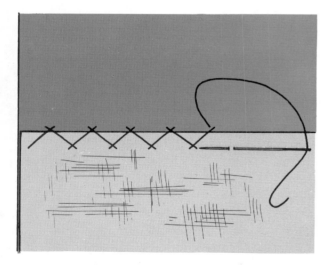

Catch-stitch. This stitch can be used over an edge to hold it flat or inside the hem as described on page 185. Work from left to right, but insert the needle from the right. Take a very short stitch, one or two threads, in top layer of fabric. Continue to alternate up and down, keeping the upper and lower rows of stitches the same distance. Do not draw the thread tight as you work.

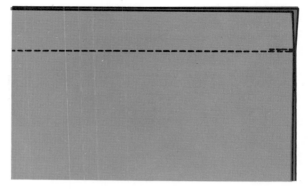

Plain seam. The most commonly used of all seams and the basis for many other types of seams, it is usually made 5/8 inch wide, and is stitched with a regulation machine stitch. The plain seam is used in all sections of a garment. Choose from the following seam finishes the one that is appropriate for your fabric.

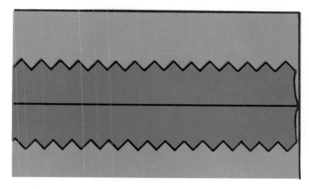

Finishes for plain seams. If you are going to line the garment, the seams do not have to be finished. A plain seam is finished to prevent raveling, to strengthen the seam and to give a neat appearance to the wrong side of the garment. Pinking the seam allowance with pinking shears is the most popular finish for a plain, pressed-open seam.

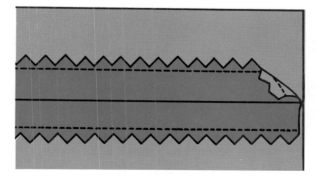

Stitched and pinked. Stitch 1/4 inch from the edge of each seam allowance; then trim the edges with pinking shears.

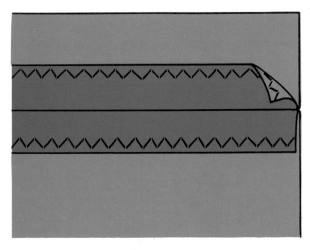

Zigzagged or overedged. Finish each seam edge with a medium-width zigzag stitch or with an over-edge stitch such as a zigzag blind-stitch. For more detailed instructions, see page 43.

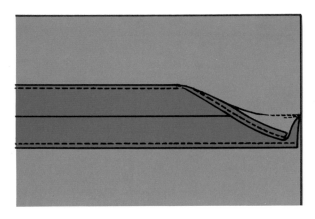

Clean finished. Use on light and medium weight fabrics or fabrics that ravel. Stitch 1/8 inch from the edge of each seam allowance. Turn edge under on stitching line; stitch close to folded edge.

Overcast. This seam finish is done by hand or with a combination of machine and hand stitches.

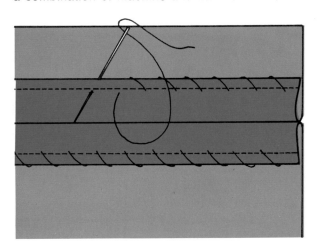

1. Working usually from right to left, make slanted over-and-over stitches along the edge of each seam allowance. Keep the stitches easy so that the edge of fabric is not drawn up.

2. Machine-stitch 1/8 inch from the edge of each seam allowance. Make overcast stitches as described above, inserting the needle just under the line of machine-stitching. If both seam allowances are pressed to one side, overcast the two edges

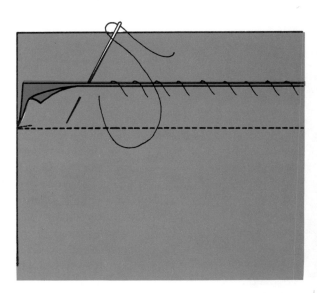

together. When the garment is underlined, you can catch the seam allowances to underlining with the stitches.

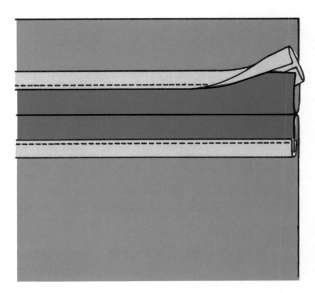

Bound. Encase the edge of each seam allowance with bias seam binding, and edge-stitch so that both edges of seam binding are caught with the one row of machine-stitching.

Types of Seams

Topstitched seam. This seamline effect can be done in two ways. First, stitch a plain seam.

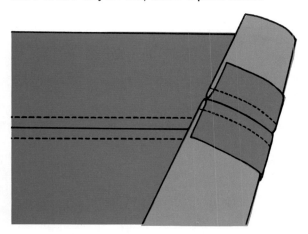

1. Press seam open. From the right side, stitch an even ¹⁄₈ to ¹⁄₄ inch on each side of seamline, stitching through the seam allowances.

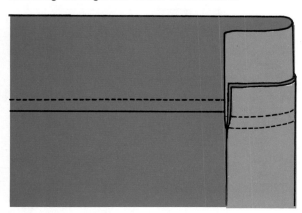

2. Press seam allowances to one side. From the right side, stitch ¹⁄₈ to ¹⁄₄ inch from seamline through the three thicknesses.

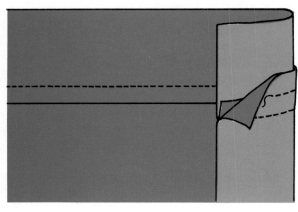

Welt seam. Stitch a plain seam; press both seam allowances to one side of seamline. Trim the under seam allowance to a scant ¹⁄₄ inch. From the right side, topstitch ¹⁄₄ inch from the seamline, catching the untrimmed seam allowance on the under side. The welt seam is decorative, good for heavyweight fabrics when a flat seam is desirable. A <u>double welt seam</u> is made by first making a welt seam and adding a row of topstitching close to the seamline.

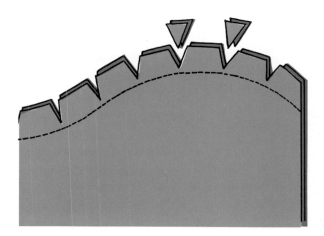

Curved seam. It is found within the garment when sections with curved edges are seamed together. Staystitch the curved edges ⁵⁄₈ inch from edges. Pin together, easing fullness if any and stitch. Clip the seam allowance of the outer curve and notch the seam allowance of the inner curve at intervals for the seam to lie flat. See Chapter 15 for pressing curves.

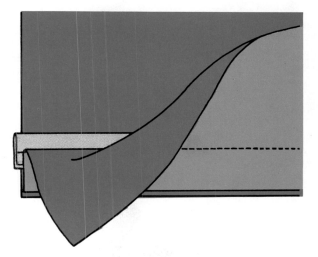

Piped seam. Use a piece of ready-made bias binding or a bias strip of fabric folding it lengthwise through the center; then press. Place the folded bias between seam edges with the fold overlapping the seamline, extending toward the garment. Pin, baste and stitch the seam. Press all edges to one side. Either flat or folded braid can be used in straight seams. It is used to give a decorative edge to collars, cuffs or faced necklines.

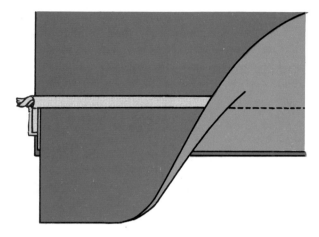

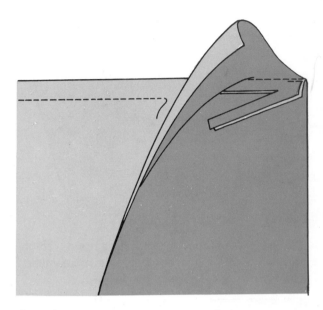

basting. An accent seam, it is used in blouses, skirts and suits of medium to heavy fabrics.

Corded seam. Use ready-made covered cord, or make covered cording as instructed on **page198**. Pin and baste the cording on the right side of fabric, matching the stitching of the cording to the seamline and with the corded edge facing toward the garment. Lay the other section right side down over cording and pin. Stitch seam, stitching through four thicknesses using a cording or zipper-foot. Press all edges to one side. This is a decorative seam or edge, very similar in its usage to the piped seam.

French seam. This is the preferred seam for most sheer fabrics. With wrong sides together, stitch $1/4$ inch from the seamline. Press as stitched, and then press seam allowances to one side. Trim the seam allowances to $1/8$ inch. Turn right sides together, fold and press on the stitching line. Stitch on the seamline to enclose the raw edges.

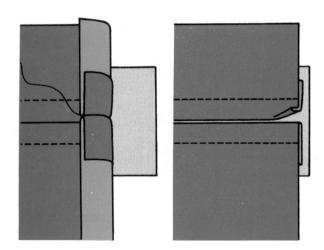

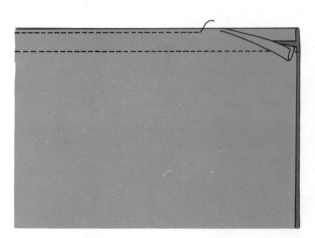

Slot seam. This seam is made with an underlay which can be either a strip of self fabric or a fabric of a contrasting color. Machine-baste the seam and press open. Clip one side of basting at 1 inch intervals. Cut a strip of the underlay fabric equal to the length of the seam and $1^{1}/_{2}$ inches wide. Center right side of fabric strip over the seam on the wrong side and pin. Work from the right side, and baste an even distance from the seamline on each side. Topstitch about $1/4$ inch on each side of seamline. Pull the long thread to remove the machine-

Mock French seam. Stitch a plain seam. Turn in the raw edges of the seam allowances toward each other, matching the folded edges. Stitch the turned edges together close to folds.

Triple-stitched seam. Almost invisible, it is excellent for sheer fabrics. With right sides together, stitch $1/8$ inch from the seamline in the seam allowance. **(a)** Press seam allowances to one side along the stitching line. Stitch close to fold, stitching

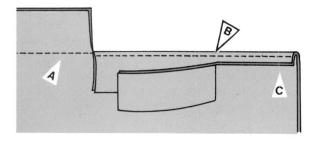

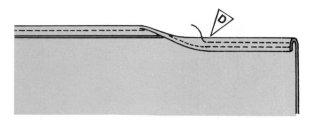

through four thicknesses. **(b)** Trim seam allowances close to stitching line. **(c)** Turn stitched fold over trimmed edges and stitch close to fold **(d)**.

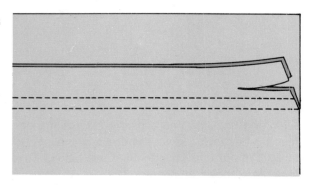

Double-stitched seam. This is a good seam for sheers and laces. Stitch a plain seam. Stitch again ⅛ inch from the seamline, in the seam allowance and trim close to second stitching. For detailed information see page 166.

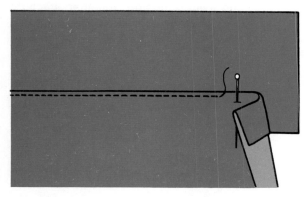

Decorative lapped seam. Turn under the seam allowance on top section and press. Overlap the under seam allowance, matching fold to seamline and pin. Topstitch close to fold, stitching through the three thicknesses. For seaming yokes to gar-

ment sections where an accent is desired, this seam is a good choice.

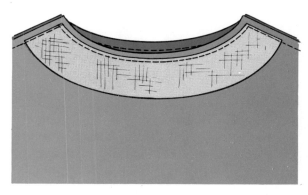

Flat felled seam. Stitch a plain seam either on the wrong side or on the right side, depending on which side you want the fell to be. Press seam open; then press both seam allowances to one side. Trim the under seam allowance to ⅛ inch. Turn under the raw edge of top seam allowance, and pin or hand-baste over the trimmed edge. Topstitch close to the fold.

This is a neat, attractive seam for double-faced fabrics, sport clothes and reversible garments.

facings

Fitted facings. All fitted facings, whether for neckline, armhole or waistline, are handled in a similar manner. A fitted facing is cut on the same fabric grain, and cut to match the shape of the garment section to which it will be applied.

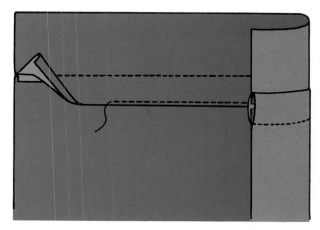

Interfacing is used between the garment fabric and the facing to add body to shaped edges. The fabric's weight and individual characteristics determine whether or not interfacing should be used.

Cut the interfacing, using the pattern pieces for the facings and cut on the same grain as the facings. Trim the outer corners of the interfacing, and pin to the wrong side of the front and back units. Machine-baste ½ inch from outer edges; trim interfacing close to stitching line.

Facing attached before zipper. Press under the left end of facing (lapped side) 1⅛ inch and the right end (narrow side) ½ inch.

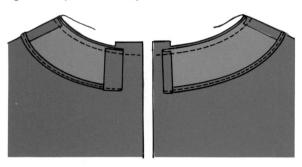

Pin facing to garment with right end 1⅛ inches from back edge and left end ½ inch from back. Stitch neckline seam; trim and grade seam allow-

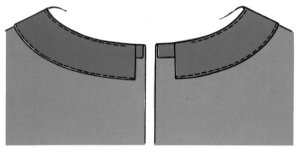

ance. Understitch, beginning and ending 1 inch from folded edges of facing. Press under the seam allowances of the neck edge beyond facing ends.

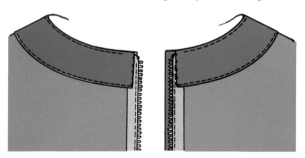

Insert zipper following lapped application in Chapter 7. Trim ends of zipper tape. Turn ends of facing down over zipper tape, slip-stitch in place.

Neckline facings are stitched together at the shoulder seams. Clean-finish unnotched edge (outer edge). With right sides together, matching centers and seamlines, pin and stitch to neckline edge of garment. See instruction details in Chapter 8.

Sleeveless armhole facings are handled in the same manner as described above. Detailed instructions are also given in Chapter 8.

Waistline facing. This facing can be used instead of a waistband to finish the waistlines of skirts and pants. The type of placket in the garment determines whether the waistline facing can be applied in sections or as an all-in-one facing. Instructions for applying facings to front and back units are given in Chapter 12.

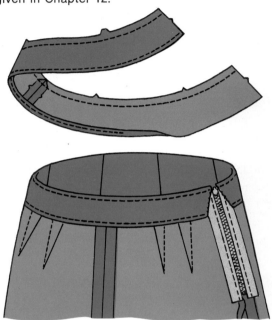

All-in-one neckline and armhole facings are perfect finishes for a sleeveless dress or blouse. Detailed photographs for attaching this type of fitted facing are shown in Chapter 8.

How to turn a facing. A facing should be smooth and flat along the edge, and it should stay in place permanently. If the edge to be faced is curved or on the bias, staystitch it. If the garment fabric is loosely woven, or if it stretches, staystitch the edge of the facing. With right sides together, stitch the facing to the garment. Trim top seam allowance to ¼ inch and bottom seam allowance slightly less.

On curved edge.

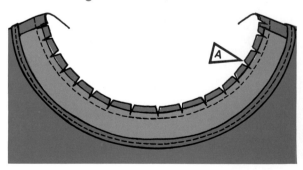

(a) If faced area is curved, clip the seam allowances on the curve.

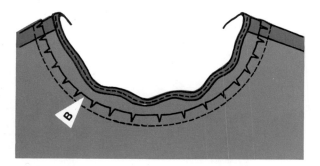

(b) Press seam allowances toward the facing.

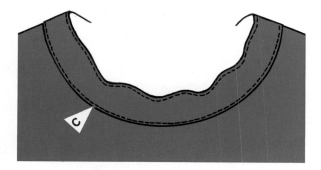

(c) With right side of garment up, understitch the facing to the seam allowances, stitching close to the seamline. Turn facing to wrong side, and roll seamline to the underside so that it does not show on the right side. Press carefully. Tack the facing to the garment at seams. See <u>Understitching</u> in Chapter 8 for photographs of this technique.

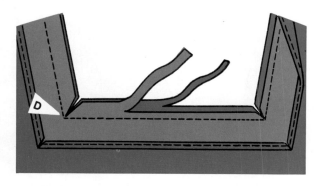

Squared opening. Apply fitted facing to a squared opening in the same manner as for a curved edge. Stitch the seam, reinforcing corners with shorter stitches **(d)**. Trim seam allowances; clip to the corners. Press, understitch and turn facing to wrong side as instructed above.

Overlapping corners on faced openings. If a blouse or shirt will be worn outside the skirt or slacks, or if a garment fastens all the way to the hem in front or back, the hem at the bottom of the garment should be finished with a neat, enclosed corner.

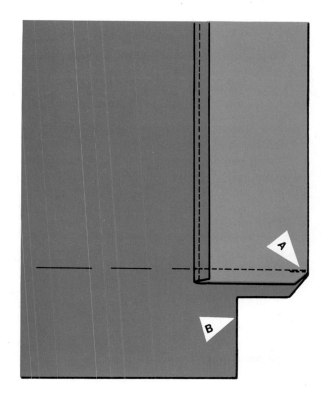

(a) With the facing turned to the right side, stitch facing to garment on the hemline. Trim the corner at folded edge.

(b) Trim edge of facing below stitching line to about a $\frac{1}{4}$ inch width. Trim garment edge slightly wider, trimming from the folded edge to within $\frac{3}{4}$ inch of the inner edge of facing.

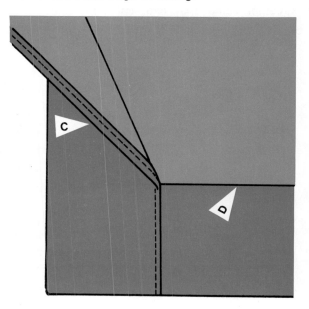

(c) Press trimmed seam open; turn facing to wrong side and press.

(d) Turn and press the remainder of the hem, and finish it as desired.

Scallops

Unless a garment is lined to the edge, the scallop stitching line (seamline) is marked only on the pattern piece for the facing. There are two ways to transfer the outline of the scallops to the fabric.

Transfer the markings by pinning or basting the pattern over the facing, and stitch along the scallop line drawn on the pattern. After stitching, tear away the tissue pattern.

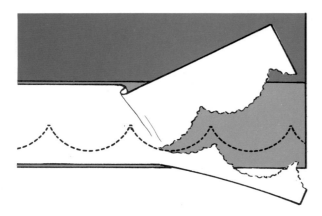

The alternate way is to transfer the scallop lines to the fabric with dressmaker's tracing paper and a tracing wheel. Dots for matching should be marked on both the facing and the garment section of the fabric. The edges of the pattern are not scalloped because it is easier to pin two straight edges together, rather than two scalloped edges, when you attach the facing to the garment. Stitch along the scallop line marked on the facing, through both

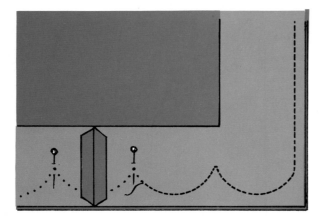

thicknesses, and trim excess fabric. Use 15 to 20 stitches per inch, and stitch in a smooth, curved line. At the points, where the ends of the scallops meet, take one or two small stitches straight across each point. The total distance across each point should not exceed $1/8$ inch.

If interfacing is used, trim it close to the stitching. Eliminate bulk by trimming the garment seam allowance to $1/4$ inch ($3/8$ inch if fabric ravels).

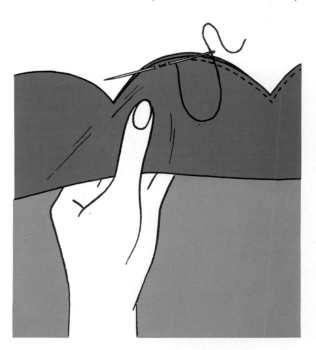

Trim the seam allowance of the facing slightly narrower. Carefully clip to the stitching at the points. Notch the curves so that seam allowances will lie flat when facing is turned to the wrong side. Turn facing to wrong side; roll edges of scallops between your fingers to bring out the edges. Press carefully, first on facing side, then on garment.

Since it is impossible to understitch by machine on a scalloped edge, hand understitch with small running stitches through the facing and seam allowance, using care not to sew through to the right side of garment. This will keep the facing from rolling to the right side.

hems

Hem Finishes

Some hem finishes have been described in earlier chapters with more detailed instructions, but all are shown here for easy comparison.

Clean finished. Stitch ¼ inch from the cut edge. Turn the edge under on the stitching line, and stitch close to the folded edge. Also see page 71.

Stitched and pinked. Stitch ¼ inch from the cut edge; then trim the edge with pinking shears.

Zigzagged. Stitch ¼ inch from the free edge of hem, and use a plain zigzag stitch along the edge, but do not allow the stitches to extend over edge.

On <u>double knits</u>, where "give" is important to the fabric, omit the straight stitching. A plain zigzag stitch or a multiple-stitch zigzag can be used along the free edge of the hem. Trim the edge, but be careful that you do not cut the stitches.

Lace or seam binding. Lap the lace or binding ¼ inch over the cut edge. Stitch close to the edge of lace or binding with straight or zigzag stitch.

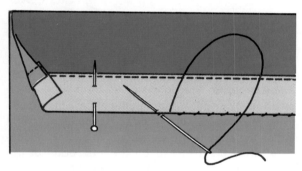

Bound. Finish the hem edge with 1 inch wide bias strips of underlining fabric or with ready-made binding. Cut and seam together enough bias strips to go around the skirt. With right sides together,

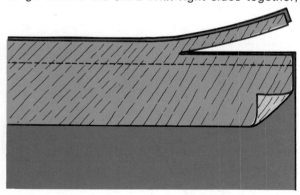

pin the bias to the hem with the edges even. Stitch ¼ inch from edge; trim to ⅛ inch. Fold strip over the raw edge to the wrong side of hem; press.

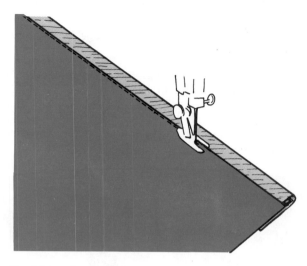

Machine-stitch from the right side, inserting the needle in the well of the seamline so that stitching is almost invisible. Press; slip-stitch. See Chapter 10.

Types of Hems

Standard hem. The steps for measuring and marking a hem are outlined in Chapter 7. See Chapter 15 for information on pressing hems.

Eliminating hem fullness. There are two ways to eliminate fullness at the upper edge of the hem. The choice of method depends on the fabric and the curve of the hem.

Method 1. This technique is used for medium and heavyweight fabrics when the hem is very flared and when the fabric will shrink when steam is used.

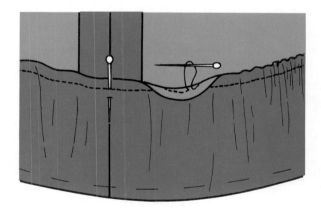

Machine-baste ¼ inch from the cut edge of hem. Turn hem up to position, matching the seams. Lay the garment flat, hem side up, so that ripples will show where there is extra fullness. Draw up the bobbin thread with a pin at each ripple, and distribute the fullness evenly. Insert a piece of brown paper between the hem and the garment; steam-press to shrink the fullness as much as possible.

On firm fabric, pink the upper edge of the hem, and blind-stitch it to the garment. If the fabric ravels, apply bias seam binding to the edge by machine. Slip-stitch to the garment.

Very flared hems in synthetic and non-shrinkable fabrics are handled in the same way as above except that you steam-press to flatten the fullness.

Method 2. Use this method for medium to lightweight, non-shrinkable fabrics.

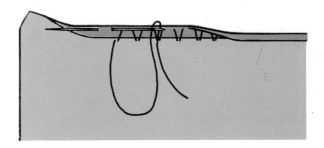

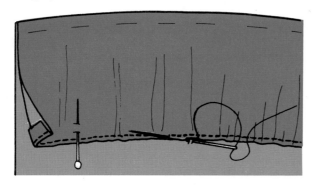

Clean-finish the hem with a row of staystitching $1/4$ inch from the edge. Turn hem edge to the wrong side on the stitching line. Set the machine for a regulation stitch and ease-stitch $1/8$ inch from the fold edge. Turn hem up to desired position, matching seams. Where ripples appear, draw up the bobbin thread with a pin as described in <u>Method 1</u>. Blind-stitch hem in place.

Faced hem. Cut the facing to the desired length and hem width plus seam allowances. The facing

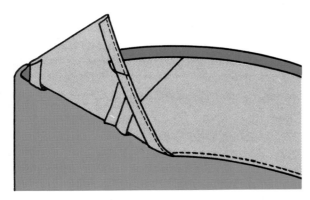

should be cut on the same grain as the garment. For straight skirts cut a straight grain facing; cut on the bias for flared skirts. Circular skirts use a facing cut to the exact shape of the lower edge.

With right sides together, stitch the lower edge of the facing to the skirt in a $1/4$ inch seam. Press the seam open. Turn the facing to the wrong side, using the width of the seam as the turning point. Clean-finish the top edge of the facing; slip-stitch.

Rolled hem. Staystitch $1/8$ to $1/4$ inch from the edge, and trim close to the stitching. Roll hem twice between the thumb and forefinger, making the width of the roll less than $1/8$ inch. Slip-stitch the hem

Stiffened hem. Horsehair braid is used on sheer fabrics to give them needed body or to make full skirts stand out.

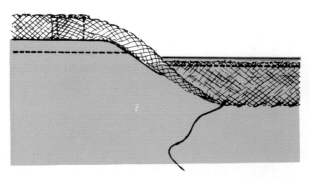

Place braid on the right side of the skirt $3/8$ inch over the lower edge, lapping the ends. Stitch close to edge of braid. Turn braid to wrong side, rolling under the skirt fabric for about $1/8$ inch. If necessary, draw up a thread on the free edge of the braid to shape it to the skirt. Hand-stitch.

Interfaced hem. Cut bias strips of interfacing 1 inch wider than depth of hem and as long as needed to go around the hemline of a jacket or coat.

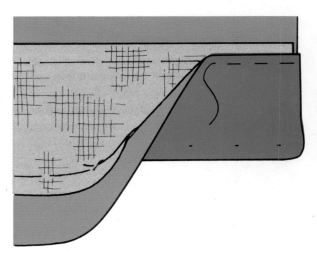

Place the garment wrong side up with the hem edge toward you. Pin the interfacing between the body of garment and hem with the lower edge of bias $\frac{1}{2}$ inch below the hem fold line. Lap the ends over the front interfacing.

Use long stitches to sew the interfacing to the garment along the top and bottom edges. Take very short, shallow stitches in the garment fabric so that the stitches are invisible on the right side and rather long stitches visible on the interfacing side. Fold hem to position, and use a long running stitch to secure it to the interfacing. Hand-sew the edge of front facing to hem.

Tailor's hem. Machine-stitch around hem edge about $\frac{1}{4}$ inch from edge, using about 10 stitches per inch; pink the edge. If fabric ravels, overcast

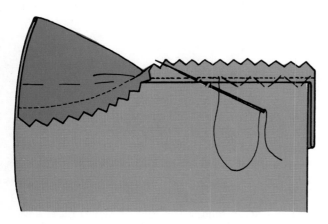

the edge instead of pinking, or apply seam tape. Draw up the bobbin thread, and baste hem in place about $\frac{1}{2}$ inch from top edge. Fold hem back about $\frac{1}{4}$ inch, and blind-stitch to skirt. Press edge flat over the stitches. This hem is especially good for jersey and other soft woolens.

Catch-stitched hem. Fold hem back to right side of garment letting hem edge extend at least $\frac{1}{4}$

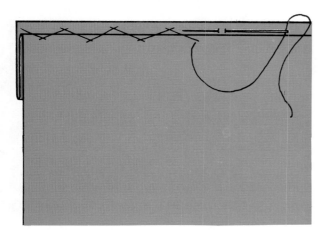

inch. Catch-stitch to skirt. Press edge flat over stitches. This hem is excellent for knits because it gives with the fabric. It is also good for heavy fabrics because the inside hemming keeps an impression from showing on the right side of the garment. If fabric ravels, overcast the hem edge before catch-stitching.

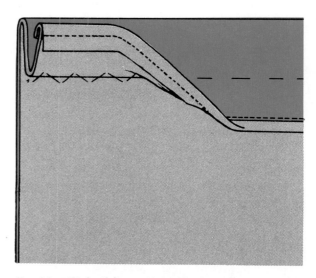

Double-stitched hem. Use this hem on an underlined garment for extra support, and to prevent the hem from rolling to the right side. Pin along bottom fold; then hand-baste center of hem around skirt. Fold back the top of hem along the basting, and blind-stitch hem to the underlining. Do not draw the stitches tightly. Turn top of hem up, and make the second row of blind-stitches between the bound edge and underlining. Remove basting.

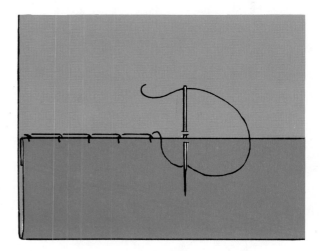

Lockstitch hem. Work from left to right. With a knotted thread secured in the hem, take a small stitch in the garment (1 thread) and then a stitch in the top edge of hem (2 or 3 threads) about $\frac{1}{4}$

inch to the left of where the thread was fastened. Draw needle through, over the looped thread as shown. Continue in the same way around the entire hem. This is a good hem to use on garments that expect hard wear and need extra strong hems.

Eliminating Bulk in Hems

Seams in plain skirts. Between the hem fold line and the edge, trim one seam allowance in hem ¼ inch and opposite seam allowance in skirt the

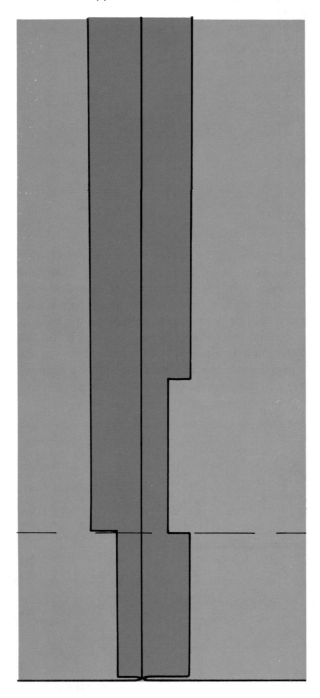

same amount. When the hem is turned up for finishing, an effect similar to layering of seams will result.

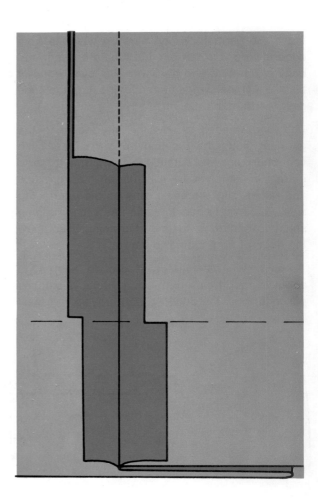

Seams in pleated skirts

When a seam falls in the fold of a skirt pleat and it is pressed to one side, clip one seam allowance to the seamline at the top of hem. Press open the part of the seam which is in the hem area; then trim the seam allowance from hem fold to edge as described for plain skirts.

the press-ons

Bonding materials, which join one fabric layer to another, are among the newer sewing aids. They can be used for applying interfacings and trims, putting up hems and mending.

The bonding agent is made of heat-sensitive material which melts under the heat of an iron. These materials will withstand washing and dry-cleaning, and they are suitable for knits as well as woven fabrics because of their flexibility. Test the bonding material you plan to use on a scrap of the fabric before applying it to the garment.

Because the heat required to apply these products varies greatly, it is important to read the detailed directions that come with each type in order to get perfect results.

Bonding materials are available in two forms, narrow strips or by the yard on a paper backing.

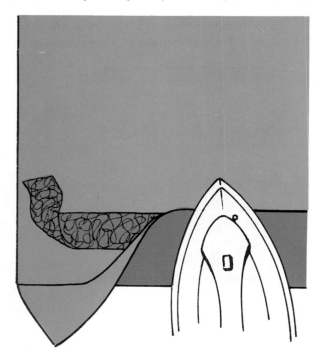

Apply strips by cutting a piece to the desired length and placing it between two layers of the fabric (a hem is illustrated). With a dry iron, at the setting for cotton, press firmly for ten seconds. Do not slide the iron back and forth! Avoid touching bonding materials with the iron; they will stick to it. After the fabric has cooled, test the seal by trying to lift an edge. If it is loose, press again for several seconds on each side.

Paper-backed bonding material, which can be cut to any shape, is practical for bonding shaped inter-

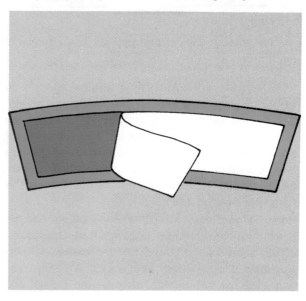

facings to the fabric for front facings, collars, cuffs and waistbands. Cut the bonding material to the desired shape, and mark seamlines. Trim $5/8$ inch seam allowances. Paper side up, place rough surface against wrong side of facing. Press firmly with a dry iron for three seconds; let cool and peel away paper.

Place the bonded side of facing over the wrong side of garment section. Press with a steam iron for ten seconds. Plenty of steam is necessary for proper bonding. A damp cloth may be used if extra steam is needed on bulky fabrics.

Iron-on interfacings, woven or non-woven, come in a variety of weights with a bonding material on one side. Because they add stiffness to the fabric, they work best in small areas such as collars, cuffs, waistbands and pocket welts.

Cut the interfacing to the desired shape, and mark seamlines. Trim interfacing seam allowances to $1/8$ inch because they are difficult to trim after pressing. Read the accompanying instructions for the correct heat setting for application.

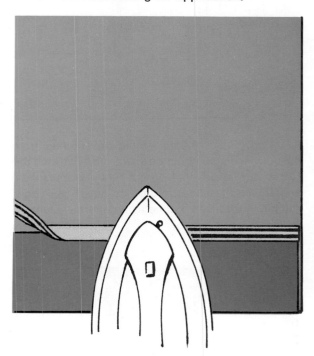

Iron-on seam binding has bonding lines along each edge. Before applying to a lightweight fabric, make a test to see that the bonding lines do not show on the right side. Center binding over cut edge with the bonding side down. With a dry iron, set for wool, press lightly at intervals to tack. Remove pins. Press firmly until both bond lines appear on the surface. Continue around hem.

pleats

Marking and Making. On the pattern, pleats are marked with a fold (or crease) line usually indicated by a solid line. The line to which the fold is lapped is indicated by a broken line. Arrows usually indicate the direction in which pleats are to lap. Transfer these lines from the pattern to the wrong side of the fabric. Then baste-mark, using a different color thread for the two different lines to avoid confusion.

Working on the right side of the fabric, lap the fold line to the broken line, keeping the upper edges even so that the pleats will hang correctly. Pin and baste in place along the folds; press lightly. Stitch as indicated by the pattern, remove basting and final press.

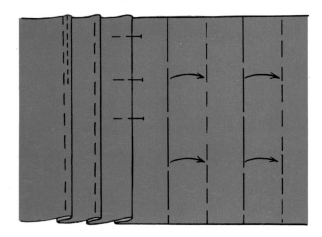

Stitching pleats. Pleats should be stitched from the bottom up; stitching downward may stretch the fabric. For fabrics that do not retain a press well, edge-stitch the under fold of the pleats (**a**). Edge-stitching may also be done as a decorative feature on the outer edges (**b**).

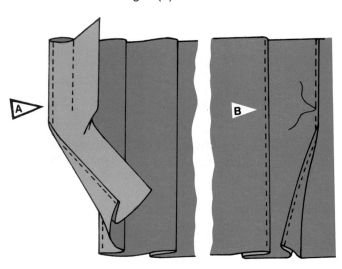

Types of Pleats

Straight or knife. Pleats all turning in one direction. They should lap from right to left. These are illustrated under the marking and making section.

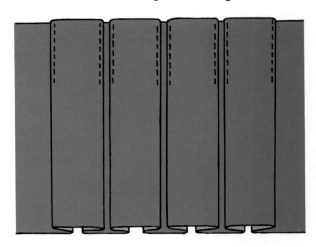

Box pleats. Two straight pleats, turned away from each other.

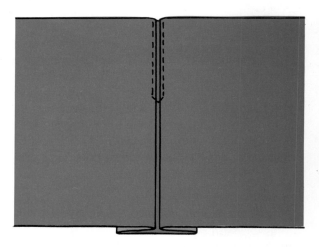

Inverted pleats. Two straight pleats, turned toward each other.

Hems in pleated skirts. On a straight skirt, it is easier to make the hem first, then make the pleats. On shaped skirts, make the hem after you have made the pleats, but before the final pressing. If shortening is needed on a straight skirt after it has been completed, it should be done at the skirt top. See page 186 for details on handling a seam in the hem of a pleated skirt.

Hems in garments with unpressed pleats can be put in after the garment is completed. Unpressed pleats should be pressed for approximately 1 to 1½ inches down from the waistline seam. See page 159 for information on pressing pleats.

18 details make the difference

Almost without exception, the style and individuality of a garment are determined by the design details which are added to the basic body shell. They are the first things to catch the eye when you are wearing the garment, so make them with great care.

Sleeves, pockets and collars, for example, are constructed as separate units. When they are finished, and you have just breathed a sigh of relief, you must then apply them to the garment for which they were made, and of which they will become an integral part.

collars, cuffs and sleeves

Although the shape and size of collars vary greatly, they fall into three basic types: The shaped collar which lies flat; the straight collar which rolls, and the straight collar which stands up. The basic construction details are the same for all. Interfacing is used with most collars because the crispness and body which it adds improves the appearance.

Detachable collar and cuffs. This type of collar or cuff often is removed for cleaning, so be sure to select a style and a fabric that can "take it".

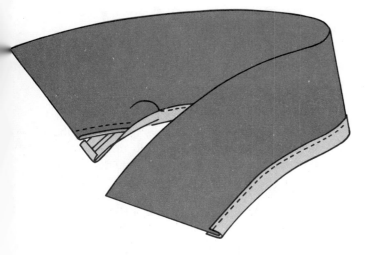

Construct the collar according to instructions. Stitch the neckline edges together on the seam-line; trim the seam to $1/4$ inch. Bind the raw edge with a bias strip or with ready-made bias seam binding turning in ends. Attach the collar to the garment with basting or with snap fasteners. When attaching a light collar to a dark dress, use the socket half of black snap fasteners on the dress and the ball part of silver snap fasteners on the underside of collar.

sleeves

Construct the cuffs according to the instructions. Stitch the raw edges together on the seamline; trim seam to $1/4$ inch. Bind the raw edges as for the collar, turning in one end at the seam. Attach the cuffs as done with the collar.

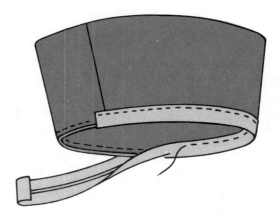

Turned back cuff. Seam the ends of cuff together, and press seam open. Press under $5/8$ inch seam allowance on one edge of cuff to the wrong side,

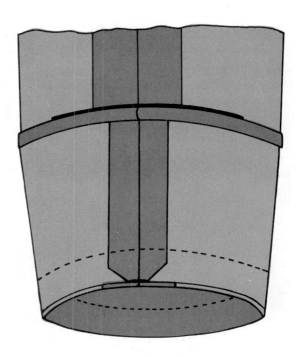

trim to ¼ inch. With the raw edges even, stitch the right side of cuff to the wrong side of the sleeve, matching the seams. Fold the pressed edge to the

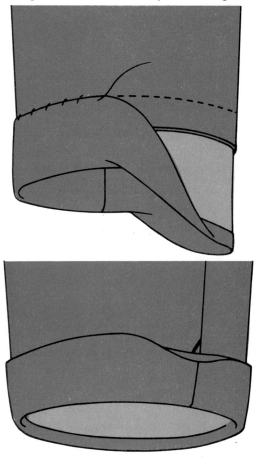

right side, and hem by hand along the seamline; press. Fold the cuff to the right side of sleeve, and tack at the underarm seam of sleeve.

Elasticized lower edge. A hem casing is used for wide sleeves or for full sleeves of various lengths. Make a plain hem, or finish the lower edge of

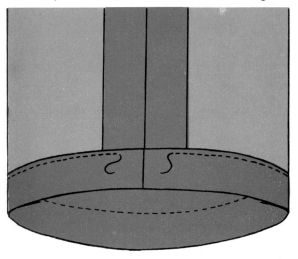

sleeve with a facing sufficiently wide to permit narrow elastic to slide through easily. Stitch close to the edge of the hem or facing. Leave an opening

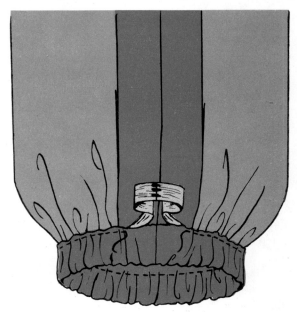

at the underarm seam. Draw the elastic through the casing, using a bodkin or a safety pin. Lap and sew the ends of elastic securely either by hand or by machine. Sew opening closed.

Pleats in a gathered or puffed sleeve. If a pleated effect is desired, follow these directions.

With right sides together, pin the sleeve in armhole. Pin the top-of-sleeve mark to the shoulder seam, matching notches and underarm seams. Make small pleats in sleeve cap until sleeve fits armhole. Pin, then baste, to hold pleats in place; stitch. Press the seam toward the sleeve if you want the pleats to puff upward; for pleats to drape downward, press the seam toward the shoulder.

pockets

Pockets fall into three basic categories: The applied or patch pocket which is stitched to the right side of garment; the insert pocket which is placed in a seam of the garment and the set-in pocket for which a slash or special opening is made in a section of the garment.

Set-in pockets come in a wide range of styles; follow the directions on your pattern instruction sheet. Patch pockets often can be added to a garment even though the pattern does not call for one. Instructions are given below for an unlined patch pocket, a lined patch pocket and for one style of an inserted pocket.

patch pockets

There are many shapes and sizes of these pockets—square, rectangular, curved at the lower corners—and they range from the very small ones on a child's garment to enormous, spacious ones on a full-length coat for an adult. Some are lined; some are finished with flaps. The general method for making and attaching all patch pockets to the garment is the same.

Unlined pocket with rounded lower corners. At the top edge, turn 1/4 inch to the wrong side and stitch. Turn top edge to right side on fold line to

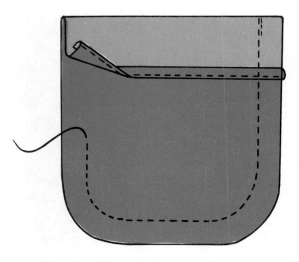

form a hem facing. Starting at top of hem fold, stitch around the pocket on seamline, backstitching at both ends.

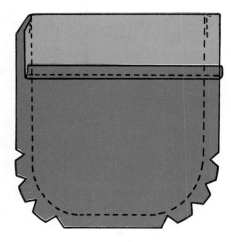

Trim corners and seam allowance of hem facing. On the curves clip in notches up to the stitching

so that when the edge is turned under, there will not be any overlapping of the clipped edges. Turn hem facing to the wrong side and press. Press seam allowance to wrong side, easing machine stitching to the underside so that stitching will not

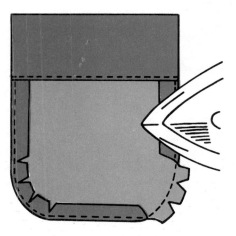

show when pocket is attached to garment.

Unlined pocket with square lower corners. Follow the first two steps for the pocket with rounded corners above. Miter the corners; see page 202. Turn and press the seam allowance to the wrong side, easing the machine stitching to underside.

Lined patch pocket. The lining is cut according to the pocket pattern, but the depth is cut to extend only from the bottom of the pocket to the fold line for the hem facing.

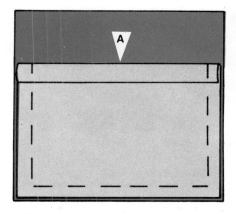

a Press under 5/8 inch on upper edge of lining. Right sides together, baste lining to pocket, keeping sides and lower edge even.

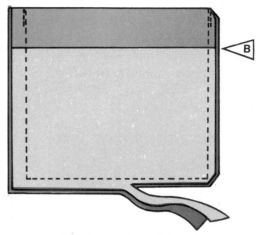

a Edge-stitched. Machine-stitch close to the pocket edge on side and lower edges. Reinforce upper corners or draw thread ends through to wrong side of garment, and fasten with tiny hand backstitches.

b Top-stitched. Machine-stitch $1/4$ to $3/8$ inch from the side and lower edges, reinforcing upper corners or securing thread ends as described above.

c Invisible application. Baste the pocket on the right side, keeping basting an even distance from the pocket edge. Turn to the wrong side of garment, and hand-stitch, using the basting as a guide. Use a small backstitch, taking the stitches through the lining or seam allowance only.

b Turn upper edge down along fold line over the lining to form a hem facing. Starting at top of hem facing, stitch down one side, across bottom, and up the other side, backstitching at both ends. Trim seam allowance; trim square corners. Turn right side out and press.

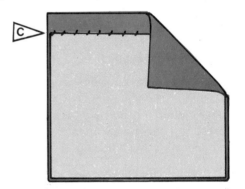

c Slipstitch the lining to hem facing.

Attaching patch pockets. Place pocket right side up on the right side of garment. Pin and baste.

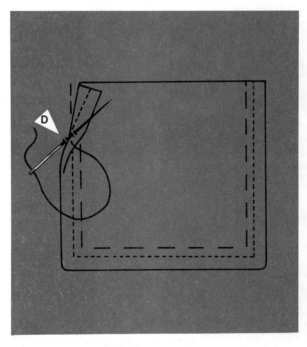

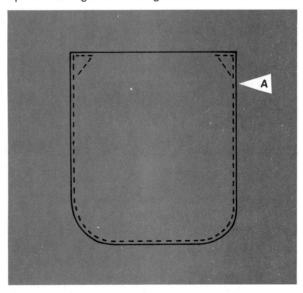

d Slipstitched. Baste the pocket on the right side about $1/2$ inch from the edge. From the right side, start at one upper corner taking several stitches to reinforce it. Slipstitch the pocket turning back the edge slightly so that stitches will not show. To end, reinforce the second upper corner as you did the first one.

Pocket in a seam

a With right sides together and small dots matching, stitch pocket sections to extensions on garment sections. Trim seams and press them open.

b With right sides together, pin the garment sections to one another matching small and medium dots. Stitch along the seam line pivoting on the dots at the inner corners, continue to stitch around pocket sections and lower seam. Reinforce the corners with small stitches for about 1 inch on each side of corners.

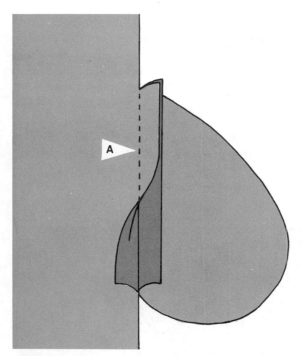

c Clip seam allowance of the back section at the end of the pocket as shown. Press the pocket towards center front, pressing a neat fold on the front section from the right side. Press seams open above and below clipped seams.

If garment fabric is bulky, cut the top pocket section of a lighter weight or lining fabric.

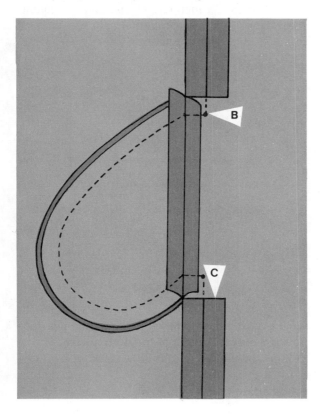

buttons and buttonholes

Buttons and buttonholes can be highly decorative in addition to their purpose. Extreme accuracy is necessary when marking your fabric if the buttons and buttonholes are to be placed precisely.

buttons

Thread of the proper type for sewing on buttons is determined by the weight of the fabric. Use a double thread, knotted at the end. For general use a heavy duty mercerized can be strengthened by coating it with beeswax. Silk buttonhole twist is a good choice for fine fabrics. Use "button" thread for heavyweight fabrics or when extra strength is needed.

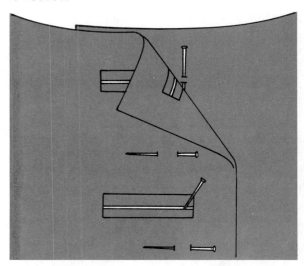

Placement. Lap the garment edges, matching center front or center back markings; pin. For horizontal buttonholes place a pin at the outer end of the buttonhole into the fabric underneath. Position the button $\frac{1}{8}$ inch to the left of this pin mark.

Sewing on buttons. A button which is to go through a buttonhole, should have a shank or stem to allow room for the extra fabric between the button and garment. A thread shank is needed when a button does not have a shank.

Bring needle and thread to the right side of the fabric, and take a small stitch to secure the thread and knot. Bring the needle through the button and place a toothpick or kitchen match across the top of button to allow for the shank, then bring needle through button and back into the fabric.

Continue sewing back and forth over the pick or match. Remove pick and wind thread firmly around the threads under the button forming a shank. Draw the needle to the wrong side of fabric and fasten with several stitches.

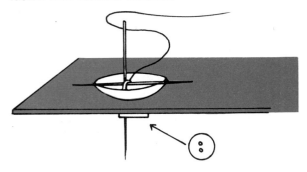

Reinforcing buttons. If the button is to be used under heavy strain, or if it is to be used on soft fabrics, it should be reinforced. On the inside of the garment, directly under the button location, place a small, flat button or a square of firm fabric. Sew through the button or fabric when attaching the outside button.

Measuring a button. Cut a strip of paper about ¼ inch wide, and wrap the strip around the button at its widest part. Pin ends of paper together under the button. Without unpinning, remove the paper

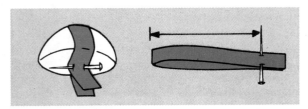

strip. Smooth strip flat so that there is a fold opposite the pin. The distance from the fold to the pin is the length of the buttonhole. Note: When button has a shank, <u>do not</u> pin paper strip around the shank; it will make the measurement too large.

buttonholes

Length. See page 82 for cutting and applying interfacing strips to a bodice front. The same principles apply regardless of where the buttons and buttonholes are to be used. Buttonholes are usually ⅛ inch longer than the width of the button, but there are certain exceptions to this rule. When very small buttons are used, the difference should be less than the ⅛ inch; when a thick or heavyweight fabric is used for a coat, and the button is covered with the same fabric, or the button has a high design (such as a ball button), the buttonhole should be slightly larger than the ⅛ inch differ-

ence. It is suggested that you make a test buttonhole of the same fabric as garment.

Marking. Mark the horizontal and vertical buttonhole lines with dressmakers' tracing paper on interfacing. Pin the interfacing to the garment, and baste-mark through to the right side of fabric.

bound buttonholes

Strip method. Although interfacing is shown in these illustrations, this method can be applied to a garment without interfacing. Mark buttonhole lines as instructed above.

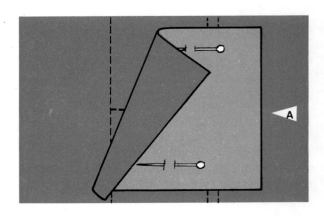

a Cut a strip of fabric on the straight grain, 2 inches wide and 1 inch longer than the buttonhole mark. With right sides together, pin the strip to garment, matching grainlines.

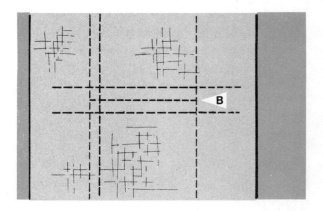

b From the wrong side, using a regulation stitch, stitch over the baste-marked lines on the interfacing for the exact length of the buttonholes. Machine-baste ¼ inch on both sides of this line. Let stitching extend about ½ inch beyond buttonhole mark at both ends.

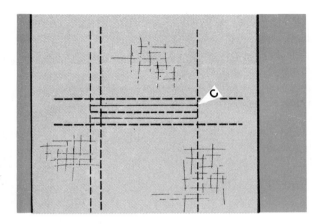

c Halfway between center buttonhole line and baste-stitched lines, draw pencil lines the exact length of buttonhole.

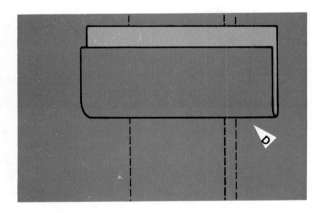

d On right side of garment, fold one edge of fabric strip back over the machine basting toward the buttonhole center. Press. Repeat on other edge.

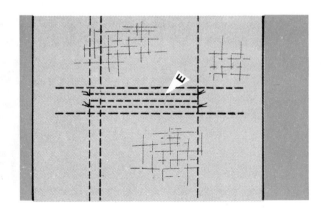

e Turn garment to wrong side. On the interfacing, using 20 stitches per inch, stitch on the pencil lines on each side of the buttonhole line, through garment and folded fabric strip. Pull thread through to wrong side and tie. Remove basting.

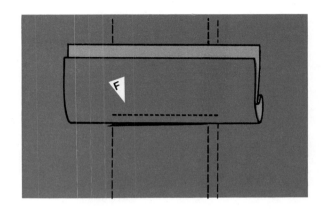

f Illustration shows how this looks on the right side.

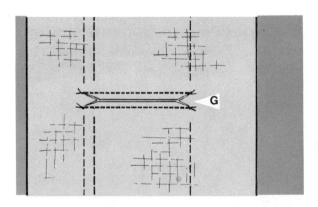

g On wrong side, start at center and slash through patch and garment to within $3/8$ to $1/4$ inch from ends of stitching. Clip diagonally into corners, all the way to the stitching forming triangles.

h Turn patch to wrong side through slash. Press patch away from opening. Make an inverted pleat at ends with folded edges meeting at center of buttonhole.

Place garment right side up on machine. Fold the

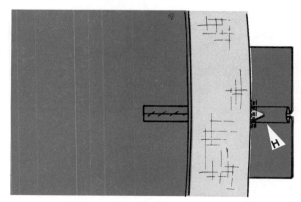

garment fabric back so that the patch end and the triangular piece can be placed under the machine needle. Using 20 stitches per inch stitch across base of triangular piece and inverted pleat. Repeat several times. Baste edges of opening together.

Window method. Mark buttonhole lines as described above.

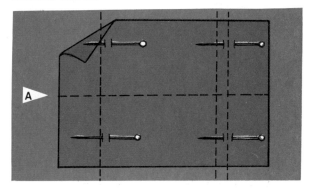

a Cut a piece of organza or lightweight fabric the same color as garment, about 1½ inches wide, and 1 inch longer than the buttonhole mark. Center strip and baste over buttonhole marking on right side of fabric.

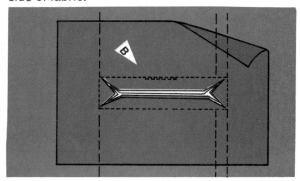

b Using 15-20 stitches per inch, stitch ⅛ inch on each side of basting, squaring stitching across ends. Start stitching at center of buttonhole marking on one side and stitch to the end. To square stitching at the ends, pivot on the needle at each corner, taking the same number of stitches across each end. Take about five overlapping stitches at the starting point.

Slash between stitching lines from the center to within ¼ inch of each end. Clip to the four corners, forming a triangle at each end. Do not clip stitching.

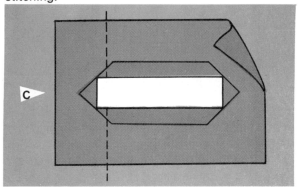

c Turn the organza piece through slash to wrong side. Press seam and organza away from opening, forming a "window". Make sure that the organza does not show from outside; this is the size of the finished buttonhole. Remove basting.

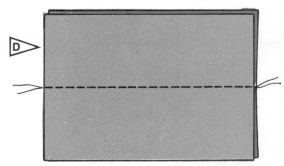

d Cut two straight pieces of the garment fabric 1½ inches wide and 1 inch longer than the buttonhole. Cut the pieces on the bias for stripes, plaids, etc. Press each piece in half, lengthwise. Open each piece and with right sides together, machine-baste them together along the pressed fold. Remove this basting when the garment is finished.

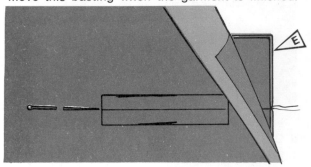

e Re-fold each piece, wrong sides together; press. Place basted piece over "window" on wrong side of garment with seam at the center. Pin at ends as shown.

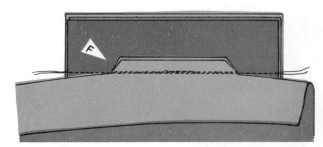

f Turn away garment from buttonhole, exposing seam. Using 15 to 20 stitches per inch, stitch over previous stitching, through seam, organza and basted pieces on long edges, extending stitching to end of piece.

g Stitch across each "triangle" through organza and pieces; press. See page 195, illustration **h**.

Finishing the back. There are two methods that can be used to finish the back of the buttonhole.

Slash method

a After completing buttonholes, attach the garment facing. From the right side, put pins straight through center of each end of the buttonhole to mark the length on the facing. Slash facing on a straight line between the pins, and make a short clip at center of each edge of slash.

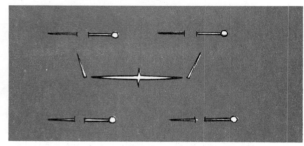

b Turn in the edges and hem securely in place, making an oval on the facing side as shown. If desired, the facing may be slashed and clipped in the same manner as the outside of the garment was done. In this case, the marking pins should be put into the four corners of the buttonhole; the edges and triangular ends are then turned in and hemmed in place to make a rectangle.

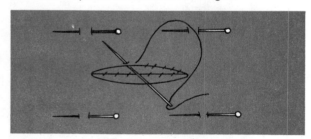

Window method. Finish the back of the buttonholes on the facing before attaching it to the garment. Work steps a, b and c from the window method under bound buttonholes. When garment is finished, slipstitch opening of facing over buttonhole.

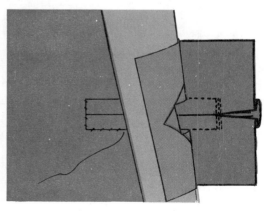

worked buttonholes

By machine. Most zigzag sewing machines can make buttonholes without an extra attachment, but standard machines require a buttonhole attachment. Follow the manual for specific instructions, and always test your buttonholes on a scrap of the same fabric you are using for garment.

By hand. Hand-worked buttonholes are also done after the garment is finished. Mark the buttonholes as instructed previously. Depending on the fabric, use regular thread, heavy duty thread or buttonhole twist. Use a single thread.

a Using small stitches, stitch about 1/16 inch from mark as shown.

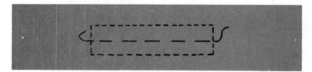

b Starting at center, slash buttonhole on center mark to ends. Overcast the edges.

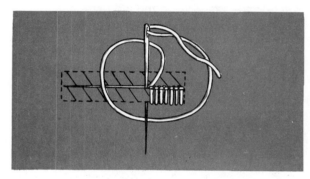

c Work the buttonhole stitch over the edges, working from right to left as follows:
1. Start at end and insert needle into slit bringing it out below stitching. Bring thread from needle eye around and under needle point, from right to left.
2. Draw needle up to form a "purl" on the edge. Do not pull the thread tightly. Continue, placing stitches close together so purls will cover edge.
3. At end towards garment edge, form a fan as shown, keeping the center stitch of the fan in line with the cut.

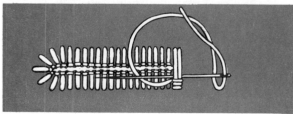

d Make a bar at the end opposite the fan by taking several stitches across the end and working blanket stitch over the threads and through the garment cloth.

button loops

Button loops are used when a decorative finish is desirable. For fabrics such as lace, they are preferable to buttonholes. The loops can be made in various ways; from bias self-fabric or a coordinated fabric; from ready-made satin tubing or fine braid, or they can be worked loops of silk buttonhole twist. They combine best with ball buttons.

Fabric loops. Make tubing from bias strips of fabric filled with its own seam allowances or filled with a cable cord. Adjust the garment pattern before you cut if you are substituting loops for buttonholes. The left front, the section to which the buttons will be sewn, is cut exactly like the pattern. Mark the center front of the right front, the section to which the loops will be sewn. Add $5/8$ inch for seam allowance, and draw a new line for the cutting line. Adjust the right front facing in the same way. Loops are sewn on the center front line. Always make a test loop to see how the fabric works, and to determine the loop size needed.

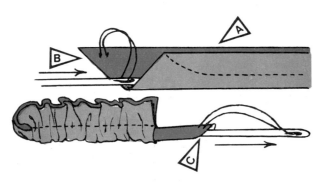

Self-filled tubing. Cut true bias strips $1^1/8$ inch wide. Fold bias in half, lengthwise, with right sides together. Stitch $1/4$ inch from fold, stretching the bias slightly while stitching. Slant the stitching toward edges of bias at one end as shown **(a)**.

To turn the bias right side out, use a heavy needle, threaded with 4 or 5 inches of heavy thread. Knot the thread ends and fasten securely to one end of bias **(b)**. Insert needle, eye forward, through bias fold. Work the needle through the tube, turning bias inside out **(c)**.

Corded loops. If you are using a lightweight or delicate fabric, it may be desirable to cord the tubing for added strength. Use a cord of appropriate size for the fabric. Determine the width of the bias strip by folding fabric over the cord and pinning it snugly. Cut $1/2$ inch beyond the pin. Unpin and measure the width of the cut piece. Cut true bias strips of this width and of the needed length.

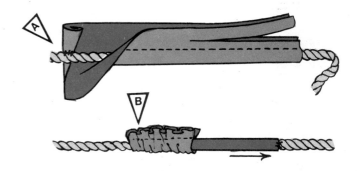

Cut a length of cord twice the length of the bias. With right sides together, fold strip over one-half of cord. Secure end of bias at center of cord either by hand or by machine **(a).** Stitch close to cord, using a zipper or cording foot. Start the stitching about $1/4$ inch from cord and taper in, stretching bias slightly as you stitch. Trim seam allowance to $1/8$ inch. Turn bias right side out over cord by pulling the cord end that is covered and working bias back over the uncovered cord **(b).**

Attaching Loops
Method 1. Use cut loops when the buttons are large or the loops are spaced some distance apart along the edge of the opening.

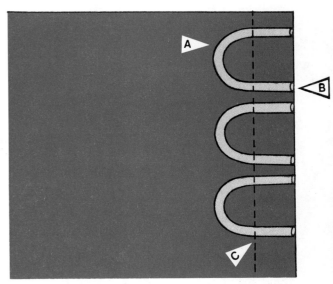

a Cut individual loops, adding $1^1/4$ inch to each length for seam allowance.
b On right side of fabric, baste loops on the seam allowance in the correct location with the ends even with the garment edge.
c Stitch across ends of loops, stitching 1/16 inch from seamline inside seam allowance. With right sides together, pin facing over loops. With garment side up, stitch on $5/8$ inch seamline, using the first

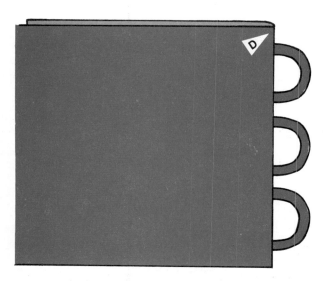

line of stitching as a guide. Trim seam allowance.
d Fold facing to inside along the seamline and
press. Loops will extend beyond garment edge.

Method 2. When the buttons are small and placed
close together, use a continuous strip of narrow
tubing. On a sturdy piece of paper, draw a line,
⅝ inch from one edge to represent the seamline

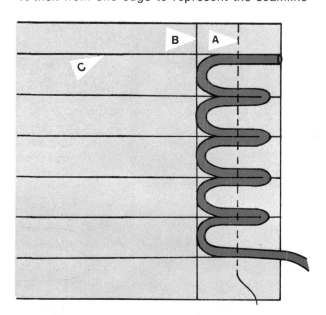

(a). Draw another line to the left of the first one **(b).**
The distance between the two lines equals the
width of the loop. Across these two lines, draw
lines equaling the length of each loop **(c).** Form
loops between markings, as shown. Baste along
seamline to secure loops.

Pin the paper with loops to the right side of the
garment, matching edges and with loops facing
away from the edge. Stitch over loops on seamline.

Tear away paper; attach facing and finish as instructed under Method 1.

Loops also can be sewn to the garment after it is
finished. Mark a continuous tube dividing it into
correct lengths for the buttons. Mark garment
edge. Matching the marked points, sew loops with
small stitches, making sure that the seam of the
tubing is turned to the underside.

Braid loops give still another effect. Use braid as
a substitute for self-fabric loops when the fabric
is bulky. Attach the loops following one of the
methods previously described.

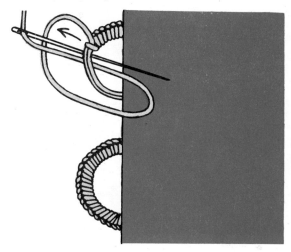

Thread loops made of silk buttonhole twist make
small, attractive loops; they are quick and easy
to do if you are using just a few small buttons.
Mark the loop locations on the edge of the garment,
opposite the buttons. Sew several strands of thread
on the garment edge, making them loose enough
for the buttons to pass through. Work a blanket
stitch over thread strands, working with the eye
of the needle forward, as shown.

Frogs

Decorative frogs can be made of purchased cord or of self-fabric corded tubing (see page 198 for directions on making tubing). Pin the frog into the desired design, securing each loop with small stitches on the underside. Slipstitch the frog to the garment, leaving one loop extending beyond the garment edge for buttoning. Chinese ball buttons are commonly used with frogs and can be made of the same cord.

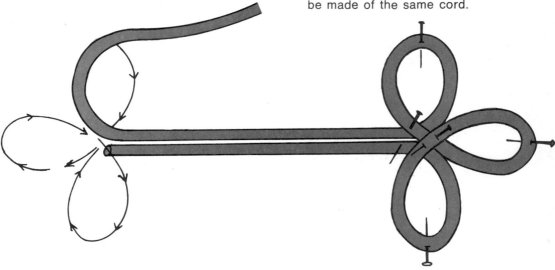

Chinese Ball Buttons

These can be made of purchased cord or make corded tubing (see page 198). The size of the ball will depend on the thickness of the cord. About 8 to 10 inches of a $\frac{1}{4}$ inch cord makes a small button.

a Loop cord as shown.

b Loop again over and under first loop.
c Loop a third time, weaving through other two loops. Keep loops open while working.
d Ease together, shaping into a ball. Trim the ends and sew them flat to underside of ball.

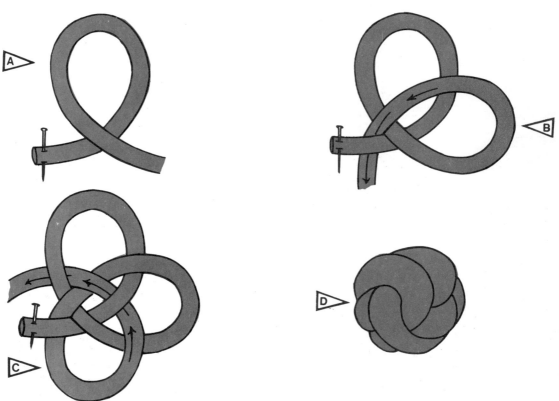

other fastenings

Hooks and Eyes

These fasteners are used when there may be some strain on the closure. On overlapping edges, use a straight eye; on edges that meet, use a round eye. A thread eye may be substituted for the metal eye on softer fabrics, or in closings without strain. Match edges of closing, and mark the position of hook and eye. Stitches should not show on right side of garment so carry the thread between the fabric layers.

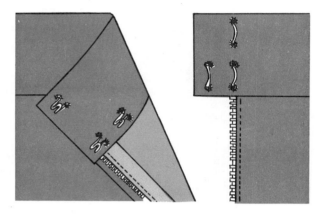

On lapped edges, sew hook ⅛ inch from edge on the overlap side. On edges that meet, sew hook ⅛ inch from right hand side. Take several stitches at end of hook; then through the underside to the eyelets, and make stitches around the holes.

On lapped edges, use a straight (bar) eye. Place the eye just under the bend of the hook with the eye curve facing the edge of the closure. Sew around the holes, using overhand stitches. When edges meet, use the round eye, extending it beyond the edge of the closure. Sew around the holes, using overhand stitches.

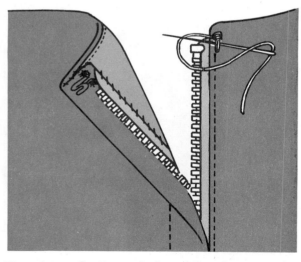

Thread eye. On the underlap of the closure, make

two or three overlapping strands of thread at the desired point. Use a blanket stitch and work over these strands same as for thread loop.

Snaps

These fasteners are used on closures having very little strain. Sew only through the facing and interfacing so that the stitches do not show on the right side. Place the ball section of snap on the overlap, about ⅛ inch in from edge. Use three to six overhand stitches (depending on the snap size) through each hole, carrying the thread under the snap to the next hole.

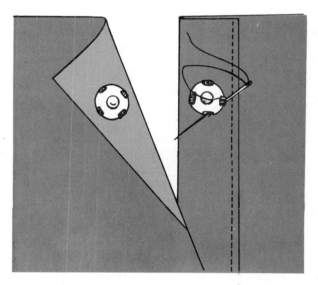

Lap the closing. Mark position of socket section with chalk or by placing a pin through the center hole of the ball section. Attach the socket section in the same manner as the ball section.

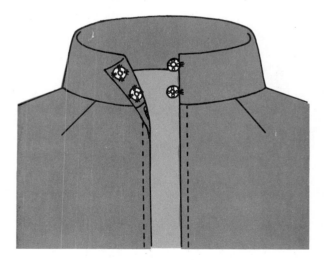

Hanging snap. This gives a neat closure where two edges should just meet, as in the center back opening of collars. It can also be used instead of a hook and eye at the neckedge of a zipper application. Sew the ball section through just **one** holes to the edge of the right side. This leaves the snap free to fit under the socket section. Mark the position of the socket section on the left side and sew it close to edge.

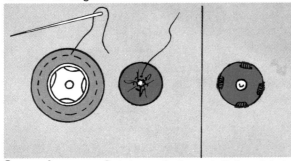

Covered snaps. Cut two circles of lining fabric twice the size of the snap. Make small running stitches by hand along the edge of each circle. Do not fasten or break the thread. Place the snap section face down on the circles. Pull up the thread on each circle and secure with several stitches. Sew to the garment. Snapping and unsnapping the sections will bring the ball through the fabric.

mitering

Mitering Corners on Pockets

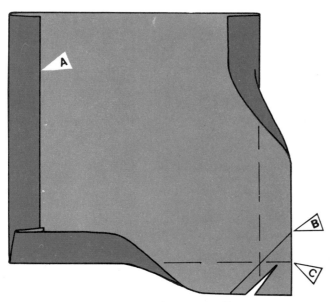

a Turn under and press the seam allowances.
b Open out the pressed seam allowances, and fold corner on a diagonal line running through the point where two pressed lines meet; press.
c Trim corner about ⅛ inch from the pressed diagonal edge.

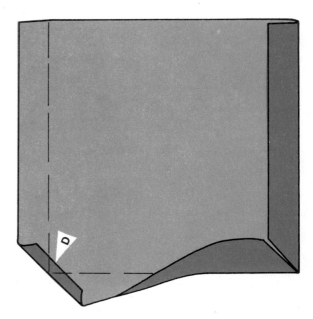

d Fold trimmed corner to the wrong side on the diagonal crease. Fold the remaining seam allowances on the pressed lines.

Mitering Loose Corners

Press the seam allowances, and trim the corner as in mitering corners on pockets (**a, b, c**).

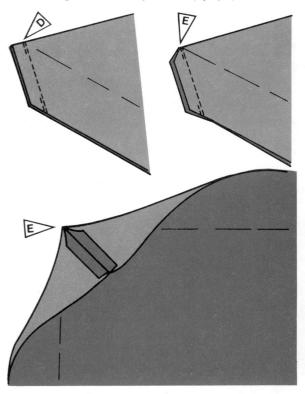

d Fold corner with right sides together, matching the trimmed edges of the diagonal fold. Stitch on the diagonal fold line.

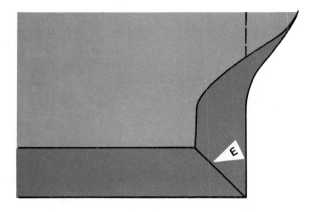

e Clip point of fold to the stitching; press seam open. Turn seam allowance to wrong side; press.

Mitering a Band Trim
a Topstitch both edges of ribbon or band in place along the finished edge of the garment, stopping at the lower edge.

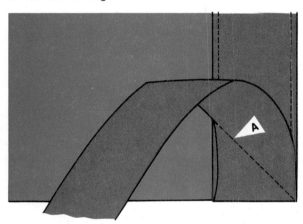

Fold the remaining trim back on the stitched trim and press the fold. Fold and press the trim again toward the edge to which it will be applied, forming a diagonal crease.
Stitch on the diagonal crease, through the trim and the garment.
b Continue to apply trim, topstitching both edges.

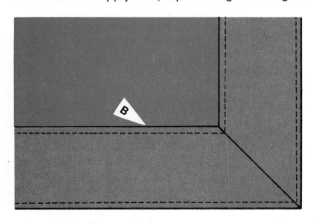

topstitching

Topstitching is a construction technique that may also be used as a decorative finish. It can add an accent to the lines of a simple garment. The stitching must be straight and even. Unless you have an accurate eye, use one of the following guides for stitching an edge:

Throat plate of sewing machine with markings in eighths of an inch.

Seam guides that attach to the bed of sewing machine.

Attach strip of adhesive tape to the machine at the desired distance from the needle.

For topstitching that is not along an edge, or is not in a straight line, hand-baste a guide line and stitch along line. The quilter attachment is also excellent for this use. Adjust it to the desired width.

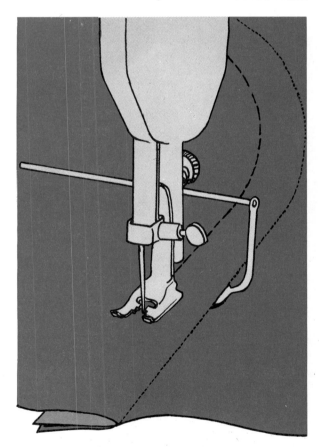

The type of thread used will be determined by your fabric. The regular thread with which you are sewing your garment serves well for lightweight fabric. On medium or heavyweight fabrics, or for more prominent topstitching, use buttonhole twist. Lengthen the stitches and/or adjust the tension for best results. Always topstitch on right side to get a better looking stitch. Test on fabric scrap.

Stitching that is to be done on an edge that will also show on the underside, the turn back of a lapel for example, is done as follows. Topstitch the facing-side of lapel, but stop the stitching at point of the turn back **(a)**; continue stitching so that the topstitching will be on the outside when garment is worn. Where the stitching begins and ends, leave thread ends long enough to be inserted in a needle, worked to the inside and fastened.

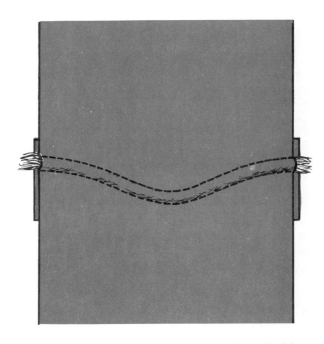

Method 1. Make one or two rows of topstitching along the edge or seam. Pad the area between the edge and the stitching or between each row of stitching, using several lengths of wool yarn. Use a bodkin or a heavy needle (eye forward) to insert yarn from the end of stitching.

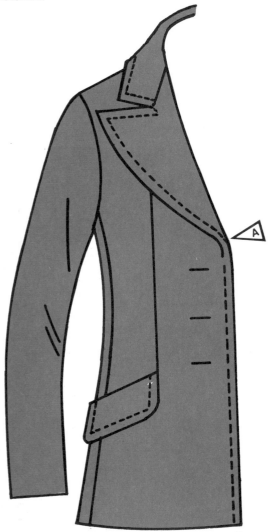

The "Designer Touch" can be attained on patch pockets by topstitching the pocket before it is attached to the garment, and then slipstitch the pocket to the garment so that the stitches are invisible. Many designs feature one or more rows of machine-stitching with a longer than average stitch. Use either matching or contrasting thread.

The soft, rolled look along an edge, featured in many couturier garments, can be achieved in two ways:

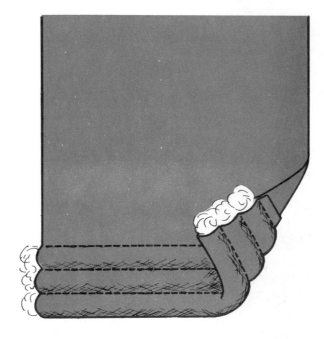

Method 2. Use a layer of lambswool interfacing, cut as wide as the desired padded edge will be plus $1/4$ inch. Lay the lambswool inside the facing or hem turn. Make two rows of basting to prevent slippage, and it will be easier to do the topstitching. Do not make the rows of stitching less than $1/2$ inch apart.

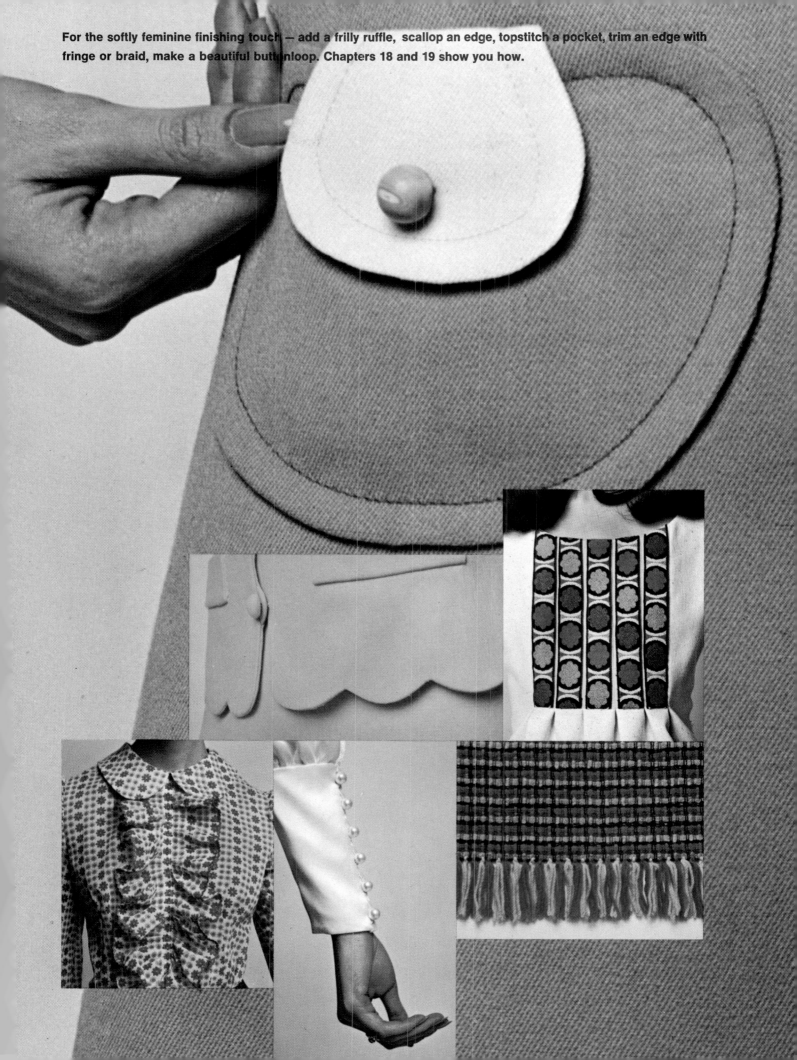

For the softly feminine finishing touch — add a frilly ruffle, scallop an edge, topstitch a pocket, trim an edge with fringe or braid, make a beautiful buttonloop. Chapters 18 and 19 show you how.

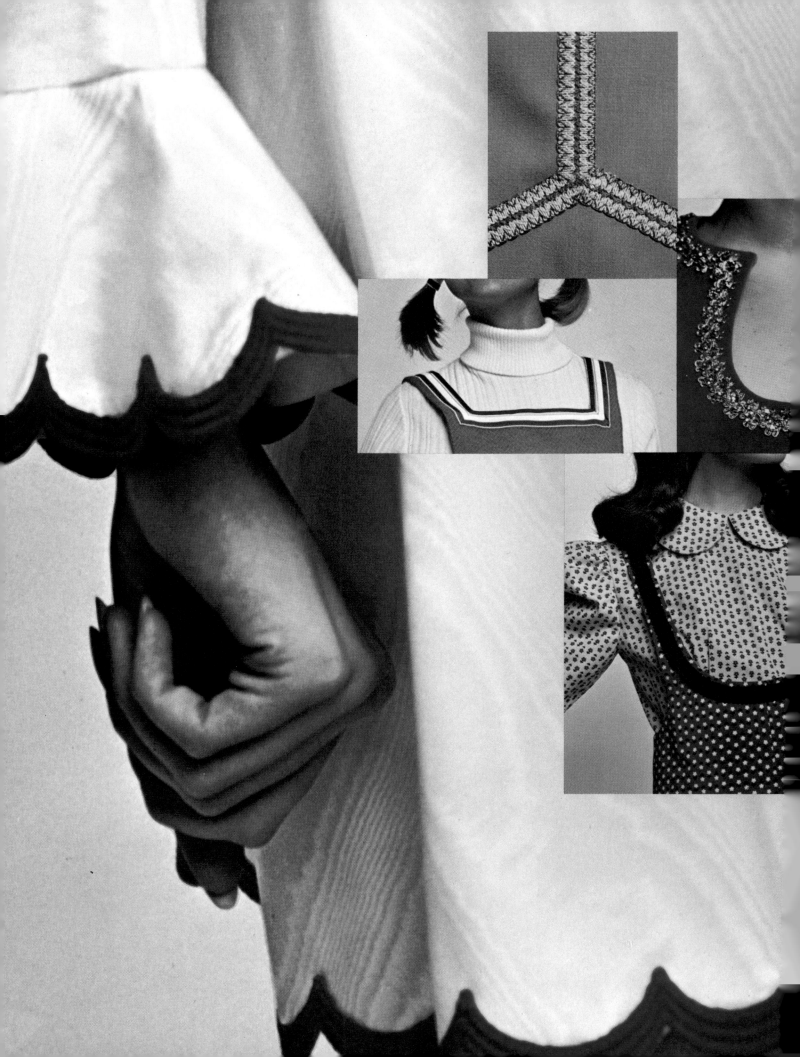

Often the simplest decorative touch is just what you need to complete a fashion look. Here we show a delightful array of ways to give the fashions you sew your personal touch. Try topstitching — or edgings of lace, embroidered ribbon, rick-rack and braid. And, elegant metallics and jewels. Chapter 19 has them all.

There are all kinds of marvelous belts and closures to accent your individuality — tie belts, ribbon sashes, braid and jeweled belts, and special closures like frogs or tabs are all described in Chapters 18 and 19.

the personal touch

When you selected the pattern for your garment, you were sure that its design suited your figure and personality. The addition of a belt, a ruffle, topstitching or binding might be just the needed touch to give it that highly individual, one-of-a-kind appearance of having been created especially for you.

belts

A belt is an accent that can give a dress a perfect finishing touch or co-ordinate a skirt and shirt. A self fabric belt with an eye-catching buckle, a belt of a contrasting fabric or a tie belt made of attractive ribbon are simple to make. Belt kits, complete with instruction, are also available.

Experiment with a strip of fabric or brown paper fitted around your waist to help you decide on the proper width and length of the belt.

Smooth Belt. Commercial belting, available in various widths, can be covered with any fabric to make a smooth tailored belt. The width of the belting should be the same as the intended width of the finished belt. Cut the belting equal to the waist measurement plus 6 inches for the overlap. Cut one end of belting at a right angle for the point. Cut a strip of fabric on the lengthwise grain. Use a selvage edge, if available, especially when you are using a heavyweight fabric. The width of the fabric should be double the width of the belting plus $^3/_4$ inch, ($^1/_2$ inch if the selvage edge is used), and make the length equal the belting measurement plus $^3/_4$ inch.

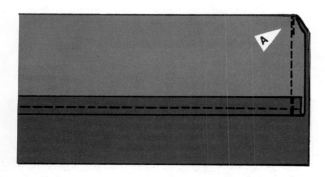

On one lengthwise edge, turn $^1/_4$ inch to wrong side and stitch close to the fold. (If the selvage edge is used, do not turn under the edge.) Fold one end in half lengthwise, right sides together, with the turned edge or selvage $^1/_2$ inch from the raw edge. Pin and stitch in $^1/_4$ inch seam, backstitching to secure each end (**a**).

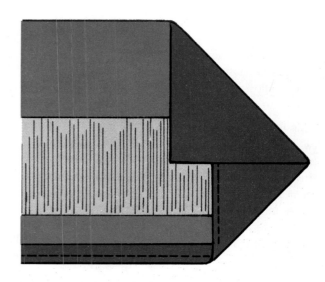

Press seam open and turn right side out. Insert the pointed end of belting into the fabric point. Fold the raw edge over the belting on lengthwise grain and press (**b**). Fold the finished edge or selvage over the raw edge. Pin so that the fabric is drawn

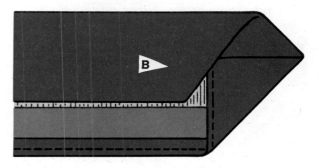

snugly over the belting (**c**). Hand-sew securely in place. Attach the unfinished end of belt to buckle as instructed under buckles.

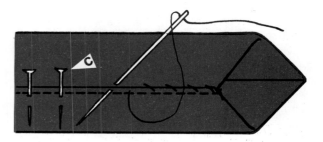

Crushed Belt. Soft, crushed looking belts of fabric, leather or leather-like fabric are much in fashion. It is a practical one to make if you are short of fabric or are using leather or a leather-like. Use a coordinated fabric for the backing or facing. For heavyweight fabrics or for the leather types, use a lighter weight fabric such as satin or sturdy taffeta. Interfacing is usually needed, but do not choose one that is too stiff or it will not give a crushed look.

The fabric for the right side of the belt should be the width of the finished belt plus $1\frac{1}{8}$ inch for seam allowances. The length should equal the waistline measurement plus 8 inches for overlap.

Cut the backing and interfacing to the finished width plus $\frac{7}{8}$ inch, and make them the same length as the fabric strip. The backing is cut slightly narrower so that the seamlines will be on the underside of the finished belt. Cut one end of all strips on an angle. Trim corner of interfacing. Machine-baste interfacing to wrong side of backing, $\frac{5}{8}$ inch from edges. Trim interfacing to stitching (**a**).

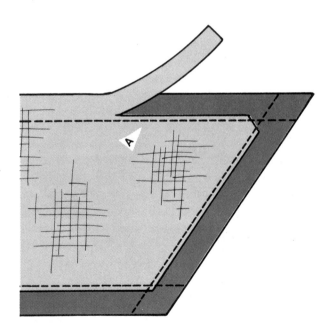

With right sides together, pin the backing to the belt fabric, keeping the long edges even. Stitch $\frac{5}{8}$ inch seams on both sides. The belt fabric will have ease because it was cut wider. Trim and grade seams, and press them toward backing (**b**).

Stitch the angled end. Trim seam allowances and corners (**c**). Press. Turn right side out through the open end.

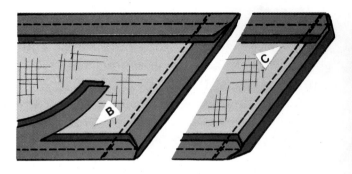

For this type of belt, the width of the buckle, not the inner bar, usually is equal to, or is narrower than the belt width. The narrower the buckle, the

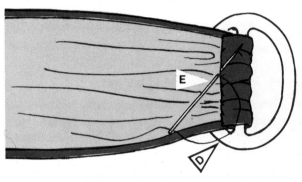

more crushed the belt will look. To attach the buckle, pleat the unfinished end (**d**), and fit it over the inside bar. Turn under the raw edge and stitch it securely in place (**e**).

Tie Belt. Tie belts are usually made of self fabric or a length of ribbon. Experiment with a piece of ribbon around the waist to determine the correct length of the tie ends. Interface the belt only in the waistline area to prevent it from curling. Select a sturdy interfacing.

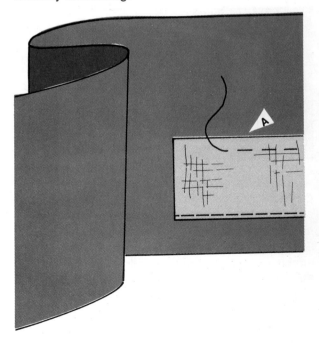

Cut the fabric strip on the lengthwise grain double the finished belt width plus 1⅛ inches for seam allowances. The length should be equal to the waist measurement plus the length of both tie ends. Cut the interfacing 1 inch shorter than the waist measurement and one-half as wide as the fabric strip. Pin interfacing to the wrong side of fabric, centering it over the waistline area. Machine-baste ⅝ inch from raw edge. Trim interfacing close to stitching. Sew in place with small stitches ¼ inch from the center (**a**). Fold strip in

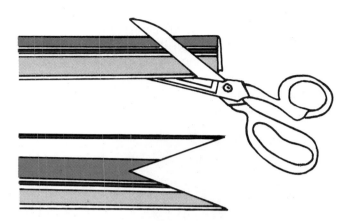

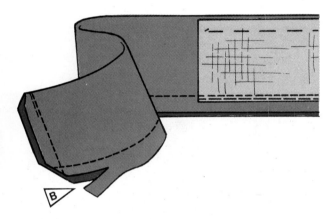

half lengthwise and with right sides together stitch raw edges in ⅝ inch seam, leaving an opening for turning at center back. Trim seams and corners (**b**). Turn belt to the right side; slip-stitch edges of opening (**c**).

shorter than the waist measurement. Round off the corners, center the interfacing on the ribbon and press in place. Cut the ribbon ends diagonally to prevent raveling.

Buckles. Buckles are featured items, as varied and interesting as pieces of jewelry. They are made of metal, bone or plastic to match any color, or they can be covered with jewel-like stones. Kits are available for covering buckles with self fabric.

A regular buckle comes either with or without a prong; the inside bar is slightly wider than the finished belt width except when it will be used for a crushed belt.

A buckle without a prong is attached by folding the unfinished end of the belt over the center bar to the wrong side; turn under the raw edge and sew securely in place by hand or machine.

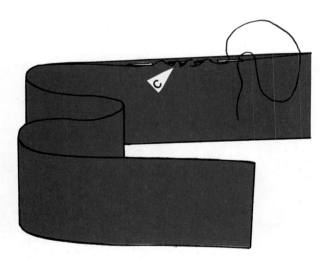

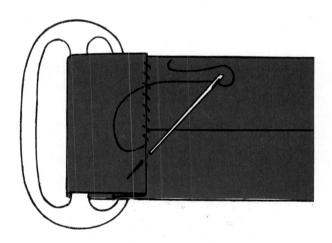

Ribbon Belts. Many beautiful ribbons can be made into excellent tie belts. Use a strip of iron-on non-woven interfacing to prevent the waistline area from curling. Cut interfacing strip slightly narrower than the width of the ribbon and 1 inch

A buckle with a prong is attached as follows: Make an oblong hole about 1 inch from the un-finished end of the belt. Use a stiletto to punch two holes, and cut from one hole to the other to make the oblong opening (**a**). Use a short over-casting stitch to finish the opening. Insert prong through the opening. Turn under the raw edge and sew securely. Try on the belt to determine the position of the required eyelets, and mark two

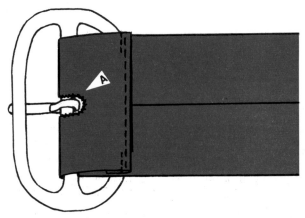

or three locations. Punch the holes with a stiletto and finish them with a buttonhole or blanket stitch, or make machine-worked eyelets on a zigzag machine. Metal eyelets can also be used but are not recommended for fine or delicate fabrics.

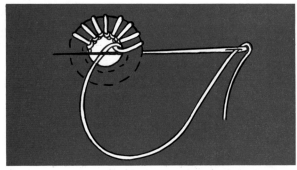

Belt Carriers. Usually attached to the garment at the side seams, belt carriers hold the belt in place. They can be made from self fabric tubing or thread. Mark position on outside of garment.

A fabric carrier is made from a length of bias tubing, the belt width plus 1 inch. Turn each end

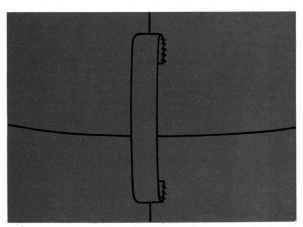

under ¼ inch, and press the folds. Pin the carriers in position on the garment, centering them over the waistline seam if there is one. Sew securely in place.

A thread chain carrier is made with the same chain stitch that is used to make a chain tack and lingerie strap holders. Use double strands of silk buttonhole twist thread, knotted together; fasten the thread securely on the wrong side. Bring needle through to right side at the mark for the top of carrier. Take a small horizontal stitch in the top mark, and draw up thread to form a 2½ inch

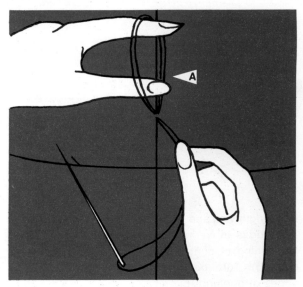

loop (**a**). Hold the needle in right hand; insert index finger and thumb of left hand through the loop, take hold of the needle thread, and draw the thread

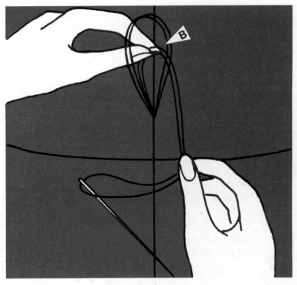

through to form another loop (**b**). Hold the second loop open while you draw the first loop down close

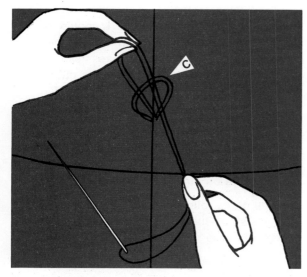

to the garment (**c**). Reach through second loop, and draw out a third loop. Continue to draw up a loop, drawing through a new loop until the chain is of sufficient length. Draw the needle through

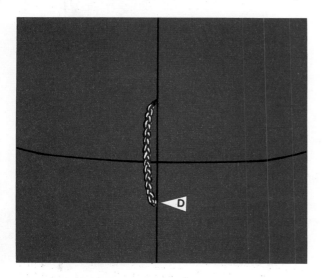

the last loop made and tighten (**d**). Sew this end at the bottom mark to complete the carrier. Make secure on the wrong side.

Lingerie strap holders are placed on the shoulder seams of garments to prevent lingerie straps from

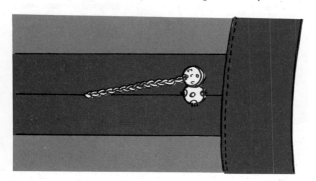

showing. Start a thread chain about ¼ to ½ inch from the sleeve seam or armhole edge. Fasten the chain with a small snap fastener ¼ to ½ inch from the edge of the neckline.

binding

Binding can be purchased ready-made, or you can cut it by hand. It must be cut on the true bias if it is to fit smoothly and be easy to handle. The finished width of binding is usually ¼ to ½ inch. When binding garment edges such as necklines or armholes, staystitch ¾ inch from the raw edge, and trim away the ⅝ inch seam allowance which will not be needed.

Bias Strips
Cutting. Fold fabric on the true bias, lengthwise and crosswise threads running parallel to each other. Refer to Fabric Grain in Chapter 4. From the fold, mark off widths for the strips in parallel lines and cut (**a**). The ends of the strips must be on the straight grain, and the ends to be joined together must be parallel to each other (**b**).

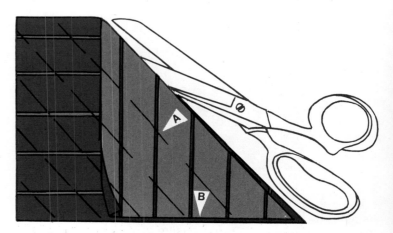

Joining. With right sides together, lap ends so that strips are at right angles to each other. Stitch on the straight grain, starting and ending at point where strips cross (**c**). Press seam open and trim to ¼ inch. Trim extending points (**d**).

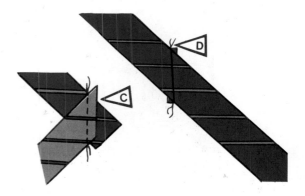

Continuous bias can be cut when a long strip of bias is needed. Prepare a rectangle of fabric on the straight grain. On the wrong side, mark a true bias line (line 1) from the upper corner to the

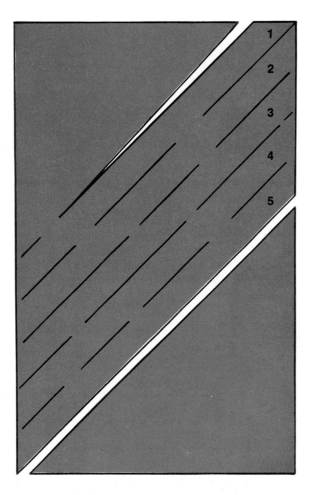

opposite side. Measure from this line the width of the bias, and draw a second line parallel to the first. Continue to measure and mark until you have sufficient length. With right sides together, form a

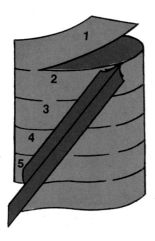

tube by folding rectangle so that the lines on the lengthwise edges match. Line 1 should extend above the other lines as shown. Pin edges and stitch, making a $1/4$ inch seam. Press seam open. Start to cut on line 1, and continue to cut around the tube on the marked lines.

Binding Methods

Here are a few suggestions to help you make perfect bindings. If possible, start the binding in an inconspicuous place. Pin in place for stitching. Always baste on curves or angles.

Use one of the following methods for final joining of a bias strip. Bulky fabrics leave about 2 inches of the bias strip unstitched at the starting point.

Stitch around the garment, and stop slightly before reaching the starting point: cut bias strip, leaving about 2 inches. Fold the garment so that the ends of strips can cross each other at right angles. Stitch strips together on grain close to the garment. Press seam open and trim. Finish stitching binding to garment.

For lightweight fabrics simply lap the ends. Fold $1/2$ inch of strip to the wrong side, on the straight grain and stitch. As you near the end of this stitching line, lap the second end over the folded end, and cut the excess bias on straight grain. Finish stitching to garment.

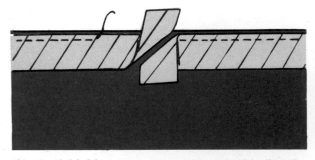

Single fold bias tape. If ready-made binding is used, open it out on one fold. With right sides together, and raw edges even, stitch to the edge to be bound. Fold the binding over the raw edges to the wrong side and hem to stitching.

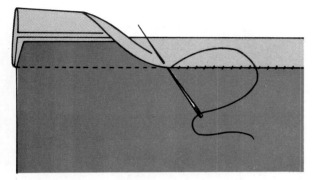

If you made the binding strips, cut the true bias four times the desired width of the finished binding. Press under the seam allowance (one-fourth of the width). With right sides together, stitch binding to edge in a seam one-fourth the width of the strip. Turn binding over seam to wrong side and hem to stitching.

Double fold bias tape. This binding is ready-made. Encase the edge with the bias with the wider fold

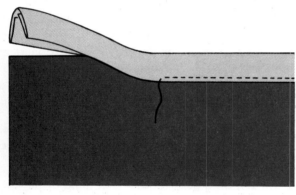

to the wrong side. Stitch along the edge on the right side so that the bottom fold of binding is caught in the single row of stitching.

French binding. This binding is used for sheer fabrics and lingerie. Cut true bias six times the desired width of the finished binding, and fold

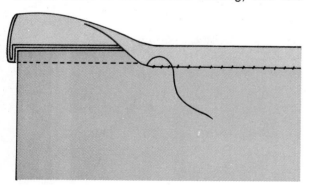

lengthwise, wrong sides together. Stitch raw edges of bias to right side of garment, making a seam one-third the width of the folded bias. Turn folded edge over seam and hem in place on wrong side.

Binding by machine. A special machine attachment can be used for a topstitched application of ready-made or hand-cut bias strips. Refer to your machine manual for directions.

Corners

Binding an inside corner. With right sides together baste bias binding to the edge to be bound, stretching the bias at the corner. Stitch to the

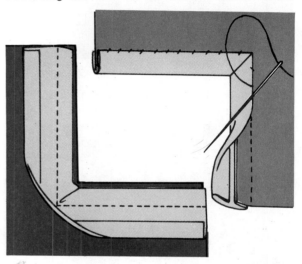

corner, and leave the needle in the fabric while pivoting to turn corner. Turn binding to wrong side, mitering the binding at the corner on the top and bottom. Slipstitch the folds at corner; hem to stitching.

Topstitched binding. Clip corner diagonally 1/8 inch. Enclose one edge of inside corner with bias

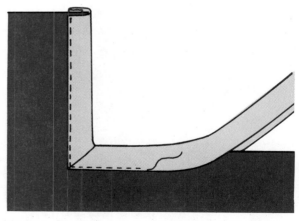

binding. Stitch to corner, pivot on needle. Form a miter in binding, and continue stitching along the second edge of corner.

Binding an outside corner

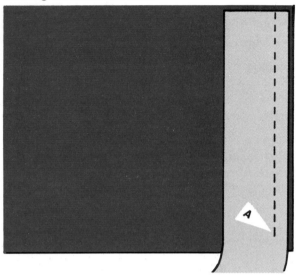

a. Right sides together, stitch bias binding to one edge as far as corner. Raise needle from fabric.

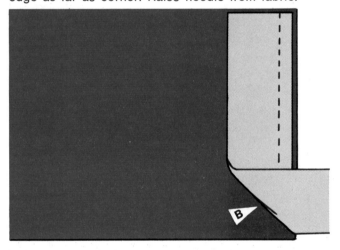

b. Turn binding at right angles to stitched edge to form a diagonal fold at the corner.

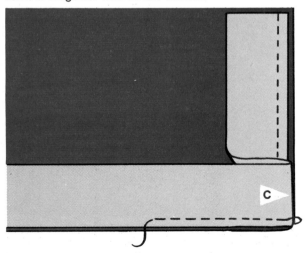

c. Turn folded binding back on itself; bring fold

edge of binding to raw edges forming a small pleat. Lower needle into binding at corner, letting thread extend over fold. Stitch second side.

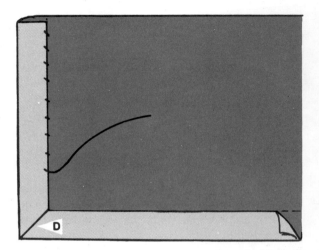

d. Press binding toward edges, pinning the miter to hold it in place. Turn binding to wrong side, and form a miter at the corner. Turn under raw edge and hem to stitching. Slipstitch the miter.

Topstitched binding. Enclose edge of fabric with bias binding and stitch through all thicknesses to about $1/2$ inch from corner. Turn binding at corner to make a miter on both sides. Pin folds. Continue stitching to fold of miter. Pivot on needle and stitch along second side. Slipstitch the miter.

rick rack

Rick rack is a simple braid, available in various widths and colors. It is especially attractive for children's garments and casual clothing.

Apply flat on a garment, using straight or narrow zigzag machine-stitching. Stitch through the center of the braid.

It may be applied in several ways. Turn edge of fabric to be trimmed to the wrong side and press. Lay fold over rick rack so that only the points on one edge are visible; topstitch (**a**).

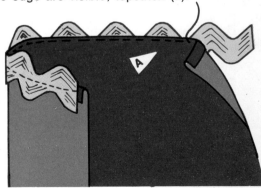

Lay rick rack on the right side of fabric close to raw edge and stitch through center of rick rack.

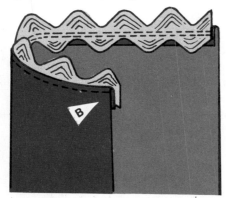

Press to wrong side along stitching. Topstitch close to turned edge (**b**).

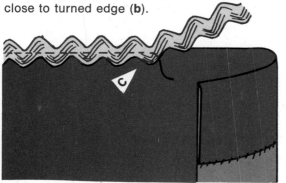

Place rick rack on the right side of a finished edge, and stitch through the center (**c**).

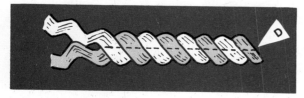

Two interlocking strips of rick rack in a single color or in contrasting colors can be used. Machine-stitch the same way as for a single strip (**d**).

ruffles

Ruffles, cut on the crosswise grain or on the true bias, fall in softer folds and are the most satisfactory type to use on garments.

The width of a finished ruffle should be in proportion to the garment. Cut strips to the desired width plus a seam and hem allowance. Ruffles are usually made of a single thickness of fabric, but they can also be a double thickness, especially if the fabric is sheer. For a double layered ruffle, cut strips double the width of the finished ruffle plus two seam allowances. Fold in half, lengthwise, and treat as one layer of fabric. It does not require a hem.

Fullness guide for ruffles. Narrow ruffles need less fullness than do wide ruffles; sheer fabrics need more fullness than heavier fabrics. For very full ruffles cut strips three times the length of the finished ruffle; average fullness requires double the finished length, and slight fullness needs only one and a half times the finished length.

Cut bias ruffles by following one of the two methods used for cutting bias bindings. Before gathering the ruffles, hand roll one edge of strip or machine-stitch a narrow hem. A decorative edge can be added by using a zigzag-stitch pattern or a narrow lace edging.

Gather ruffle strips by machine, stitching one row on the seamline and a second row of stitching 1/8 inch from the first within the seam allowance. Use heavy-duty thread on the bobbin.

When gathering long ruffles, divide the fabric length into quarters, and gather each quarter separately. This procedure makes it easier to space the gathers evenly, and lessens the danger of breaking the bobbin thread when it is pulled. Before the ruffles are attached, mark the garment area into quarters, and adjust one-fourth of the ruffling to one-fourth of the garment area.

Ruffles can also be made by machine, using the ruffler attachment which is adjustable for pleating, or gathering. Refer to machine's instruction book.

Sewing on the Ruffles

Ruffle on an edge. This method of application can be used on faced edges such as on collars and cuffs. Draw up the ruffle. With right sides together pin gathered edge of ruffle to the edge of the top section of collar or cuff, matching the seamlines. Distribute the gathers evenly, and allow slightly more fullness at the corners. When used on a collar or the front of a blouse, the ends of the

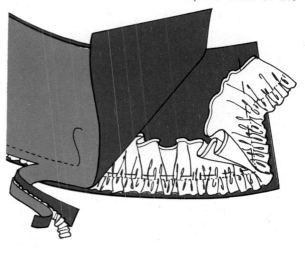

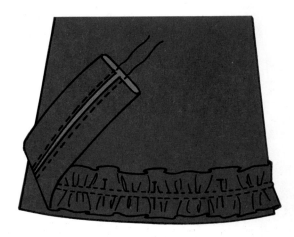

ruffle should be tapered. Baste. Pin right side of facing over ruffle, and stitch along seamline through all thicknesses. Trim corners and grade seam allowances. Turn to right side and press. If a ruffle is used at the neckline, finish the ends before applying the ruffle.

Ruffle in a seam. The method of application for this ruffle is the same as that for applying a ruffle to an edge. After stitching the seam, press seam allowances away from the ruffle or press open, depending on how you want the ruffle to fall.

Ruffle applied with a bias strip. Because facings are eliminated, this is an excellent method to use for applying ruffles to heavier fabrics. With right sides together pin the ruffle to the garment edge,

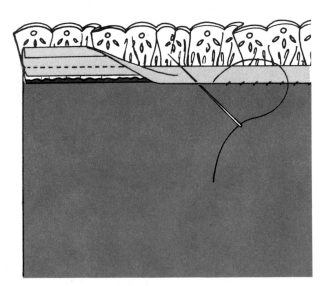

matching seamlines. Distribute fullness evenly. Baste a bias strip, right side down, over the ruffle. Stitch on the seamline. Trim seam; turn bias to the inside, turn under the raw edge, and hem.

Double ruffles. A custom touch can be attained by using double ruffles on the hems of dresses, the bottom of sleeves, a bodice or blouse front. Cut the fabric strips to double the width of the finished ruffle and to the desired length. On the wrong side chalk mark the center for the full length of the strip. If ruffles are to be attached to the hemline, seam ends of the strip to form a circle. Turn the lengthwise edges to the wrong side so that they meet at the center chalk mark. Pin in place.

From the wrong side make two rows of machine basting. Make each row about $1/8$ inch from the raw edges at the center of strip. Draw up the bobbin thread until the circle fits the hemline. Pin the ruffle, wrong side down, over the right side of garment, and adjust gathers. Topstitch twice, stitching close to, but not on the gathered lines. Remove the gathering threads.

Circular ruffles. These ruffles are made from circles of fabric. The fullness is introduced when the inner curve of the ruffle is straightened. To make a paper pattern for the ruffle, draw a circle, the circumference of which will equal the length of

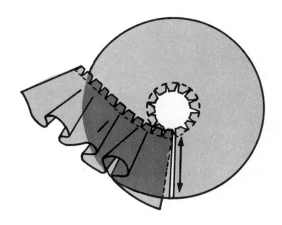

the ruffle. Measure out from the edge of the circle a distance equal to the desired width of the ruffle plus ¹/₂ inch, and draw a second circle around the first. Mark the grainline on the ruffle with a straight line through the center. Cut out the pattern, cutting through the outer circle on the grainline to cut out the inner circle. Lay the pattern on the fabric, matching grainlines and pin. Cut through the circle on the grainline cutting out the small circle. If necessary, cut more than one circle, seaming them together to get the desired length

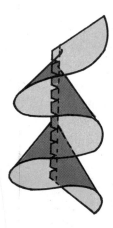

of ruffle. French seams should be used for organdy and other sheers. Staystitch the ends and outer curve ¹/₈ inch from the edge, and finish with a narrow hem, either by hand rolling or by machine. You can also attach lace to the edge.

Staystiitch ¹/₄ inch from the inner curve; clip curve to within 1/16 inch of the stitching so that seam allowance will lie flat when the ruffle is stitched on garment. With right sides together and with the bottom edge of ruffle turned up, pin staystitching line of ruffle to garment and stitch. When the ruffle is turned down, the stitching will be concealed.

sequins and beads

To apply ready made sequin and bead motifs, just slipstitch in place. Sequins and beads are also available packaged individually. The thread will be less likely to twist if it is waxed.

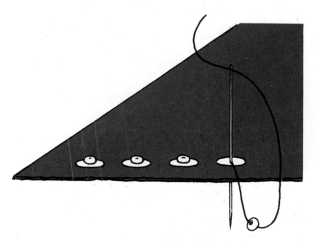

Single sequins are sewn on with a bead in the center. Bring needle up through fabric to right side; put a sequin on the needle and then a bead. Slide them down onto the fabric; take a stitch over the bead and back through the center of the sequin through to the wrong side of fabric.

Sequins in rows can be used to outline a motif. Start with tiny backstitches on the wrong side of fabric. Working from right to left, bring needle to right side and add a sequin, its right side up. Hold sequin flat, taking a stitch over the edge directly to the left, and bring needle to right side, one-half the width of a sequin ahead. Place a second

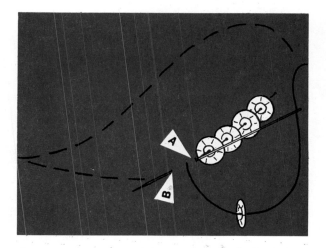

sequin on needle, wrong side up. Take a backstitch, inserting needle at front edge of first sequin (**a**) and bringing it out at (**b**). (The under stitch from **a** to **b** should be equal the width of a sequin.)

As the thread is drawn up, turn the sequin over so that its right side is up. Continue to add sequins in this manner.

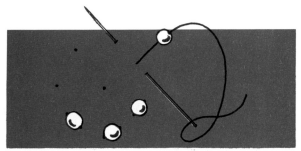

Single beads can be sewn on with a backstitch, working from right to left.

Beads in rows can be used as an outline or as individual motifs. Mark the outline lightly on the right side. Thread beads on a heavy duty thread, and

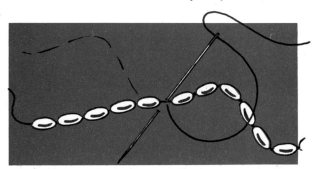

sew them to the fabric between the beads. If motifs have short lines, use a heavy duty thread, and sew on the beads in groups (4 to 6 beads to a group). Fasten securely on wrong side.

tucks

When tucks are included in a pattern, they may be used either to bring needed fullness to an area of

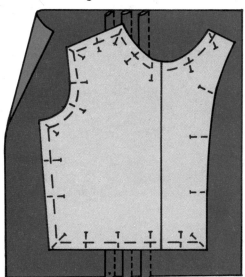

the garment or just to decorate the garment. Follow pattern instructions for marking and stitching.

If you plan to introduce tucks into a design, determine their placement, width and spacing in relation to your figure. Whenever possible, tuck the fabric before cutting the garment. Tucks used for decoration should always be on grain.

Use tracing paper and a tracing wheel or chalk pencil to mark tucks accurately. Pressing tuck creases lightly makes it easier to stitch the tucks accurately. When you are making hand-sewn tucks, make a cardboard gauge to indicate the depth of the tucks and the distance between them. Use fine hand or machine stitches for tucks. Machine-stitched tucks can be done on a zigzag machine, using a decorative stitch instead of a straight stitch.

The machine tucker helps to make tucks that are uniform. Refer to your instruction manual. A seam guide will also help in getting the tucks even.

Types of Tucks

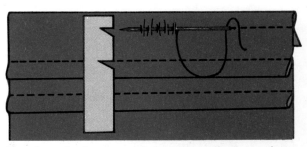

Hand-run tucks are preferred for delicate or sheer fabrics, but a similar effect can be attained by machine. Crease on the tuck lines, and make small running stitches close to the crease.

Pin tucks are very narrow hand-run tucks about 1/16 inch wide, frequently used on babies' wear.

Cross tucks are made by marking and stitching all the tucks on the lengthwise grain. Press all tucks in one direction; then mark and stitch all tucks on the crosswise grain and press.

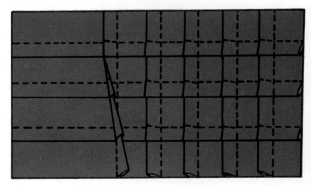

Fringe

You can apply fringe on a garment, insert it in a faced edge or stitch it along hem edges. Ready-made fringe can be bought by the yard. It comes with a heading which is usually meant to show. Just stitch it on the garment.

Self Fringe. Tweeds, plaids, sheer woolens and many other fabrics will fringe. Test on a fabric scrap first to see the effect.

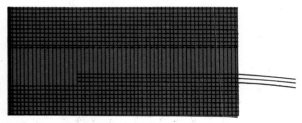

Cut the edge to be fringed perfectly straight along either the lengthwise or crosswise grain. Measure in from the edge the desired length of the fringe and pull a thread. Just above this pulled thread, make a line of machine stitching. Then pull the thread next below the first one pulled and continue pulling threads to the edge. Starting in this way at the top of the fringe and working down keeps the threads from tangling.

Floss or yarn fringe. Cut a length of heavy paper the desired width of the fringe plus ½ inch and as long as needed. Fasten and wrap the yarn around

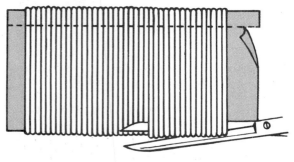

the gauge, laying the strands touching each other but not overlapping. Machine stitch across one long side about ½ inch from the edge. Cut through the strands on the opposite side. Tear away the

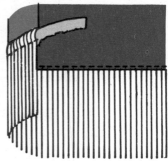

lower part of the paper. Turn under and topstitch the edge of the garment to the top of the fringe. Remove remaining paper.

Knotted fringe. Before fringing an edge, make a test tassel to decide best length and thickness. There are two methods for making knotted fringe.

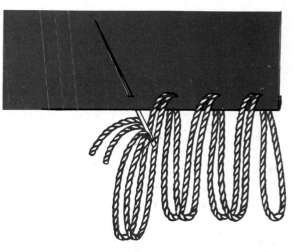

Narrowly hem the edge to which fringe will be attached. Thread a large darning needle with two or more strands of yarn or floss. Turn under the edge to which the fringe is to be attached. Working from right to left, bring needle up through turned edge of fabric. Take stitches about ¼ inch apart, leaving loops of the desired length between stitches. Cut loops and knot the yarn of each one. Trim lower ends evenly.

Cut a paper gauge the width and length the fringe is to be. Wrap gauge with yarn and secure the end. At one edge, cut through several strands. Insert a crochet hook into the finished fabric edge; with the hook, pick up the cut strands at the uncut edge and pull through the fabric. Pull the cut ends through the loop to fasten.

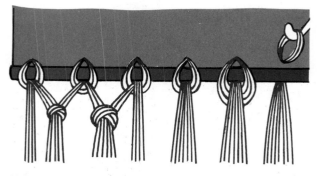

Knotted fringe can be turned into a Mexican look by knotting together the halves of two adjacent tassels. Several rows of such knots give an especially hand crafted look.

index

index